State of Suffering

STATE OF SUFFERING

Political Violence and Community Survival in Fiji

Susanna Trnka

Cornell University Press

Ithaca and London

First published 2008 by Cornell University Press
First printing, Cornell Paperbacks, 2008

Printed in the United States of America

Library of Congress Cataloging-in-Publication Data
Trnka, Susanna.
    State of suffering : political violence and community survival in Fiji / Susanna Trnka.
        p. cm.
    Includes bibliographical references and index.
    ISBN 978-0-8014-4640-5 (cloth : alk. paper) — ISBN 978-0-8014-7498-9 (pbk. : alk. paper
    1. Political violence—Fiji.   2. Ethnic conflict—Fiji.   3. Fiji—Politics and government.
4. Fiji—Ethnic relations.   5. East Indians—Fiji.   I. Title.
    DU600.T74   2008
    996.11—dc22
2008019289

Cornell University Press strives to use environmentally responsible
suppliers and materials to the fullest extent possible in the publishing
of its books. Such materials include vegetable-based, low-VOC inks
and acid-free papers that are recycled, totally chlorine-free, or partly
composed of nonwood fibers. For further information, visit our website
at www.cornellpress.cornell.edu.

Cloth printing   10 9 8 7 6 5 4 3 2 1

Paperback printing   10 9 8 7 6 5 4 3 2 1

For John

Contents

State of Suffering

1 Violence, Pain, and the Collapse of Everyday Life

On May 19, 2000, armed gunmen led by indigenous Fijian businessman George Speight burst into the Fiji Parliament and took hostage forty-four members of Parliament, including the prime minister. They sought to overthrow the democratically elected Labour government and remove from office Mahendra Chaudhry, Fiji's first, and to date only, Indo-Fijian prime minister. For the next six months, Fiji was plunged into turmoil. Crowds swept through the nation's capital, looting shops and businesses. Schools were shut down. Indo-Fijian homes and Hindu temples were set alight. Like most of the political rhetoric that accompanied the coup, much of the violence targeted Indo-Fijians, some of whom were mugged, physically assaulted, or raped.

The Indo-Fijians in Nausori with whom I was living and conducting fieldwork during the coup were profoundly shaken. Unable to go to work due to the government-imposed curfew, they spent their days inside, with their doors locked and bolted in case of attack, listening to the radio and exchanging every scrap of news in the hope of collectively being able to shed some light on the situation. They spoke incessantly about the violence, relating accounts of physical assaults that had happened to them or to their relatives, and trying to figure out who might be targeted next. For months, they lived in terror that the country was going to devolve into anarchy. Some worried that it might be the beginning of an anti-Indian genocide.

One of the many who bore the brunt of the violence is a woman I call "Shanti," whose story is among those told in this book.[1] Shanti fled her

1. With the exception of well-known political and community leaders, all of the names of my interlocutors are pseudonyms, as is the name of the village in which I was based during the bulk of my fieldwork.

home and farm in the interior of Viti Levu after she was held at knifepoint and threatened with rape by a band of youths. A few days after the attack, she came to stay in a small village in the Nausori area. The accounts she gave of her assault were partial and incoherent, invoking vivid images of violence but uncertain about to whom they had happened. The villagers who rallied around Shanti were left to collectively piece together various accounts of what might have happened to cause her such trauma. Months passed and despite the increasing safety of the Nausori area, Shanti refused to step out of the house to walk her children a hundred yards down the road to the local school. Five years after she was assaulted, she had permanently settled in the village, her new home fortified with a cement and barbed wire fence and three attack dogs.

This book is about what happens to a community of ordinary people when their lives are irrevocably overturned by violence. It explores how people collectively react to, interpret, and ascribe meaning to the terror that overwhelms their lives. In the pages that follow, I focus on the social processes through which violence is embodied, articulated, and silenced by those it targets and consider the following issues: How is political violence both embodied and disembodied by those it targets? What kinds of pain are shared in times of violence and what kinds are suppressed in the struggle to regain a sense of social "normalcy"? How might pain come to be seen as part of one's ethnic identity and invoked as part of the lobbying for political rights? Finally, what forms might a community's struggle to articulate widespread trauma take? In addressing these questions, I examine how a moral discourse that linked together pain, "race," and physical labor became the primary means through which many Indo-Fijians attempted to ascribe meaning to the chaos that engulfed them, and what happened when their explanations fell short. I also suggest how studies of political violence might better take into account communitywide processes of coping with and ascribing meaning to moments of acute trauma.

A Tumultuous History

The events of May 19, 2000, were neither Fiji's first nor last political coup. Thirteen years earlier, in 1987, Fiji experienced its first overthrow of an elected government when Lieutenant Colonel Sitiveni Rabuka executed not one but two military coups. As of this writing, Fiji has gone on to earn itself the moniker of a nation plagued by "four coups in twenty years," with the most recent coup, this one led by Commodore Frank Bainimarama, taking place in December 2006.

The events of 2000 were unique, however, in terms of the longevity and severity of the crisis and its impact on Fiji's political future. The hostage crisis that began on May 19, 2000, lasted for fifty-six days, but the coup-related violence didn't come to an end until mid-November 2000, nearly six months after Speight took over the Parliament Complex. During this period, four potential governments wrestled for control of the nation, the country was put under an evening curfew, schools and businesses were often closed, and food was hoarded in anticipation of shortages. The economic effects of the 2000 crisis were felt almost immediately as garment factories shut down and tourism, and the inflow of tourist dollars, ground to a halt, sending thousands to join the ranks of the jobless.

Following May 19, 2000, outbreaks of violence between civilians, rebels, and the military occurred across the country. Never before and never since has postcolonial Fiji experienced such levels of violence. Much of the civilian violence was directed against Indo-Fijians, their homes, businesses, and properties. It was fueled by a racialized, anti-Indian rhetoric that promoted images of Indo-Fijians as *vulagi,* or foreigners, who had usurped the rights of the *taukei,* or indigenous Fijians, to govern Fiji. Hand-in-hand with taukei assertions of "indigenous rights" were condemnations of non-Christians and calls for Fiji to restore its status as a Christian state.[2] The violence was, however, highly racialized; targets were not limited to Hindus and Muslims but Indo-Fijian Christians were also attacked. Not far from the village in which I was working, a Methodist school run primarily by Indo-Fijian Christians was partially burned down.

The anti-Indian violence was particularly intense in Naitasiri, Speight's home province, where Indo-Fijian families were physically assaulted, had their houses burned down, and were driven out of villages and off of their farmland. Many of those who fled made their way across Viti Levu to Lautoka where they spent months living in tents, making up Fiji's first "refugee camp."[3] The refugees' predicament was the most dramatic, but in towns and villages across the nation many Indo-Fijians were similarly subject to racial abuse and physical assault. Not surprisingly, Indo-Fijians of all religious and

2. The taukei movement mobilizes its members around the concept of indigenous Fijian political paramountcy. The term *taukei* has various political and cultural meanings that will be explored in detail in chapter 2.

3. Technically, this was a camp for displaced persons. It was, however, locally referred to as a "refugee camp."

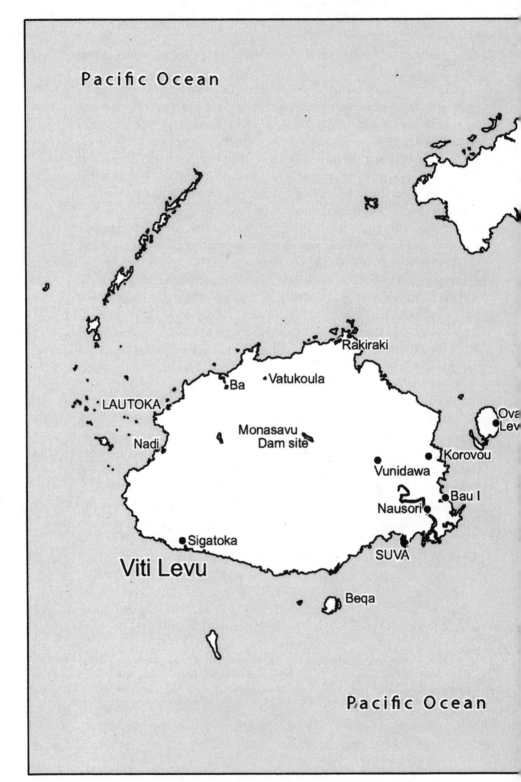

Pacific Ocean

Rakiraki

Ba • Vatukoula

LAUTOKA

Ova Lev

Nadi

Monasavu Dam site

Vunidawa

Korovou

Bau I

Nausori

Sigatoka

Viti Levu

SUVA

Beqa

Pacific Ocean

Map of Fiji

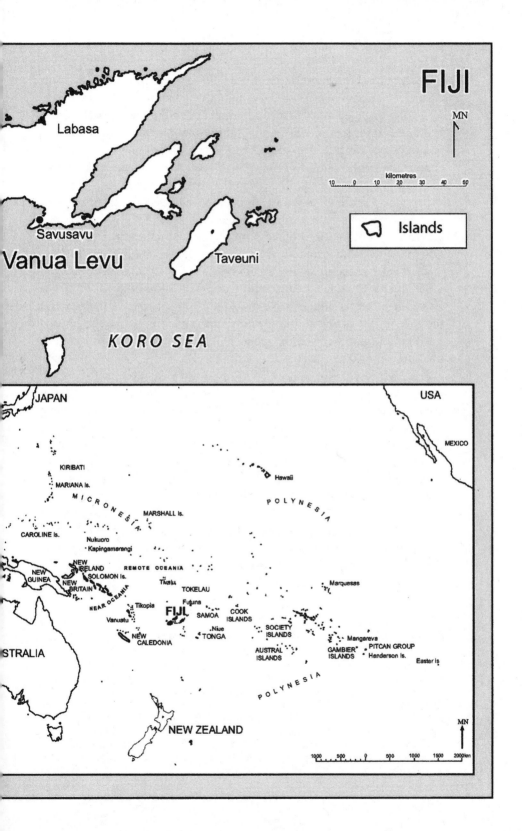

socioeconomic backgrounds were afraid to leave their homes, and as a result curtailed their employment, social activities, and children's schooling.

The fighting died down in mid-November 2000, but the political tension continued. Prior to May 2000, most political analysts had assumed that Fiji had recovered from the two coups of 1987 and was not only committed to democratic politics, but many suggested, was embarking on a new era of multicultural government.[4] The coup of 2000 put an end to these hopes by opening up a space of radical political and social insecurity that has lasted ever since. Speight never made it into power, but neither was the previous government restored into office. Instead, a new military-backed civilian government, led by Prime Minister Laisenia Qarase and initially installed by Commodore Bainimarama, went on to win Fiji's elections in 2001 and 2005. But its electoral successes were based on promoting policies that alienated its former military supporters. Tensions between the military and the government escalated until Bainimarama violently ejected the government out of office in December 2006, plunging Fiji into another round of political confusion.

Since May 2000, uncertainty over Fiji's future has never abated. While the economy, and in particular tourism, had begun to slowly recover, the events of 2006 set it back again. Many in Fiji have continued to feel acutely insecure about their safety and those who can have joined the exodus out of the country. In the first four years following the 2000 coup, an estimated 23,000 people, out of a total population of approximately 775,000, have migrated, most of them to Australia, New Zealand, the United States, and Canada.[5] As with the bulk of the victims of coup-related violence, the overwhelming majority of those leaving—more than 85 percent according to the Fiji Islands Bureau of Statistics—have been Indo-Fijians. This book is about the Indo-Fijians who have left and those who have stayed, and how the events of 2000 plunged their lives into a chaos from which they are still recovering.

4. Examples include political historian Brij V. Lal (2000a) and anthropologist Robert Norton (2000b).

5. This figure is based on official immigration statistics from the Fiji Islands Bureau of Statistics, which are available only up until August 2004 (Fiji Islands Bureau of Statistics, personal communication). A comparison with immigration figures for the four years *prior* to May 2000 reveals a 19 percent increase in the number of Indo-Fijians permanently leaving Fiji following May 2000, a factor that has contributed to an overall decrease in Fiji's Indo-Fijian population. An even higher increase in immigration has been suggested by the deposed prime minister, Mahendra Chaudhry, who stated that by May 2005 (i.e., five years following the 2000 coup) approximately 35,000 people had permanently left Fiji (see Marau 2005).

Political and Economic Positioning of Indo-Fijians in Fiji

Indo-Fijians, also popularly referred to as Indians, are the second-leading ethnic group in Fiji.[6] Their numbers in Fiji are steadily decreasing, but at the time of the 2000 coup, they composed approximately 44 percent of the population, with indigenous Fijians composing another 51 percent.[7] Indo-Fijians predominate in business enterprises and in many areas of commercial agriculture, including sugarcane, the country's leading agricultural export. Their economic and political leverage has been, however, constrained by arrangements designed to favor indigenous Fijians. The bulk of the land in Fiji—today nearly 87 percent—is inalienably owned by indigenous Fijian landowning units (Reddy and Lal 2002). This land can be rented, but not sold, to non-indigenous Fijians, making most of the Indo-Fijian population reliant on renting land for their homes and for the maintenance of their livelihoods. Governmental power, both in terms of political office and leadership in the civil service, has also been dominated by indigenous Fijians. The military is composed almost entirely by indigenous Fijians and, along with the police force, has had indigenous Fijian (or foreign, but not Indo-Fijian) leadership.[8] In addition to this, there has been a history of coups—in 1987 and in 2000—carried out in the name of protecting "Fijian rights."

The majority of today's Indo-Fijians are the descendants of indentured laborers who were brought to Fiji to work on the colonial sugar plantations. The indentured laborers, or *girmitiyas* as they called themselves due to the "girmit," or agreement, they signed with the British, were released from bondage following five years of hard labor and most settled in Fiji.

Indenture ended in 1920, but despite their efforts to secure fair political representation from the British, Indo-Fijians were kept on the sidelines of national politics during the remainder of colonial rule. Nor did things greatly improve when Fiji became independent in 1970 as political leadership was transferred from the British into the hands of primarily Eastern, indigenous Fijian chiefly elites. Political power remained with

6. The social science literature tends to employ the term *Indo-Fijians,* or, in older texts, *Fiji Indians,* for people of Indian ancestry in Fiji. However, in everyday speech, members of this group commonly to refer to themselves as "Indians." Government documents in Fiji also frequently use "Indian." I use both "Indian" and "Indo-Fijian" interchangeably.

7. Members of other groups, including Australians, New Zealanders, Chinese, Rotumans, and other Pacific Islanders, made up the remaining 5 percent. All figures are from the Fiji Islands Bureau of Statistics (1996).

8. For a discussion of how this contributed to the coup, see chapter 2; also Kelly and Kaplan 2001a; Rakuita 2002.

them until the victory of the multi-ethnic Fiji Labour Party (FLP) in the 1987 elections.

Within a few weeks of the Fiji Labour Party government taking office, however, Fiji's first coup was carried out, under the leadership of Lieutenant Colonel Rabuka. Rabuka rallied support for an overthrow of what he called an "Indian-backed" government in order, he stated, to return power to Fiji's rightful rulers: indigenous Fijians.[9] Rabuka was successful, though he had to stage a second coup in the same year. He was later twice elected, under an ethnically skewed constitution, as Fiji's prime minister.

While Indo-Fijians' political history reflects a continued battle against political marginalization, their economic history tells a different story. Since the end of colonialism, many, but certainly not all, Indo-Fijians moved to the forefront of Fiji's economy, either through sugarcane farming or by running independent businesses. The result was that while many Indo-Fijians were skeptical of the government and the ruling party, they felt keenly involved, even responsible, for Fiji's economic development. As we shall see, during the 2000 coup many Indo-Fijians made a direct correlation between the girmitiyas' (and their own) physical industriousness and national development, viewing the growth of shops and other businesses in Suva's downtown as the fruits of their labor. While the nation as a whole was "developing," so too was their position in it, despite political inequities and their lack of security over land. In fact, in the years following the 1987 coups, many Indo-Fijians felt that they could successfully work toward their economic aspirations as long as they kept a low political profile (Kelly 1998).

But in 1999, a new constitution and growing dissatisfaction with Rabuka's leadership prompted a multi-ethnic cross-section of voters to re-elect the Fiji Labour Party. This time, the party was headed by an Indo-Fijian, the former trade unionist Chaudhry. Chaudhry's acceptance of the position of prime minister was the final blow to the still-widespread expectation that leadership would remain in the hands of indigenous Fijians.

Political Tensions Come to a Head (Again)

Chaudhry lasted only one year as prime minister. On May 19, 2000, the exact day of the first anniversary of Chaudhry's inauguration, he and his government were taken hostage inside the Parliament. The 1999 Labour government

---

9. In addition to his desire to restore the previous Alliance government, it has also been noted that Rabuka was likely biased against a government led by a Fijian from the West (see, for example, Teaiwa 2000). For an extended discussion of political differences between eastern and western provinces, see also Norton 1990, especially chapter 4.

never returned to office, though some of its members, including Chaudhry himself, were later appointed as government ministers in Commodore Baini- marama's military-imposed interim regime.

Much has been written about the various factors that led to the 2000 coup, among them the undermining of business interests by the Chaudhry government, personality politics among those ousted from office, and esca- lating concerns over indigenous Fijians' land rights.[10] But a great deal of mystery still remains regarding exactly who was behind the 2000 over- throw. While it has been widely acknowledged that Speight himself was only a front man acting in the interests of an unknown party or parties, in- tense controversy surrounds who else was involved in the planning and execution of the coup and who bankrolled the action.

Also hotly debated is the issue of what sort of a punishment—if any—is appropriate for those found guilty of colluding in the coup, an issue that led up to the most recent round of political turbulence. In 2005, Fiji's post- coup prime minister, Qarase, proposed the highly controversial Bill for the Promotion of Reconciliation, Unity, and Tolerance, which would have granted amnesty to some of those found guilty of coup-related offences, potentially including members of the military who had attempted mutiny against Bainimarama. Bainimarama's ire over the Reconciliation bill, along with other actions of the Qarase government, resulted in his instigation of yet another political coup, following which he installed himself as Fiji's newest prime minister.[11]

Unanswered Questions

Given the ongoing interest generated by Fiji's ever-changing political scene, much scholarly attention has gone into examining the events and personali- ties that constitute the country's troubled political history. Numerous stud- ies have assessed the impact of the 1987, 2000, and 2006 coups on Fiji's economic development and examined the possibilities for a return to demo- cratic governance.[12] A related line of scholarship has focused more generally on critically interrogating the role of "race" and ethnic conflict in the history

10. For a more detailed discussion of the lead up to the 2000 coup, see chapter 2.

11. During the military takeover of the government on December 5, 2006, Bainimarama took executive control of the government away from President Ratu Josefa Iloilo and initially installed a military doctor, Jona Senilagakali, as Fiji's prime minister. One month later, how- ever, Bainimarama reinstalled Ilolio as president. President Ilolio then named an interim administration in which Bainimarama was appointed prime minister.

12. For analyses of the 1987 coups see Akram-Lodhi 2000; B. Lal 2000d, 1992, 1990; V. Lal 1990; Lawson 1991; Premdas 1995; Rutz 1995; Scarr 1988; Sutherland 1992. Sources on the 2000

of Fijian politics.[13] Such studies are invaluable for our understanding of Fiji. But it is the purpose of this book to expand the scope of this scholarship by presenting a viewpoint that has been largely overlooked, namely an analysis of how the coup-related violence has been lived out by Fiji's citizens.[14]

We cannot fully understand the significance of Fiji's ongoing political turmoil without some comprehension of how the grassroots citizenry perceives and responds to the violence they have been forced to live through. How do people attempt to ascribe meaning to events that initially strike them as incomprehensible? Why do members of victimized communities circulate rumors and fantastical stories that heighten their feelings of panic? How do communities respond to individuals who cannot find a means of expressing their pain and terror? While this book cannot do justice to the range of peoples and perspectives involved in Fiji's numerous political upheavals, my aim is to contribute to this enterprise by focusing on the reactions of Indo-Fijians in Eastern Viti Levu to what has been Fiji's bloodiest round of terror. By doing so, I hope we can better understand how Indo-Fijians view their history, what the Fijian nation means to them, how they partake in the politics of racial divisiveness, and how they resist it.

A detailed analysis of citizens' responses to the 2000 political crisis in Fiji also contributes to the wider literature on nation-making in the Pacific. In recent years, there has been a growing body of inquiry into how Pacific states are constituted, the place of indigenous politics in the Pacific, and issues of political instability in the Pacific region.[15] Because of its South Asian migrants, Fiji is in some respects a unique case, but its history is of wider importance, as it

coup include Field, Baba, and Nabobo-Baba 2005; Kaplan 2003; Kelly and Kaplan 2001a; B. Lal 2003b, 2002b, 2000c, 2000d; Leckie 2002a, 2002b; Merry and Brenneis 2003; Robertson and Sutherland 2001; Teaiwa 2000; Tomlinson 2002b; Trnka 2005a, 2005c, 2004, 2002a, 2002b, 2002c, 2002d. More recent sources focusing on the aftermath of the 2006 coup include B. Lal 2007; Madraiwiwi 2007.

13. Some notable texts include Hermann and Kempf 2005; Kaplan 2004, 1993, 1988; Kaplan and Kelly 1994; Kelly 1998, 1995a, 1995b; Kelly and Kaplan 2001a, 1999; B. Lal 1999, 1995; V. Lal 1990; Lawson 1991; Teaiwa 2000.

14. Among the few scholarly accounts of the 1987 coups to offer ethnographically informed treatments are Kelly 1998, 1995a; and specifically on the coups' impact on women, both Lateef 1990 and Leckie 2000. There is also a wealth of fictional and biographical accounts of 1987, including Dean and Ritova 1988; Griffen 1997; Nandan 1991; Sharpham 2000; A. Singh 1992; Thomson 1999. Focusing on the events of 2000, there has been an edited volume (Trnka 2002a), a documentary film (L. Thomas 2002), and two collections of personal reflections (Field, Baba, and Nabobo-Baba 2005; Lal and Pretes 2001) that speak to this topic.

15. Examples include Foster 2002, 1995; Koli and Muckler 2002; Linnekin and Poyer 1990; Lockwood 2004; Merry and Brenneis 2003; N. Thomas 1997.

holds a prominent position in the Pacific and the economic repercussions of the country's political troubles have been felt throughout the region. An increasing number of Fijian citizens have, moreover, responded to the political turmoil by relocating to other parts of the Pacific, in particular Australia and New Zealand. Both of these factors make a deeper understanding of Fiji's political crises critical beyond the country's borders.

While, however, the specific individuals and events discussed in this book are particularly relevant to the Pacific, the broader issues of violence, pain, and ethnic identity that they raise are of interest to any region. Despite the increase in scholarship on political violence, questions still remain as to how groups collectively respond to and attempt to reconstitute social life in the face of nationwide trauma.

In thinking about these issues, I have focused on three areas of critical concern: violence and the boundaries that separate extraordinary moments of upheaval from everyday life; pain; and the constitution of ethnic identities in the modern nation-state.

Living on the Boundaries of Political Violence

The past decade has seen a growing anthropological literature on violence. Political anthropology has assessed the role of violence in the constitution of the state, with a number of scholars recently following the lead of political philosopher Giorgio Agamben (2005, 2002, 1998) to interrogate the impact of a sustained "state of exception" on our understandings of the place of violence in state governance and identity construction.[16] Ethnographers of structural violence have also given us vividly detailed examinations of how people experience ongoing violence in a variety of settings. Examples include Nancy Scheper-Hughes (1992) on "the violence of every day life" among the poor in Brazil; Philippe Bourgois (1996) on the structural effects of racism and cultural marginalization on drug dealers in Harlem; and Pierre Bourdieu and Alain Accardo (1999) on the daily struggles of the poor and other disadvantaged groups in France. These accounts vividly attest to situations where violence is normalized and experienced as part of daily living.

Intertwined with such regularized forms of violence are moments of intense and unexpected violent crises. These events, particularly when limited in duration, have a different dynamic. Despite their profound and

16. See, for example, L. Cohen 2004; Das 2004; Das and Poole 2004a, 2004b; Fassin and Vasquez 2005; Ferme 2004; Feuchtwang 2006; Pandolfo 2005. Others have focused more directly on refining Foucault's work on governmentality, pain, and violence (e.g., Feldman 1994; Mbembe 2003).

often enduring effects on daily life, the crises themselves are experienced as momentarily taking one outside of the boundaries of "ordinary life." Anthropological accounts of what are locally perceived as *extra-ordinary* moments of crises and the outbreaks of fear, panic, and in some cases, terror that they generate have focused on how such violence impinges on the subjectivity of victims and perpetrators; the cultural, historical, and political factors that shape how such violence is enacted; and the processes through which these events are remembered, repressed, or actively memorialized.[17]

Looking across these accounts, two characteristics of the experiential domain of violent crises emerge: the phenomenological reorientation of time and the struggle to grapple with experiences that surpass ordinary categories of action, affect, and meaning-making. Both of these points have been developed by anthropologist Veena Das in her work on "critical events," a term that I find particularly useful for discriminating between the experiential qualities of crises and what is taken as the "everyday," but that I would also like to further expand on here.

In her work on various turning points in Indian history, including the Partition and the 1984 anti-Sikh riots in Delhi, Das uses the concept of "critical events" to delineate moments that seem "almost hostile to the continuity of time" during which social life is suspended as people search for and "invent" new interpretations of events (1995, 200; see also 2007). Similar insights into how crises instigate a sense of a rupture in time have been suggested by Achille Mbembe and Janet Roitman (1995) in their analysis of a severe economic downturn in Cameroon and in Charles Briggs's (2003) examination of a deadly outbreak of cholera in Venezuela. All four authors describe these events as being experienced as moments out of time, appearing to those caught up in them as coming out of nowhere, without referents and outside of a known historical or social context. Seemingly without a temporal anchor, these moments are marked as Other to ordinary life. Mbembe and Roitman vividly characterize this experience as it was lived out in Cameroon:

> The sudden nature of this intrusion is well illustrated by popular expressions: "the crisis fell on our heads" and "I've got the crisis." This experience, which is at once intimate and dramatic, gives rise to narratives that no longer locate the crisis in an evolutionary history; that is to say, in a casual descrip-

17. There is a huge range of texts but some of the works that shape my analysis here include Aretxaga 1997; Daniel 1996; Das 1995, 2007; Das, Kleinman, Ramphele, and Reynolds 2000; Das, Kleinman, Lock, Ramphele, and Reynolds 2001; Feldman 1991; Greenhouse, Mertz, and Warren 2002; Kleinman, Das, and Lock 1997; Malkki 1995; Pandey 2001; Poole 1994; Strathern, Stewart, and Whitehead 2005; Tambiah 1996; Warren 1993b. This is by no means, however, a comprehensive list.

tion of an event that develops over a relatively long period of time. The experience and the imaginary of time that results are of a condensed, compressed and abrupt nature. Because of this contraction, the transformations taking place are not necessarily correlated to precise factors and historical references, even if one is aware that these elements do in fact exist. For lack of these referents, the crisis is exiled to the domain of inexplicable. (1995, 338)

As some of these authors also attest, the extremely unsettling experience of being plunged involuntarily into a "time outside of time" leads people to attempt to recontextualize "the crisis" into a broader historical time frame. Das suggests that in the midst of crises, the past takes on the quality of being unfinished and reopened as part of the present (2007, 1998). Particularly in situations where a similar sense of emergency (or emergencies) are part of local memory, moments of violence and social upheaval thought to have been relegated to the past return, almost as if the interval between the past and the present has vanished. To adapt Mbembe and Roitman's depiction of these dynamics, "evolutionary time" does not disappear but it too becomes fragmented and distorted so that the spaces in between violent events collapse as the past is recast into the present. The past is thus reopened in order to rethink its import for a present that seems strangely out of context and out of time. Ironically, it is because the present is felt to be distinct and *unlike any other time* that people struggle to fit the events they are living through into a larger context; as a consequence, the crisis that *was* becomes part of the crisis that *is*. Das has vividly shown how this occurs with images of the Partition of India in 1947 seeping into the midst of the 1980s anti-Sikh riots (2007).

The Fiji case is particularly enlightening in this regard because of the relatively short duration of the violence; the upheaval that followed Speight's entry into Parliament lasted just under six months. As a result, people never lost sight of a sense of something *outside* of the events they were experiencing, something other than the violence, locally referred to as "normalcy." The various efforts they undertook to restore this sense of "normalcy" into their lives will be discussed in detail in this book, but for now my point is that the 2000 crisis and the violence it instigated were never "normalized." Instead, the events of the 2000 coup were experienced as transporting people out of "ordinary time" and into the realm of the fantastical. Simultaneously, they instigated a rethinking of the past, as the 2000 coup came to be actively contextualized not in terms of the everyday flow of time but in relation to two prior events of extreme upheaval—the history of indenture and the coups of 1987.

One aspect of the phenomenological reorientation of time that has not received as much attention is the issue of tempo. In the midst of crises, the *lived* space of time is altered. As I discovered during the coup of 2000, there were moments when time seemed to move "fast forward" with one event tumbling into the next, hurtling people from one emotional and psychological space into another, before they could gather their bearings. At other points, there was a sense that "nothing" was actually happening but that violence loomed all around; in the midst of the fear and panic, people focused on preparing themselves for what was to come. In both of these spaces, the sense of daily rhythm was lost. There was no time to rest. Momentary breaks in this space of fear, through humor for example, provided rare and welcomed moments of relief. When the fear and panic finally died away, they were replaced by a deeply penetrating boredom. People could not return to their daily activities but found themselves listlessly waiting for the next thing to happen—be it another wave of chaos or the cessation of the crisis. As important as the sense of a loss of historical context and the lack of a temporal anchor are to the phenomenology of crises, so too are these changes in the tempo and tenor of daily life.

One area where the dramatically altered sensibility of time is most evident is in the difficulty people have in narrating the crisis. The disruption in their sense of "normal time" often leads to the production of fragmentary accounts in which links between events, particularly a sense of cause and effect, are absent. As Briggs tells us of the men in the delta community of Mariusa in eastern Venezuela,

> Instead of detailed descriptions of specific episodes laid out in chronological sequence and deftly connected by logical connections (*because* . . . , *in spite of* . . . , and the like), Mariusan men could only provide fragmentary and disjointed stories [of the cholera epidemic]. . . . The Mariusans were adept at using the sense-making power of storytelling to reinforce established cognitive and social orders. What happened to these narrative skills when cholera entered their lives? Why were the men in particular capable of telling only stories that they knew were grossly inadequate to depict their experiences and encourage their tenacity? As they related their stories . . . [they] were clearly attempting to make sense of their most baffling and terrifying moments—but terror can make a mockery of sense-making. (2003, 76–77)

Briggs attributes the Mariusan men's bafflement to their fractured sense of time, which makes the construction of linear narratives almost impossible. But as so many of these accounts attest, there is another, closely related factor that also contributes to making narration so challenging; intense crises not only alter the phenomenology of time but also the social categories of action, affect, and meaning-making through which the world is lived.

Whether they disrupt a form of sociality in which violence is rare or one in which particular forms of violence are considered part and parcel of daily life (Das 2007), violent crises are marked by their ability to throw taken-for-granted categories of social life into question. Das suggests that intense crises cause a "failure of the grammar of the ordinary," forcing a reevaluation of the categories through which experiences are thought, felt, evaluated, and given meaning. New modes of action come into being, opening up the possibility for new cultural forms and a necessary redefinition of previous categories of affect and meaning (2007, 8).

In a different context, anthropologist Marshall Sahlins's work on early encounters between British sailors and Hawaiians similarly emphasizes that while deeply embedded cultural values and social relations are retained and reenacted in moments of crisis, their usefulness is often challenged by the events at hand. In extreme circumstances this results in an unforeseen transformation of both cultural categories and related social structures (Sahlins 1981).

Anthropologists and social historians have given us a great deal of insight into how such revisions of the "taken-for-granted" categories of social life impact the subjectivities of individuals as well as how these radical revisions are enacted within cultural groups or within the nation-state.[18] This book acts as an addition to this literature by examining how the 2000 coup instigated collective reevaluation of what it means to be part of "the Fijian nation," local understandings of inter-ethnic "friendship," and perceptions of the ethnic identities of "Indian" and "Fijian."

Another aim of this text is to extend anthropological analysis of the *interpersonal* dynamics at play in such situations. Despite increasing attention to the intersubjective aspects of violence, anthropological and historical accounts of political violence tend to grant prominence to analyses of structural and symbolic transformations, changes in the public sphere, and broad discursive trends. In contrast, our understandings of the interpersonal negotiations through which meaning-making and affect are forged in the midst of crises remain more fragmentary.[19] I have tried to address this issue by focusing on a self-constituted community—an Indo-Fijian village, or *gaon*—and examining how on a day-to-day level, people's interactions with one another assist,

18. For sources, see the previous footnote.
19. Much of the recent work on subjectivity and violence, including many of the texts listed in footnote #17, endeavors to rectify this imbalance.

impede, and otherwise influence their efforts to make sense of and attribute meaning to crises. I have also endeavored to show how affects such as fear, confusion, and suffering are collectively constituted and how this occurs not only through widespread responses to nationwide phenomena (such as the shock caused by some news reports of the crisis) but also through interpersonal communications that stimulate certain forms of affective response. One of the means that I have found particularly useful for thinking through the interpersonal domain of these experiences is by considering how the 2000 coup gave rise to various collective embodiments, articulations, and silences of pain.

Pain

Much of this book is an examination of multiple forms and meanings of pain. As part of my assessment of the 2000 coup, I consider the pain caused by political chaos and social turbulence, the pain of corporeal violence, and the pain of witnessing large-scale economic destruction. I examine how people struggle to assess who are the likely victims of physical violence, who are the assailants, and what happens when these assessments are found to be at odds with the realities of violence. I look at how shops and businesses have come to symbolize Indo-Fijian labor and to embody Indo-Fijian pain when they were destroyed; explore how pain is proudly invoked as a marker of physical labor and a claim for Indo-Fijian political rights; and analyze collective enactments of pain through the sharing of violence narratives. I also suggest how pain is collectively silenced in an effort to return to social "normalcy." In doing so, I draw from a well-developed literature that questions both the shareability and communicability of pain.

There are many testimonies to the all-encompassing and alienating quality of pain. Hannah Arendt famously asserted in *The Human Condition* that

> the most intense feeling we know of, intense to the point of blotting out all other experiences, namely, the experience of great bodily pain, is at the same time the most private and least communicable of all. Not only is it perhaps the only experience which we are unable to transform into a shape fit for public appearance, it actually deprives us of our feeling for reality to such an extent that we can forget it more quickly and easily than anything else. There seems to be no bridge from the most radical subjectivity, in which I am no longer "recognizable," to the outer world of life. (1958, 50–51)

Literary critic Elaine Scarry has similarly argued that extreme pain transports the sufferer to a state beyond or outside of language. According to

Scarry, this incommunicable aspect of pain is dehumanizing and, echoing Arendt, experientially separates the subject from his or her social universe. As Scarry puts it, physical pain "does not simply resist language but actively destroys it" and thus "achieves its aversiveness in part by bringing about, even within the radius of several feet, [an] absolute split between one's sense of one's own reality and the reality of other persons" (1985, 4).

Various anthropological studies of those subjected to physical and psychological trauma have drawn on Arendt and Scarry's insights to depict pain as instigating a breakdown in communication between sufferers and nonsufferers and forcing a radical removal of the sufferer from society. E. Valentine Daniel describes acts of torture as part of collective violence in Sri Lanka as creating a "hyperindividualized self compacted in pain" (1996, 144). In his examination of sufferers of chronic pain, Byron Good similarly suggests that they live in a "separate world" which he describes, directly invoking Scarry's terminology, as "a world unmade by pain" (1992, 42).[20] Whether its initial source is physical or psychological, intense pain can moreover permeate the mind and the body of the sufferer so that the entire self is afflicted (J. Jackson 2005, 1994; see also Dormandy 2006).

Ethnographic accounts also, however, raise the possibility of languages of pain as a means of reintegrating subjects into the social world.[21] In his work on chronic pain patients in the United States and in China, Arthur Kleinman refers to pain as a "rhetoric of complaint" and an "idiom of distress," suggesting how sufferers actively engage in the possibility of communication through their expressions of pain (1992, 175, 170). Nadia Seremetakis (1990) has also shown how Greek mourning laments act to turn an individual woman's pain into a collective act of grieving, bringing women together through their mourning rituals.

How can we reconcile these different accounts? It seems to me that there are two distinct issues in Scarry and Arendt's suggestions of pain's isolating qualities. One is the question of whether pain can be communicated from one person to another and the second is whether pain can be shared. While Scarry, in particular, conflates these two, ethnographic evidence suggests it might be more fruitful to consider them separately.

20. There are many other examples one could consider, particularly in medical anthropology. See Das 1996a, 1990b; B. Good 1994; J. Jackson 2005, 1994, 1992; Johansen 2002; Kleinman 1992, 1986; and various contributors to Das and Kleinman's edited series on social suffering (Das, Kleinman, Lock, Ramphele, and Reynolds 2001; Das, Kleinman, Ramphele, and Reynolds 2000; Kleinman, Das, and Lock 1997).

21. These include Brodwin 1992; Cole 2004; Das 1996a, 1990b; Desjarlais 1992; Good, Good, Kleinman, and Brodwin 1992; Hooper and Ong 2005; Kleinman 1992; Seremetakis 1990.

In terms of communication, Scarry suggests that pain is distinct from all other emotions and sensations in that pain "more than any other phenomenon, resists objectification in language" (1985, 5). It is a fallacy, however, to suggest that other bodily sensations can somehow be fully communicated from one subject to another. Can love ever be fully articulated? Or sorrow? Some forms of pain may indeed be unique in their isolating qualities due to their intensity, duration, and the profound effects they have on the body, but the alienation this results in is due to factors other than pain's resistance to articulation.

Instead, I suggest that just as with other emotional and physical states, we must consider how pain is partially articulated through various forms of expression. During the 2000 crisis, such articulations included not only narratives of violence, expressions of despair, and racist diatribes but also jokes, rumors, and silence. All of these were partial, creative means of articulating pain. Some followed routine patterns of speech, others visibly involved a *struggle* for words or did not involve spoken language at all but were conveyed by silent gestures. Rather than attempting to assess whether these discourses enabled the full and complete transfer of one person's experience of pain to another (Scarry 1985), I suggest that through language itself, a form of communicable pain was constituted (Wittgenstein 1958; see also Das 1996a, 2007).

In doing so, I again draw inspiration from the work of Veena Das. Devoting her attention to the issues of language, alienation, and pain, Das offers an alternative to Scarry and Arendt's assessments by placing individuals' experiences within the broader framework of how pain is responded to by social groups and institutions. In her analyses of both the riots of the Partition (1996a) and the riots following the assassination of Indira Gandhi in Delhi in 1984 (1990a, 1996b), Das examines not only individuals' narratives of pain but also the language of the media and of the state; she parses through victims' retrospective accounts of the riots, the slogans that the rioters chanted, media coverage, and the bureaucratic forms used by police and relief workers in their official assessments of the violence. Das's examination of such a wide array of materials reflects her concern that individual victim's expressions of pain cannot be analyzed in isolation but must be put into the contexts of how languages of pain are actually enacted (cf. Wittgenstein 1958), in this case by the members of their families, other victims, those responsible for the violence, and the various institutional bodies with which victims must contend. In doing so, Das concludes, as I understand her, that expressions of pain are an act of communication that is both fallible and simultaneously possible. As she puts it, "The sentence 'I am in pain' becomes the conduit through which

I may move out of an inexpressible privacy and suffocation of my pain. This does not mean that I am understood" (1996a, 70).

The wide range of possible comprehensions of pain, and the severity of their implications, becomes clearer if one looks at Das's case materials. In her examination of the victims of the 1984 anti-Sikh riots, Das devotes a large section of her text to a detailed discussion of the plight of a woman who loses her husband and son in the riots (1990b). Unable to recover her sense of living in the present and to find meaning in her relationships with surviving kin (including her daughters and father-in-law), she continually relives the events of the tragedy until she ends up committing suicide. This particular woman's story is counterpoised against those of many other survivors who Das depicts as forming a "community of women healers" and undertaking a "collective mourning" (1990b, 361, 362) that allows them to move away from the past and reengage with the present and with an imagined future. Even though they too suffered extreme losses, these women were able to find ways to express their experiences by symbolically speaking through their living spaces and refusing to clean up the human remains, ashes, and blood that littered their homes, and later, by verbally making claims for the relief assistance that was offered to them. They wanted, Das writes, "to find some way by which the truth of their suffering could be made known to the world" (1990b, 363).

Das's examination of pain and the communicative aspects of language and bodily symbolism offers a way around the impasse suggested by Scarry and Arendt in that she allows for the possibility of radical alienation through pain, but also documents how expressions of pain can transform not only individuals but become the shared catalyst for new community identities and revised approaches to constructing meaningful everyday life.

In addition to the issue of pain's *communicability,* a second issue thrown into question by Scarry and Arendt's accounts is its *shareability.* Again, ethnographic evidence suggests that some forms of pain may be experienced as isolating and alienating, but there are also moments in which pain is *collectively* experienced, without it necessarily having been actively communicated from one person to another. Jadran Mimica's (1996) analysis of shared sensations of pain among the Iqwaye of New Guinea suggests that pain which is physically located in one person's body can indeed result in pain being felt by another person.[22] Mimica gives the example of a mother who feels pain as she watches her child's boil being ruptured. Mimica's

---

22. Though Mimica does not engage with Wittgenstein, this is precisely the question posed in Wittgenstein's *The Blue and the Brown Books* (1958; see also Das 1996a).

point is not that the mother and child go through the *same* experience, but that both feel pain even though the physical act is located only in the child's body. Mimica concludes that "neither sickness nor pain are modes of personal being; nor are they experiences which in their manifestations, are exclusively restricted to the person subjected to them" (1996, 225).

Another example comes from Jean Jackson's (2005, 1992) work on the embodiment of pain by chronic pain sufferers. Analyzing interactions between patients at a chronic pain center, Jackson found that when patients first entered the center, they tended to actively verbalize their pain (1992). But after about a week in residence, patients fell quiet, no longer feeling the need to state that they were in pain, nor to wince or grimace. Her interviews with patients revealed that once they realized that they were in a space where other people were similarly in pain and understood and accepted the veracity of their experience, they did not need to express it. In a similar vein, Robert Desjarlais (1992) looks at the wordless communication of pain not amongst sufferers, but between sufferers and healers. Desjarlais describes how Nepalese shamans derive a sense of their patients' pain through sensory knowledge. While they may not "fully" share their patients' suffering, shamans claim to *sense* what is wrong with their patients in their own bodies to the extent that they are able to act on it, and sometimes heal it, without the pain having to be verbalized. In all of these accounts it is *not* the act of expressing pain through language but of it being *felt* by others that makes pain a shareable experience.

My material focuses primarily on pain that is put into language, but I am similarly interested in how articulations of pain may result in its collective embodiment. In analyzing narratives of violence, I suggest that these forms of discourse not only allowed narrators and their audiences to ascribe meaning to events of violence, but also instigated a reenactment of the pain of the violence. Narrators and audience members thus came to collectively embody the pain of attacks even if they were not present during the actual event of violence. I do *not* contend that such narratives "fully" communicated victims' experiences to others, nor that the pain that others felt was the same as that felt by the victim of the attack. Rather, I wish to show how language not only conveyed the events of the violence but simultaneously stimulated collective embodiments of pain, fear, and in some cases, joyous release from the chaos.

Ethnic Identity

In addition to trying to get through the 2000 crisis, many people in Fiji were intensely engaged in attempting to ascribe meaning to the events that followed Speight's storming of Parliament. One of their underlying concerns was to come to terms with the place that "ethnic difference" might have played in both the governmental takeover and the civilian violence that followed it. In examining the conceptions of ethnicity and race that they employed to do so, I find the work of Fredrik Barth a useful starting point.

In 1969, Barth proposed a new approach to understandings of ethnicity by focusing scholarly attention on the flexibility of ethnic groups and the boundaries between them. In contrast to previous scholarship, which had defined ethnicity as an objective, static, and in-born quality, Barth proposed that we look at ethnic groups as subjective groupings with shifting and malleable boundaries. As such, he called for a move away from ethnographic attempts to catalogue the so-called "objective" cultural attributes of particular ethnic groups (such as their clothing styles, language, food, etc.) and toward analyses of the processes by which groups negotiate the ethnic boundaries that demarcate them. As Barth put it, "The critical focus of investigation from this point of view becomes the ethnic *boundary* that defines the group, not the cultural stuff that it encloses" (1969, 15).

Barth's insights into the transactional nature of ethnicity have had a major impact on studies of ethnicity and ethnic difference since the early 1970s. There have, however, been a number of developments in scholarly understandings of ethnicity since the publication of Barth's *Ethnic Groups and Boundaries*. Barth's exclusive focus on the boundaries between ethnic groups has been tempered by anthropologists who have insisted on the historical, political, and cultural importance of the "cultural stuff" that groups use to identify themselves (A. Cohen 1974; Geertz 1973; Linnekin and Poyer 1990; N. Thomas 1992). One question that they have raised is if ethnic boundaries are indeed as malleable as Barth suggested, then how are the seemingly primordial sentiments of ethnicity inculcated? Many have responded by examining how the specific attributes of ethnic-group identification are selected. Nicholas Thomas, for example, turns his attention to the historical processes by which ethnic identities are created, urging us to be aware of the dynamics that "determine what specific practices, manners, or local ethics are rendered explicit and made to carry the burden of local identity" (1992, 213). Others, such as Lisa Malkki (1995), Arjun Appadurai (1998), and Mary Weismantel (2001), have interrogated the links between perceptions of ethnicity and cultural constructions of "race," with particular emphasis on the place of the body in the construction of ethnic identity. Barth himself later noted that in his desire to move away from cataloguing "objective criteria" he may have deemphasized the

importance of the specific values and behaviors out of which ethnic identifications are made (1994).

Another critique of Barth's work was that it sidelined the relationship
between ethnicity and other forms of collective identity such as national,
regional, and local identities, religion, race, class, caste, chiefly and other
status-based rankings, sexuality and gender, all points picked up by more
recent scholarship.[23]

By the late 1980s anthropologists such as Stanley Tambiah (1989) were
calling for a radical revision of Barth's work, particularly given the rising
tide of violence that employs "ethnicity" as one of its motivating forces. Indeed, while its focus was ethnic opposition, Barth's text had very little to
say about violence. Today there is a burgeoning scholarship on ethnic conflict, much of it focusing on the interrelationship between political violence
and the constitution of ethnic identities, as well as the relationships between ethnic identification and other forms of social cleavage. Numerous
scholars have shown how political violence either exacerbates preexisting
ethnic divisions or creates new forms of ethnic opposition.[24]

My approach to the place of ethnicity in Fiji is to employ Barth's appre-
ciation of the constructed and oppositional nature of ethnic boundaries
without losing sight of the historical, political, and symbolic processes behind the selection of the "cultural stuff" that particular ethnic and racial
identities are seen to entail. In assessing the relationship between political
violence and what is locally conceptualized as "race" in Fiji, I argue that for
many Indo-Fijians their identity as "Indians" is crucial in determining how
they should navigate their way through daily life (such as in their assessments of whether or not they are likely to be targeted by violence during
times of political upheaval) and as the basis of their claims to citizenship
and the right to remain in Fiji. As we shall see in the chapters that follow,
many Indo-Fijians accepted interpretations of the 2000 and 1987 coups as
rooted in inherent racial differences between "Indians" on the one hand
and "Fijians" on the other. Indeed, it is one of the aims of this book to show
how political upheavals that are motivated by a number of various factors,
including class and regional differences and personal aspirations for political power, were represented to the populace as an "ethnic conflict" and how

23. Some of the many texts include Alonso 1994; Bax 1997; Partha Chatterjee 1993; R. Cohen 1978; John Comaroff 1987; Das 1996b; Hayden 1996; Pandey 2001; Tambiah 1989; Verdery
1994; B. Williams 1995, 1991, 1989.

24. See, for example, Appadurai 1998; Bowman 1994; Carmichael 2006; Daniel 1996; Hayden 1996; Malkki 1995; Mehta and Chatterji 2001; Sekulíc, Massey, and Hodson 2006; Volkan
2006; R. Williams 2003.

many people, *despite* their awareness of these other factors, adopted this mode of thinking.

However, in contrast to a growing literature, both academic and in the popular press, that suggests that acts of inter-ethnic violence, whatever the complexities of motivations that lead to them, are perceived by grass-roots communities as reducible to the logic of ethnic or racial differences between "us" and "them,"[25] I found that Indo-Fijians' responses to the 2000 coup were more complicated than this. For the most part, they did indeed view coup-related violence in racial terms and partake in the broader reification of racial categories. But their accounts of rural, inter-personal violence between Fijian assailants and Indian victims also raised important questions about the influence of other personal characteristics (especially age and gender), interpersonal relationships, and local histories on such events. Particularly in situations where victims and assailants knew one another, narrative accounts of interpersonal violence indicated a more nuanced awareness of the many processes that result in "inter-ethnic conflict." In accordance with an emergent line of scholarship that indicates the need to assess the more subtle *interplay* between ethnic identities, other forms of identity (including gender, class, and geographic location), and local, inter-personal relationships (Das 1996b; Megoran 2007; Neofotistos 2004; Tambiah 1996), I suggest how these narratives force us to think more carefully about how members of victimized communities respond to the variety of people who end up categorized as "the ethnic Other."

Fieldwork in the Midst of Violence

The three themes of violence, pain, and ethnic identity were central concerns throughout the course of my fieldwork, but I could never have predicted how they would manifest themselves in the events I ended up documenting. Many fieldworkers find themselves encountering incidents in the field that they could not have foreseen and had little or no intention of studying. In situations of violence, all of the challenges that come with "being there" (Geertz 1988) are furthermore compounded by the necessity of dealing with the inherent instability of intense crises (cf. Nordstrom and Robben 1995). My ethnographic experience was an acute example of this.

25. Authors who make such arguments include Appadurai 1998; Bax 1997; Bowman 1994; Daniel 1996; Jansen 2003; Loizos 1988; Sekulić, Massey and Hodson 2006; Volkan 2006.

Like most people in Fiji, I had no inkling that there was a coup in the making when in October 1999, after nine months of conducting research on Hindu community life and studying Fiji Hindi in Suva, I moved into a small village on the outskirts of Nausori Town. I lived in that village, which I call by the pseudonym of Darshan Gaon, with my husband and our three-year-old daughter, and later our second daughter who was born in Fiji, until the end of October 2000.

Located just over ten miles to the north of downtown Suva, Darshan Gaon is a thriving, multi-ethnic neighborhood. Once the site of European sugar plantations and a handful of small-scale Chinese commercial vegetable farms, residential settlement in the area blossomed as part of the increasing urban sprawl that started in the 1950s. Today, there is no longer any sugar cultivation, the Chinese vegetable farmers have moved on, and only a handful of Indo-Fijian residents rely on small-scale commercial agriculture to eke out a modest living.[26] Most of Darshan Gaon's current residents are small-time tradespeople, teachers, or minor civil servants who were attracted by the village's proximity to Nausori Town and Suva as well as the fact that it is composed of freehold land, which can be bought and sold on the open market.[27] The majority, but not all, of them are also Indo-Fijians; the results of a household survey I undertook of Darshan Gaon in mid-2000 revealed that of the 56 households in the village, 73 percent were Indian, 23 percent were Fijian, and the remainder were Pacific Islander or multi-ethnic.[28]

The first part of my time in Darshan Gaon was spent gathering material on how discourses of physical pain and the legacy of indenture inform Indo-Fijian identity. My interest in violence was firmly focused on examining the enduring impact of historical events that had occurred a century before. In addition to conducting participant observation in a nearby medical clinic, most of my days were spent in Darshan Gaon, visiting families

26. The Colonial Sugar Refinery established Fiji's first cane crushing plant in Nausori in 1880. Because the conditions for cultivating sugarcane were more favorable on the western side of the island, the plant was shut down in 1959.

27. Only 8 percent of all land in Fiji is fee simple land that can be bought by any Fiji citizen, regardless of ethnic background (Reddy and Lal 2002). Most rural Indo-Fijians must rent land that is owned by Fijian land-owning units, or *mataqalis*. Most rural Fijians live on land owned by their own mataqalis or on land they either informally borrow or formally rent from other Fijian land-owning units.

28. The most recent official statistics for the greater Nausori area are from 1996 when 66 percent of the population was estimated to be Indian as compared to 30 percent Fijian and 4 percent "Other." "Other" is a designation that is used by the Fiji Bureau of Statistics to cover a multitude of people including Asians, so-called "Europeans," and people from other Pacific Island nations.

in their homes, cooking, helping to mind their children, and getting tips on how I should better mind my own. While I got to know many of the village men, particularly during the coup when a number of them were actively involved in ensuring my family's and my own safety, most of my time was spent with Indo-Fijian women, many of whom took it on themselves to reeducate me into their vision of a proper Hindu woman.[29]

One area of their lives in which they very eagerly involved me was their religious practices. As in other parts of Fiji, religious activities in Darshan Gaon occupy a large part of residents' time and expenditure. Whether Hindu, Christian, or Muslim, many people live out not only their spiritual but also familial, social, educational, and sometimes part of their business lives through social networks that have developed out of the local, national, and transnational religious organizations in which they take part.

The bulk of Darshan Gaon's Indo-Fijian residents belong to the same religion, identifying as *Sanatanis*, or practitioners of what is locally considered the "traditional" form of Hinduism.[30] In the village there are three *mandalis*, or locally based prayer groups, whose members meet at least once a week, and sometimes more frequently, to pray and read the *Ramayana*. Some mandali members engage in almost daily interactions with one another, not only to pray, but also to plan large-scale religious functions, take part in family events such as weddings and children's birthdays, gossip, and exchange

29. During most of the political turmoil, women and men no longer felt safe congregating in public and, when not at work, spent much of their time within their individual households. Within these, there was a noticeable change in how space was arranged according to gender, a fact that allowed me much more informal access to men than I had had in the past. Previously, when my family visited other families in their homes, my husband would join the men and boys outside on the porch or under the awning of the house, while the women and I stayed inside. During the coup, however, out of concern for their personal safety as well as their desire to stay close to the radio and television for news updates, men tended to stay inside, sharing the living room with the women of the household. As a result I was able to spend a lot more time casually talking with men than I had prior to the political upheaval. Some men in the village also became much more involved in my daily activities due to their concern over my family's safety. They invited us into their homes during curfew so that we would not need to be alone in the evening. They also assisted us in ways that women, who had less access to certain kinds of resources and forms of public influence, were unable to do. When, for example, my telephone line was cut a few months into the coup, two men from Darshan Gaon, who expressed concern not only about my overall safety but also about my ability to get medical care while pregnant, went to great lengths to use their contacts at the local telephone agency to have it reinstalled.

30. The two main Hindu groups in Fiji are the *Arya Samaj*, a reformist branch of Hinduism that was founded in Mumbai in 1875 and attracts a minority of followers in Fiji, and the *Sanatan Dharm* (or "eternal religion"), which is locally considered to be the more "orthodox" version of Hinduism and attracts a much larger following. There are also various Hindu sects that have been gaining in popularity since the 1987 coups, including the Hari Krishnas and the Sai Baba mission (Kelly 1995a).

food. Religious involvement is particularly intense during large-scale festivals. In the days leading up to Holi, Ram Naumi, and Diwali, many devotees will attend one or more prayer ceremonies a day. In addition to their religious significance, these events are also sites for the exchange of community gossip, political opinion, and national and international news.

Alongside kinship ties, which link together more than a quarter of Darshan Gaon's Indo-Fijian households, these religious ties go far in creating a palpable sense of community solidarity. Most Indo-Fijian residents of Darshan Gaon proudly refer to the area as a "village," or gaon, and had no hesitation in correcting me when I initially spoke of it as a satellite neighborhood of Suva. Devi, a forty-five-year-old Hindu woman who became one of my closest companions during my fieldwork, once empathically asserted to me, "We do not live in the city. We are *gaonwallahs* (villagers)."

Over the months that I came to know them, Devi and other residents of Darshan Gaon explained to me how as gaonwallahs, they (and now I, as a member of the village, they informed me) were morally obligated to one another. Gaonwallahs must, for example, attend each other's weddings and funerals, take care of neighbors who are sick or elderly, and exchange food and labor on a casual basis. As part of this village ethos, many Indo-Fijian men and women also claimed to have intimate knowledge of one another's lives to the extent that the clothes that they wore, what they ate for dinner, how often they saw the doctor, how they prayed, or whom they did business with were all open for community comment. The webs of social interaction that bound Indo-Fijian families in Darshan Gaon together were very rarely, however, extended to their Fijian or Pacific Islander neighbors. In contrast to the intimacies they shared with other Indo-Fijian families, Indo-Fijian residents were often unclear about basic facts about their Fijian neighbors, nor did they engage in much communication or material exchange with them.

One result of the close ties between Darshan Gaon's Indo-Fijian residents was that the village became a critical site in shaping their responses to the coup of May 2000. Anxious and fearful, and at times locked in their homes for days on end due to the military curfew and their concerns over violence, Indo-Fijian residents turned to one another in this time of intense crisis. For the most part, it was their Indo-Fijian neighbors, friends, and kin with whom they shared their despair and terror and with whom they attempted to regain a sense of stability.

The Impact of the Coup

The most profound and immediate impact of the May 2000 coup on neighborhoods such as Darshan Gaon was that it opened up an atmosphere of overwhelming confusion and fear. People struggled to make sense of daily and sometimes hourly changes in a political situation that had a tremendous impact on their personal safety. In Darshan Gaon, as in other areas hit by violence, residents were forced to continually question and make new sense of the world in which they lived. I, in turn, was forced to reconsider the usefulness of ethnographic approaches to knowledge not only for the sake of ethnography, but also regarding its usefulness in assessing the safety of my informants, my family, and myself.

Due to the radical changes in social and political life following the coup, the nature and scope of my fieldwork were irrevocably altered. Instead of attending communitywide prayer ceremonies, I found myself documenting countless accounts of physical attacks. Hour after hour was spent sitting with my neighbors, trying to come to terms with the crisis. What was at stake—for them, as well as for me—in understanding the ever-changing political landscape had dramatically shifted.

The coup also affected me in some very intense and personal ways. The months following May 19 were a time of profound trauma, and like many of the people I write about, I am still haunted by some of the events that took place. I will never forget the evening my husband silently moved a machete next to our bed, should we need to defend ourselves in the night. Or the time our neighbors heard the gunfire of a rebel shootout about half a mile away. They called us up in the middle of the night to demand that I immediately flee the village while my husband, they suggested, stay behind to protect the house we were renting from them.

But by far the most terrifying experience for me was the night I went into labor with my second child and had to drive past two military checkpoints after curfew. I had been told by my doctor that the military could hardly stop a woman in labor. But it seems he did not have as much insight into the mind of an eighteen-year-old soldier as he thought. We were held up for twenty minutes while a soldier with a semiautomatic rifle questioned me about why I needed to see my doctor in the capital when there was a small maternity clinic closer by in Nausori Town. I struggled to answer him in between contractions. When he finally waived us through, my husband pleaded with him to call ahead to the next military checkpoint to warn them of our arrival. But there the whole farce was played out once again. Two days later we went through similar checkpoints in an ambulance on our way to evacuate our critically-ill newborn to New Zealand.

As my husband and I went through these experiences, our relationships with villagers in Darshan Gaon intensified. While I do not want to elide the many differences between our situations, such as the fact that I had a ticket back to my home in the United States while many of them were anxiously—and in many cases unsuccessfully—attempting to get travel visas out of Fiji, there was also a feeling that we were in it together. Each of us was scrambling to make sense of events and through our various personal connections, access to information, and familiarities of Fijian and international politics, we all had something to contribute. When a new rumor of impending violence broke out, I would call friends at the University of the South Pacific or at the Australian Embassy. My neighbors would call relatives on the other side of the island or acquaintances who worked in one of the government ministries. We would then compare various versions of similar stories that we had heard, trying to assess together which of the variations was more credible.

Because of my pregnancy, many villagers were especially protective of me. And as my pregnancy progressed into its ninth month, it became clear that even if I wanted to, I would not be able to leave Fiji and my reliance on them increased. Indeed, despite the feelings of insecurity I had about staying in the village as the violence rose and subsided, it was my feeling of being embedded in various emotional relationships of care and support with village residents that made it emotionally easier to stay rather than to leave.

In the end, it was my personal participation in these relationships, made so much more intense during the coup, that compelled me to think and write about violence as something experienced not only on a personal, familial, or national level, but in terms of how it collectively impacts a self-constituted community as well the meanings of "community" and the collective identities that they hold. The flipside to this is that my assessment of the 2000 coup is contingent on the social relations that I developed in the field. While I have, wherever possible, supplemented accounts from indigenous Fijian sources as well as from the media and from other academic sources, I have relied primarily on my experiences living and conversing with Indo-Fijian residents in Darshan Gaon and elsewhere in Nausori and Suva. No doubt the stories I would have collected and the story I would have written would have been different had I been living on the western side of Viti Levu rather than the eastern side, or had I spent most of my time in a Fijian *koro* (village) rather than in an Indian gaon.

The Layout of this Book

This book is organized into seven chapters. In chapter 2, I assess how the various parties involved in the 2000 coup employed racially inflammatory rhetoric to rally their supporters and suggest how and why a coup that was not fundamentally motivated by racial antagonism nonetheless opened up a space for anti-Indian violence.

Chapter 3 examines Indo-Fijians' first reactions to the 2000 coup, particularly their expressions of pain, fear, and their overall lack of comprehension of what was happening. Examining evocations of the fantastic, I look at how rumors gave voice to the incredulity many were feeling and in the processes added to their sense of panic. I also reflect on how jokes and other forms of humor acted as outlets for anxiety and suggested conceptual limits to how "fantastic" everyday life can get.

In chapter 4, I examine why Indo-Fijian despair in the first few weeks following May 19 focused on violence against shops and businesses (the majority of which were owned by local Indo-Fijians, Gujaratis, and foreign firms), rather than the destruction of Indo-Fijian homes, schools, and temples or even direct physical attacks against Indo-Fijians themselves.[31] Considering how shops and other commercial businesses were perceived as embodying generations of physical labor and suffering from indenture to the present-day, I observe how the value of physical industriousness and the pain it incurs play a central role in many Indo-Fijians' conceptualizations of themselves as Hindus, as Indians, and as citizens of Fiji.

Chapter 5 considers how the coup heightened perceptions of irreconcilable ethnic difference, leading some Indo-Fijians to suggest that ethnically distinct work ethics, economic practices, and levels of "civilization" were the source of the conflict. Examining the historical roots of Indo-Fijian portrayals of themselves as at the forefront of clearing away "the jungles" of Fiji and developing the national economy, I consider how the opposition of "civilized" Indian and "jungli" Fijian came into being. I also suggest how the events of the coup led many Indo-Fijians to fear that Fiji was on the brink of reverting into "jungle" again.

Chapter 6 focuses on Indo-Fijian reactions to inter-ethnic attacks that occurred primarily in rural areas. Here I examine how initial, abbreviated announcements of multiple attacks, which I refer to as "inventories of violence," were collectively recast into narrative accounts that not only attempted to give recognizable form to violent events but also stimulated collective enactments of pain. I also consider how the chaotic nature of the violence, the confusion suffered and expressed by victims who both visibly embodied the violence and, at times, disavowed its impact on their bodies,

31. There is a local distinction made between the category of "Indians" that encompasses all of those who are the descendants of indentured laborers and "Gujaratis," many of whom are merchants (or the descendants of merchants) who came over to Fiji from Gujarat on their own accord.

and the variety of relationships between indigenous Fijians and Indo-
Fijians that were represented in narratives of attack, forced Indo-Fijians to
go beyond racial stereotypes as they contended with multiple and competing ways of coping with and making meaning out of violence.

In chapter 7, I document how once the violence stopped, during a political and social period that the military optimistically called a return to "normalcy," Indo-Fijians actively attempted to forget the traumatic events of
the coup. I suggest that localized, collective efforts to keep silent and actively silence one another were therapeutic moves intended to anchor the
events of the coup into the past and allow the wounds of violence to heal.

The book closes with a reflection on the continuing impact of the 2000
coup. Eight years and one coup later, I consider how the 2000 coup's legacy
continues to shape social and political life in Fiji and consider Indo-Fijians'
prospects for the future. After more than 125 years in Fiji, the question of
what part these "foreigners" might play in their homeland still remains to be
answered.

2 The Coup of May 2000—An Invitation to Anti-Indian Violence

On July 8, 2000, a number of Indo-Fijian wedding guests from neighboring towns and villages traveled to a wedding in Korovou Town in Tailevu, about thirty miles north of Suva. As bad luck would have it, the wedding took place on the same day that Korovou Town was overtaken by rebels. According to newspaper reports as well as accounts told to me by residents of Darshan Gaon where one of the wedding party lived, the van in which the wedding guests were traveling was stopped by a group of Fijian men with cane knives. The passengers were ordered to hand over all of their belongings, including their money, watches, shoes, and eyeglasses. They were released frightened but unharmed. A few days later, police in the area stated that they knew the muggers' identities. But, the police claimed, the assailants were immune from arrest because of the amnesty provisions in the recently signed Muanikau Accord, which stipulated that all "political acts" from the date of George Speight's takeover up until July 13, 2000, were accorded amnesty ("Thugs Raid . . ." 2000, 8).

The attack against the wedding party was mild in comparison to much of the violence that was occurring in Fiji during this period. What is noteworthy, however, about this incident is how a political accord intended to provide amnesty for those guilty of coup-related offences was interpreted to include the mugging and harassment of a group of people traveling to a wedding. There was no suggestion that the Fijians who carried out the mugging were directly involved with the rebel forces. Nor was there any hint that the Indo-Fijians were doing anything other than attending a wedding. So how did an interethnic mugging come to be perceived as an excusable "political act"?

Let us begin our examination of this issue by considering the enduring role that perceptions of "race" have played in Fiji's political history.

Ethnic Relations up to 2000

The 2000 political coup and the violence that accompanied it have their roots in over a century of political turmoil that has been locally portrayed as a struggle between Fiji's two primary "races" over their right to live in and take part in the governance of Fiji.

Soon after Fiji became a British colony in 1874, its first governor, Sir Arthur Gordon, initiated the importation of Indian laborers. The purpose of the scheme was twofold: it would provide the backbone of the colony's labor force, and it would allow Fiji's native inhabitants, who practiced a subsistence-based lifestyle, to remain outside of market-based labor. Members of the colonial government expected that most of the indentured laborers, or girmitiyas, who numbered approximately sixty thousand, would leave Fiji following the completion of their contracts (Kelly 1991a). They were, however, mistaken, and the majority stayed on, later to be joined by independent migrants from Gujarat and the Punjab.

The government was left with the task of administering a colony made up not only of a diverse array of indigenous Fijian tribes, who differed from one another in terms of language, political structure, and social and religious customs, but also a variety of Hindu, Muslim, and Christian migrants from North and South India. It did so by attempting to unify and codify indigenous Fijian culture on the one hand and pitting indigenous Fijians against Indo-Fijians on the other. The result was a deeply divided society whose legacy is at the basis of the political troubles occurring today.

For decades following the introduction of indentured labor, Fijians and Indo-Fijians lived under radically different socioeconomic conditions, with most Fijians engaged in a subsistence lifestyle in rural koros, or villages, while Indo-Fijians were firmly entrenched in capitalist labor, first as indentured laborers and then as small-time farmers or business owners. The differences between the two groups were reinforced by colonial policies that kept Fijian commoners out of the labor market. Under colonial regulations, Fijians and Indians were also subject to enforced residential segregation with little opportunity to live together or to interact socially.

Some of these differences began to be stripped away with increasing urbanization and the incorporation of more indigenous Fijians into the wage labor market, initially in the 1960s and increasingly so in the early 1970s (for details, see Griffin and Monsell-Davis 1986; Nayacakalou 1963;

Ponter 1986). Today 40 percent of the indigenous Fijian population lives in urban areas (B. Lal 2003a, 674). But the social divide between Indo-Fijians and Fijians remains, in large part because of religious, linguistic, cultural, and economic practices that were encouraged by colonial policies. While there is increasing interaction between Indo-Fijians and Fijians, many still maintain ethnically segregated social and familial lives.

In both rural and urban areas there is much less contact between Fijians and Indo-Fijians than there is between residents of the same ethnic group. Both Fijians and Indo-Fijians must learn English at school, but many feel more comfortable speaking their mother tongue: Fiji Hindi among Indo-Fijians and one of the various dialects of Fijian among Fijians. Those with limited formal schooling have particular trouble communicating with anyone outside of their ethnic group. Social interactions are further constrained by many Indo-Fijians' concerns over eating "polluted" food; the majority of Indo-Fijians are Hindus, and many of them refrain from sharing food with Fijians as well as with Muslims because of concerns that they might inadvertently consume beef or food that has been in contact with beef. While there are cases of intermarriage, many people in Fiji claim never to have heard of such a thing, much less to contemplate such a possibility for themselves or for their children.

Ethnic identification continues to have a huge impact on one's economic life. The majority of land can be owned only by those who are officially identified as indigenous Fijian. Many rural areas furthermore retain ethnically divided settlement patterns with Fijians living in tight-knit koros, while Indo-Fijians are dispersed across sprawling cane settlements. Certain forms of labor are still largely ethnically segregated, there are quotas and "glass ceilings" on Indo-Fijians in public service, and some labor unions are ethnically divided. There is, for instance, a teachers' union for Fijians (the Fijian Teachers Association) and a teachers' union that is intended to be multiethnic but is made up predominantly by Indo-Fijians (the Fiji Teachers Union).

Political life is also organized along ethnic lines, with a number of the major political parties addressing their policies not to the populace as a whole, but championing the needs and perceived rights of particular ethnic groups. To a large part this is necessitated by Fiji's political structure, as more than half of the seats in the Parliament are allotted by ethnicity (B. Lal 2003a).

National identity is, moreover, popularly expressed through the relationships various ethnic groups are perceived to have to the nation, as well as to each other. The 1997 Constitution is notable for being the first to use an umbrella term for all the peoples of Fiji, defining all citizens as "Fiji Islanders." The use of this term was, however, hotly contested, particularly by some nationalist Fijians who saw it as tantamount to the theft of their Fijian identity (B. Lal 1999). Outside of references specifically to the constitution, this term is rarely employed and does not reflect the racialized ways that most people in Fiji speak of the nation and its citizens. It is more common for people to draw distinctions between Fiji's different "racial" groups and their particular relationships to the nation (see also B. Lal 1999). Among indigenous Fijians, the most commonly used term for the people of Fiji, *kai Viti*, is restricted to indigenous Fijians (Matthew Tomlinson, personal communication). Nor is there, as far as I am aware, any commonly used linguistic equivalent in Fiji Hindi to "Fiji Islanders" or even to "the people of Fiji."

At the same time as colonial policies created divisions between Indo-Fijians and Fijians, they also instigated the creation of pan-Fijian and pan-Indian identities, which remain controversial and contested to this day. Governor Gordon expressed a strong desire to "protect" Fijian culture, or rather his vision of Fijian culture. Faced, however, with a dazzling diversity of Fijian languages, systems of land use, and other customs, he initiated the unification and systematization of Fijian "tradition" through such things as the establishment of the Great Council of Chiefs (GCC), the widespread adoption of the Bau dialect, and a single system of land-ownership based on the mataqali, or land-owning unit (France 1969). Gordon's attempt to unify "Fijian culture" had mixed success. Moreover, the resulting tension between the promotion of a pan-Fijian perspective, on the one hand, and regional and tribal identifications, alongside differences in class and between those with commoner and chiefly status, on the other, has continued to have major repercussions for contemporary Fijian politics.

Indenture also created new cultural forms among the girmitiyas, including the breakdown of caste among Hindus and the imposition of a unifying language commonly referred to as *Fiji bāt* or "Fiji Hindi" (Jayawardena 1980; Moag 1977). The experience of indenture, and in particular the hardships it involved, furthermore provided the basis for a unique historical identity that has informed the self-perceptions of contemporary Indo-Fijians.

But just as there is no singular Fijian culture, there continue to be significant distinctions among Fiji's Indians. These include differences on the basis of religion. About 77 percent of Indo-Fijians are Hindus. The majority of Hindus identify with the Sanatani branch of Hinduism and distinguish themselves from Arya Samajis and members of other minority Hindu groups. Another 16 percent are Muslim, most of whom are Sunni.[1] The remainder include Christians of various denominations, Sikhs, members of minority religious groups (such as the Bahai), and those without any religious affiliation. There are also cultural differences between Indo-Fijians whose families came from North India versus those from South India. Significant class and cultural distinctions exist between the descendants of indentured laborers and Punjabis and Gujaratis who migrated to Fiji of their own free will, many coming in the early 1900s. The Gujaratis in particular are recognized as making up a large proportion of Fiji's small traders and business elite (see Ali 1980b; Kelly 1992) and are often considered by other Indo-Fijians to be more "traditional" and caste oriented, and to keep closer ties to India.[2]

The political system, both before and following colonial rule, has required, however, that political participation be conducted through the rubric of "race." Despite repeated attempts on the part of various political leaders to promote solidarities that cut across ethnic divisions, the structure of political participation and political rights in Fiji since the early days of colonialism has remained a racialized one.

A History of Racialized Politics

At the end of indenture in 1920, Indian community leaders made continued demands for improved political representation in Fiji, particularly for the establishment of a system of noncommunal (i.e., nonracial) voting (Gillion 1977). But many of Fiji's "European" residents (a category primarily composed of the British, Australians, and New Zealanders, but also

---

1. Historically, tensions have waxed and waned between Hindus and Muslims, as well as between Sanatanis and Arya Samajis. While Muslim-Hindu relations were amiable during indenture, conflicts began to surface between "free" Indians and rose to a peak in the 1920s and 1930s, resulting in 1926 in the establishment of the Muslim political lobby, the Fiji Muslim League, and in calls for separate Muslim representation on the colony's Legislative Council (Ali 1980b). In the 1920s, conflicts also escalated between the reformist Arya Samaj and the more "orthodox" Sanatan Hindus over the place of the *Ramayana* and religious idols in Hindu worship (Kelly 1991a). There have also been tensions over appropriate Islamic forms of worship between the majority Sunnis and other Muslim groups (Ali 1980b). The population statistics are courtesy of the Fiji Islands Bureau of Statistics (1996).

2. These cultural distinctions also carry political weight as voting in various elections, both pre- and postindependence, has been influenced by cultural allegiances that go beyond popular portrayals of an electorate divided between Indians and Fijians. In the 2001 elections, for example, the National Federation Party (NFP), which is described in the Fijian media as an "Indian party," was avoided by many North Indians because they saw it as focusing primarily on the needs of Gujaratis and South Indians (B. Lal 2002b, 90).

including expatriates from other European nations and from the United States) campaigned against the Indians' requests and actively incited elite Fijians to support them in opposing Indian demands. In 1923, for example, a group of European residents announced that they "will resist, and will also encourage the native Fijians to resist with all means at their disposal, the contemplated attempt to admit Indian residents of Fiji to the body politic or to granting to them any measure—however small—of political status" (as quoted in B. Lal 1992, 87). Despite the European residents' assertions, Indo-Fijians did slowly gain more access to political power, but never during colonialism did they receive the "equality with Europeans," to quote one of their placards, that they demanded (Lawson 1991).

As historian Brij V. Lal and others have argued, the overriding emphasis on cultural or "racial" differences between Indians and Fijians was not accidental but was a means by which the colonial government could mask conditions, such as their shared subjection to British dominance, that might otherwise have served to politically unify members of these two groups (B. Lal 1995, 37). The emphasis on race over class was particularly acute in response to grassroots attempts to mobilize class-based action. In 1959, for example, Fijian gas and oil workers went on strike alongside Indian workers as part of an action against expatriate oil companies. Various chiefs and Fijian leaders exhorted the Fijian strikers to stop protesting and to remember, in the words of Legislative Council member Semesa Sikivou, that the British are the Fijians' "best friends" and that they should not give in to the incitement of "foreigners" (i.e. the Indo-Fijian workers) to strike against them (as quoted in B. Lal 1992, 169). Their words were effectual; the Fijians stopped striking and soon after, racially segregated trade unions were founded (ibid., 169).

For the most part, up until 1970, the strategy of racialized politics kept the colonial government secure in its rule over Fiji as elite indigenous Fijians could be convinced that their best interests would be served by keeping up their allegiance to the British against the "threat" posed by Indo-Fijians (Kelly and Kaplan 2001b; B. Lal 1995, 1992). Indeed, many indigenous Fijian leaders expressed concern and regret over Britain's decision to end colonial rule in 1970.

Postindependence

In the postcolonial period, the politics of "race" did not disappear but was made to serve another master—the indigenous Fijian elite to whom political leadership was effectively transferred when the British departed from Fiji. In collaboration with local Indo-Fijian business leaders and international business interests, the Fijian elite shaped the form of economic and political life in the postindependence period.

Not only were postindependence politics organized along racial lines, but many political analysts have concluded that the allotment of communal seats in the nation's first constitution in 1970 gave "immediate advantage in electoral contests" to a political party that predominantly represented the voices of the indigenous Fijian elite: the Alliance Party, which retained control of government from 1970 up until 1987 (Lawson 1991, 187).[3]

Led by Ratu Sir Kamisese Mara, a high chief from the East, the Alliance lost its grip on political power for the first time in the elections of 1987, when a coalition of two opposition parties—the National Federation Party and the newly founded Fiji Labour Party (FLP)—received widespread support from Indo-Fijian voters across the nation as well as from voters of various ethnicities in western Viti Levu. For the first time since Independence, Fiji had a new prime minister; Mara was replaced by the FLP leader, Dr. Timoci Bavadra, an indigenous Fijian politician from the West.

But Bavadra lasted only a few weeks in office before he was thrown out in Fiji's first coup.

The 1987 Coups

Stirring up fears that Bavadra's multiethnic coalition was in fact an "Indian government," Sitiveni Rabuka, a lieutenant colonel in the Fiji military, justified the 1987 coups as necessary to combat "the Indian design for political domination" (Rabuka 2000, 10). Only a minority of scholars agree, however, that irreconcilable cultural or ethnic differences between indigenous Fijians and Indo-Fijians were at the heart of the 1987 coups (see Ravuvu 1991; Scarr 1988). Most analysts of the events of 1987 have pointed out that Rabuka's initial aim was to see the Alliance Party back in office, as well as to restore power to the eastern chiefly elite (Kaplan 1988; B. Lal 1995; Lawson 1991; Rutz 1995; Sutherland 1992; N. Thomas 1990a).

What is indisputable is the way that "race" was used to rally public support. The coups of 1987 were undertaken in the *name* of purported racial and religious solidarity amongst indigenous Fijians. Not only did Rabuka

3. This was despite the fact that the Alliance Party conceded defeat in the 1977 elections. The NFP won the 1977 elections by a slim majority but was slow in forming a government. In the meantime, the governor-general reinstated the Alliance Party leader Ratu Mara as prime minister, despite the Alliance Party's election loss. Siddiq Koya, the leader of the NFP, later claimed that he had been stripped of his rightful position as prime minister because he was an Indo-Fijian (Ali 1980b, 213–19; B. Lal 1992, 238–41).

claim he was compelled to stop Indo-Fijian political "domination," but he also later stated that one of his political motivations while in office was to transform Fiji into a Christian state. "I believed then," he wrote in retrospect, "that if my Indian brothers and sisters could be converted to Christianity, then the relationship between the two main communities would be less tense, and we would have more in common" (Rabuka 2000, 13).

As part of his plan to "protect" indigenous Fijians, Rabuka supported the rewriting of Fiji's constitution. The new constitution of 1990 explicitly stated in its preamble that it had been written "whereas the events of 1987 were occasioned by a widespread belief that the 1970 Constitution was inadequate to give protection to the interests of the indigenous Fijian people, their values, traditions, customs, way of life and economic well being" (Government Printing Office 1990, 498). It also imposed a variety of measures to ensure that Indo-Fijians stayed on the sidelines of governmental power.[4] In addition to an allotment of communal seats that skewed representation toward indigenous Fijians (Premdas and Steeves 1993), the 1990 Constitution reserved a number of governmental positions, including the position of prime minister and half of all judicial and legal offices as well as civil service jobs, for indigenous Fijians or Rotumans.[5]

The late 1990s were, however, a turning point. Rabuka, who had by now twice stood in elections and twice been elected prime minister (in 1992 and 1994), radically tempered his anti-Indian stance. In the words of anthropologist Robert Norton, he recast himself, out of the role of "ethnic champion" and into that of a "national leader" (2000a, 89). Responding to widespread international condemnation of the racist provisions of the 1990 Constitution, Rabuka took the unanticipated step of collaborating with the Indo-Fijian political leader Jai Ram Reddy to pave the way for a more multiethnic government. Together they played a leading role in the writing of yet another new constitution (the 1997 Constitution), and together they entered the 1999 election as coalition leaders. It was a step for which Rabuka was internationally praised but to which he also attributed his election defeat. In his own words, Rabuka later reflected,

4. This is not to deny that due to their economic clout some Indo-Fijians continued to have significant political influence. The point here is simply that Indo-Fijians were officially excluded from certain positions within the government on the basis of their "race."

5. As the native people of the island of Rotuma, which is included as part of the Republic of the Fiji Islands, Rotumans hold special status in Fiji. While they compose just over 1 percent of the total population of Fiji (Fiji Islands Bureau of Statistics, 1996), they are often included in programs that focus on improving the living standards and political and cultural rights of Fiji's indigenous people.

The poetic irony is that Mr. Reddy and I, the main architects of the 1997 Constitution, which was designed to bring about greater national unity, were essentially rejected by the voters. That was the price we had to pay for bringing in so much change in the process of Fiji's transition. Mr. Reddy was probably punished by the Indians for getting too close to Rabuka, the coupmaker. My own SVT Party lost ground because it was seen as selling out the Fijians. But our multiracial vision for the country was right and I have no regrets about embracing it. (2000, 18)[6]

The victory of Mahendra Chaudhry's Fiji Labour Party in the 1999 election was not only an electoral upset, but a stunning surprise for political analysts both inside and outside of Fiji. Part of Chaudhry's success can be attributed to a split in the Fijian vote between numerous small parties, all of which focused on the indigenous Fijian electorate. Some disaffected Fijian voters furthermore cast their vote for Chaudhry as a way of voicing their displeasure against Rabuka's inability to make good on many of his promises of higher living standards, economic prosperity, and the consolidation of indigenous Fijian political power (B. Lal 2000a; Norton 2000b; Rakuita 2003; Sutherland 2000).

Norton has explained the FLP's success as a result of the Fijian electorate's willingness to vote across ethnic lines, given the rising appeal of a platform that focused on the interests of labor and the poor. "While it would be mistaken to infer that the 1999 elections reflect a great weakening of racial or ethnic identities in national politics," Norton suggested, "it is clear that significant indigenous Fijian support for the still predominantly Indian Fiji Labour Party (FLP) was regained following the dissolution of their interest in it after the military coups 12 years ago" (2000b, 49).

Political turmoil was initially expected to follow on the heels of Chaudhry's installment as prime minister as it did in 1987. But it soon appeared as if the majority of Fiji's citizenry had accepted the "People's Coalition" government that Chaudhry put together as well as the leadership of an Indo-Fijian prime minister.[7] Many political observers hailed

6. While Rabuka has continued to espouse statements promoting a multicultural, multiethnic Fiji, he has also reiterated his strong anti-Indian bias. Despite being found not guilty on coup-related charges, there are also continuing allegations in Fiji that Rabuka was one of the covert instigators of the 2000 coup.

7. The People's Coalition was composed of three parties: the Fiji Labour Party led by Chaudhry, the Fiji Association Party (FAP) led by Adi Kuni Speed (Timoci Bavadra's widow), and the Party for National Unity (PANU) led by Apisai Tora. Labour led the coalition in terms of votes and Chaudhry was selected as prime minister.

this as the beginnings of a new era in Fijian politics (B. Lal 2000a; Norton 2000b).

Speight and company, however, had other ideas and, returning to an old theme, rallied support around fears of an Indian takeover and assertions of indigenous Fijians' "right" not to be governed by Indians.

Motivations behind the 2000 Overthrow

Many members of the public accepted Speight's explanation that the May 2000 coup was motivated by the desire of indigenous Fijian nationalists to remove Indians from political power. Journalists and local academics, however, quickly suggested that a more likely impetus came from the political and economic interests of disgruntled politicians, business leaders (including some Indo-Fijians), and members of the military forces. Over time, these ideas permeated the public's perceptions of the coup, but without dislodging the emphasis placed on "racial difference" as at the center of the conflict.

One of the difficulties in pinning down precisely which factors led up to the coup is that years after May 19, 2000, it is still unclear exactly who was involved in masterminding the ousting of the Chaudhry government. Speight willingly led the assault, but he was not the one who put the operation together. In fact, just after Speight and a group of soldiers from the military's Counterrevolutionary Warfare (CRW) unit took over the Parliament, Speight made it clear to his hostages that they would soon meet the real person behind the coup. "You will be surprised," he reportedly told them (Robertson and Sutherland 2001, 15). But despite Speight's frantic cell-phone calls, that person never materialized (Field, Baba, and Nabobo-Baba 2005; Robertson and Sutherland 2001).

Many political commentators have, moreover, suggested that a number of different factions were planning to overthrow Chaudhry and that Speight simply "jumped the queue" of potential coup makers (Field, Baba, and Nabobo-Baba 2005, 119; see also Kaplan 2003; Kelly and Kaplan 2001b). There has also been suggestion that members of Chaudhry's own party were planning to relieve him of power and install Deputy Prime Minister Tupeni Baba as prime minister in his stead (Field, Baba, and Nabobo-Baba 2005; Ramesh 2001; Robertson and Sutherland 2001).

We may never know for certain everyone who was behind the events that brought Speight into Parliament, but we do know some of the societal, economic, and political tensions that contributed to the coup. One major factor that turned the tide against Chaudhry was his government's policies toward business. Speight himself was a failed businessman who had been removed from his positions as head of Fiji Pine Limited and Fiji Hardwood Corporation and was facing charges of fraud. And he was not the only one. As Lal has pointed out, among Speight's supporters were "young business-men on the make, who rode the gravy train of the 1990s, benefited from opportunistic access to power, secured large, unsecured loans from the National Bank of Fiji, but then found their prospects for continued prosperity dimming upon the election of a new government" (2000d, 181; see also 2000c). These included business leaders from various ethnic backgrounds, among them Indo-Fijians. Indeed, speculation over particular Indo-Fijian businessmen's participation in the coup reached such an intensity during the coup that various business leaders felt compelled to place ads in local newspapers, asserting their innocence.

In addition to the support of several business leaders it is likely that Speight received the backing of disgruntled politicians eager to get back into office. A number of members of the civilian interim government, which was put into place by the military following the coup, were later investigated for their role in removing Chaudhry's People's Coalition from office in the first place. These include Vice President Jope Seniloli, Information Minister Ratu Inoke Kubuabola, and Agriculture Minister Apisai Tora. In a verdict that caused outrage across Fiji, Seniloli was convicted on coup-related charges while acting as Fiji's vice president only to be released four months into his four-year sentence. Another cabinet minister, Ratu Naiqama Lalabalavu was similarly convicted while in office. Once he served out his sentence for coup-related crimes, he was sworn directly back into Laisenia Qarase's cabinet ("Cabinet Post . . ." 2005).

Questions have also been raised over the involvement of both the police force and the military. Police Commissioner Isikia Savua was cleared of allegations of involvement in the coup by a closed-door hearing, the details of which have been not been made public. Widespread public speculation over Savua's possible role in the coup, however, continues (B. Lal 2007). There are also speculations that the CRW soldiers did not act alone but were assisted by other members of the military forces. Allegations have been raised over the role Lieutenant Colonel Filipo Tarakinikini may have played in the coup and numerous allegations have been made that the military helped distribute arms to the hostage takers after they took over Parliament. Fingers have also been pointed at former prime minister Rabuka as well as at the Fijian nationalist leader Iliesa Duvoloco.

While there is still a great deal of controversy over who exactly was involved in planning and financing Speight's takeover, various parties' interests

in seeing Speight succeed help explain why there was such widespread reluctance to put a halt to the events Speight put into motion. Considering
how they might profit from watching the People's Coalition topple, even
those who were not part Speight's campaign were hesitant to stop him.

On the grassroots level, sentiments against the People's Coalition had
been building up for some time. In the month leading up to May 19, there
had been two taukei, or Fijian nationalist, rallies protesting Chaudhry's government. The first attracted only five hundred people, but estimates of the
size of the second range from fifteen hundred to five thousand (Field, Baba,
and Nabobo-Baba 2005; Robertson and Sutherland 2001). The culmination
was a third taukei rally, which marched through downtown Suva on the
morning of May 19, 2000, marking the taukei's anger over the anniversary of
Chaudhry's first year in office. This rally was estimated to have drawn two
thousand people, some of whom then rampaged through Suva, smashing
and looting shops and businesses in the downtown shopping district.[8]

Much of the resentment came from indigenous Fijians who opposed
Chaudhry's appeal to extend the terms of leases of indigenous Fijian land.
One of the most highly contentious political issues in Fiji since the days of
colonial rule has been that of land rights. Given that Fiji's first governor set
aside 83 percent of land for indigenous Fijian ownership (later increased to
nearly 87 percent), most Indo-Fijians have no other option but to rent land
for their homes, farms, and businesses. In 2000, ongoing debates over the
demands of landowners versus tenants, along with the recent widespread
expiry of many thirty-year leases, resulted in increasing tension over the future of land tenure.[9]

In addition to fears over loss of control over land, Fijian landowners were
also concerned about the remuneration they would receive for Fiji's extensive mahogany holdings. Yet another source of popular disquiet was the
disgruntlement felt over the political prominence of the eastern provinces
and the historical dominance of eastern chiefs and political leaders, most
notably President Mara.

Given the array of likely parties and motivations involved in the buildup
to the 2000 overthrow, many commentators on the 2000 coup agree that

8. The estimate comes from *The Fiji Times*, May 20, 2000, 3.
9. In 1940, the Native Lands Ordinance established a system of land tenure administered by
the Native Land Trust Board (NLTB). At that point, the NLTB was issuing standardized ten-
year leases. Numerous Indo-Fijian farmers, however, expressed discontent over the long-term
uncertainty created by a ten-year lease, and in 1969 the Agricultural Landlord and Tenant Act
(ALTA) instituted thirty-year leases (B. Lal 1992; Lawson 1991, 82, 84). Many of these leases
expired between 1997–2001, raising concerns in the last decade over the fate of Indo-Fijian tenants and among indigenous Fijians over the future use of their land (P. Lal 2000).

the scapegoating of Indo-Fijians during the coup of 2000 was a ploy whose purpose was to mask, however ineffectively, other forms of social cleavage that contributed to the political turbulence (see Kelly and Kaplan 2001b; B. Lal 2002a, 2000c; Teaiwa 2000; Trnka 2002b, 2002d).

But if the 2000 coup was not an indigenous Fijian struggle against Indo-Fijian political domination, why did it result in the widespread terrorization of Indo-Fijians? To answer this, we need to take a closer look at three factors that promoted the violence that followed May 19, namely the protracted battle over political control, the prevalent use of racist, anti-Indian rhetoric, and direct police and military collusion.

The Struggle for Political Control

Speight's attempted coup d'état effectively opened up a power struggle between various political factions, including the rebel forces, the military, the GCC, President Mara, Chaudhry's deposed People's Coalition, and in later months, the interim civilian government.

From the first days of the conflict, the military asserted that it was in control of the security situation. But as the number of violent skirmishes around the country escalated, public confidence in the military's ability to maintain peace quickly diminished. This was particularly so among Indo-Fijians who were the most prevalent targets of intercivilian violence. Some of their sentiments were summed up by a statement issued by a major opposition party, The National Federation Party (NFP), two weeks into the crisis. Referring to the growing number of assaults and muggings of Indo-Fijians in rural areas despite marshal law, Attar Singh, a spokesman for the NFP stated, "These incidents have reached intolerable levels and must stop before people lose faith in the ability of the armed forces" (as quoted in *The Fiji Times*, June 2, 2000, 2). If we consider some of the military's ambivalent behavior toward the coup leader, it becomes clear why this "loss of faith" was eminent.

When Speight and his cadre of seven rebel gunmen stormed into Parliament, they met no resistance. According to a report in *The Fiji Times* the next day (May 20, 2000, 3), unarmed police, many of whom were monitoring the two-thousand-strong taukei march in protest of Chaudhry's first year in office, witnessed the gunmen pulling up to the Parliament Complex, but backed off when they saw that they were armed and allowed them to enter unhindered. Chaudhry later admitted that despite the high profile of the political sentiments being rallied against him, his security forces took no extra precautions on the anniversary of his first year in office.

Within a few hours of the takeover, Speight held the first of what were to become his infamous daily press conferences. On this occasion, he boldly declared himself the head of state "by the will of the indigenous people of Fiji." With no one standing up to Speight and most of the members of Parliament being held at gunpoint, it quickly became unclear who (if anyone) was in control of the government.

Later that afternoon, however, President Mara and former prime minister Rabuka, the architect of the two 1987 coups, both publicly appealed to Speight to step down. The military also denounced Speight's actions and asserted it was in control of law and order. But it soon became evident that, contrary to many people's expectations, the military's assertions of control did not extend to going into Parliament, forcing the release of the hostages, and putting a speedy end to the crisis. All eyes then turned to the GCC, a highly respected body of Fijian chiefs, who it was hoped could negotiate a way out of the political stalemate that was developing between Speight, President Mara, and the military. But the GCC, who claimed to oppose Speight but openly agreed with some of his key demands, including the suspension of the 1997 Constitution (which the GCC had previously approved) and the replacement of the Chaudhry government, similarly failed to act decisively. In the meantime, the terrain of political demands opened up as Fijians and Indo-Fijians on the western side of Viti Levu, citing fears of a nationwide economic backlash, called for a separate government for the West.

Given the military-imposed curfew and the number of armed soldiers on the streets, the military appeared to have the upper hand in the situation. The military's position vis-à-vis Speight became, however, even more uncertain as days and weeks passed without any definitive action on their part to put an end to the attempted coup. Early in the conflict, the media revealed that what had initially been referred to as a "civilian" takeover was actually a quasi-military one, as Speight's rebel cadre was made up of members of the military's elite CRW unit, with Speight the only civilian among them. It also became clear that the military was not restricting access to the hostage takers in Parliament as hundreds of Fijian civilians of all ages moved into the Parliament Complex, camping out on the front lawn, to show their support of Speight. Local and foreign journalists were also entering and exiting the Parliament compound where they were hosted by Speight and his rebels.

Many in Fiji were growing increasingly skeptical of the military's sincerity in halting the hostage crisis, and confidence in the police and military was further shaken when no one tried to stop a group of eighteen soldiers in full uniform, led by Police Commissioner Isikia Savua's brother, Major

Josefa Savua, from marching into Parliament to pitch their lot in with Speight and his forces.

At the end of May, military commander Commodore Frank Baini-marama finally made the move of taking over executive authority of the government, forcing President Mara to resign and imposing martial law. Many hoped Bainimarama would now take a decisive stand against Speight.

But despite being surrounded by the military forces, Speight continued to assert his control, occasionally even traveling in and out of the Parliament compound. On one particularly surreal occasion, Speight left Parliament to have afternoon tea with a group of Methodist Church ministers. When soldiers fired on his motorcade, two hundred of his supporters attempted to retaliate against the military, leading military spokesman Lieutenant Colonel Tarakinikini to call the shooting a mistake and to apologize to Speight's entourage.

Commodore Bainimarama also made it clear that the military had no intention of returning the legally elected government to power. Instead, he began to negotiate with Speight over possible choices for the next prime minister and other ministerial positions. Months of protracted negotiations followed as Speight, Bainimarama, and various members of the GCC debated the fates of the hostages and the hostage takers inside Parliament.

Escalating Violence

By early July 2000, uprisings in support of the rebels were occurring across the nation. Roadblocks in support of Speight sprang up across the island of Viti Levu. In a variety of locales, indigenous Fijians initiated occupations of land they laid claim to, driving away Indo-Fijian tenants, foreign tourists, and resort owners. Indigenous Fijian landowners also took over Monasavu Dam and cut off power across Viti Levu. This was also the period during which the town of Korovou was taken over by rebels. Soldiers, police, and civil servants in Korovou were taken hostage and all movement in and out of town was at the rebels' discretion (Field, Baba, and Nabobo-Baba 2005). In Labasa on Vanua Levu (Fiji's second largest island), a group of military officers mutinied and pledged their support to Speight. In light of these onslaughts, the military appeared increasingly ineffective in maintaining even the barest form of law and order. At times, Fiji seemed to be on the brink of civil war.

By now, the violence was widespread, impacting indigenous Fijians, Indo-Fijians, and others, from the streets of Suva to the rural hinterlands of Viti Levu, Vanua Levu, and numerous smaller islands. Indo-Fijians were not the only people brutalized. Armed combat took place between the predominantly indigenous Fijian members of the police and military and rebel supporters. There were also claims that indigenous Fijian civilians experienced physical abuse by the police and military during sweeps through villages in search of rebel supporters. Moreover, the structural effects of the coup, such as increased unemployment and the closure of schools, caused hardship and disruption to all residents of Fiji.

The brunt of the civilian violence was, however, ethnically focused as Indo-Fijians became the targets of physical assaults, rapes, and house burnings. Anti-Indian attacks were most prevalent in Speight's stronghold of Naitasiri Province, particularly in the areas of Vunidawa and Muaniweni. Scattered violence also occurred on the island of Vanua Levu, especially in Dreketi and in Labasa. Most of the perpetrators of the violence were disaffected Fijian youths from local koros (Fijian villages), and their targets were the residents of nearby rural Indo-Fijians settlements and villages. Large numbers of Indo-Fijians fled from these areas, settling in the newly established refugee camp in Lautoka or staying with kinfolk in surrounding areas.

We still don't know exactly how many people were brutalized. Amnesty International has estimated that "hundreds of Indo-Fijian homes and businesses were burned down or looted" and that "at least 1,000 Indo-Fijians were internally displaced or made homeless as a result of the violence and thousands were forced to leave leased properties" (Amnesty International 2001). Many incidents, however, were not reported to the police, nor did they make it onto the radio or TV news or into the three major news dailies.

The level of violence is even more difficult to assess when it comes to cases of violence against women. On July 16, 2000, the news media announced that there was one "confirmed" case of rape (FM 101 news report, July 16, 2000), despite widespread talk of numerous rapes of Indo-Fijian women occurring in the interior region of Viti Levu. A study later carried out by the Fiji Women's Crisis Centre noted that "several cases" of "race motivated" sexual violence against Indo-Fijian women had occurred in Muaniweni and Baulevu (in Tailevu, Viti Levu) and Dreketi and Batiri (on Vanua Levu), but did not specify any figures (Fiji Women's Crisis Centre 2001, 11; see also Trnka 2005d). In the course of everyday conversation about the coup, I was told of the rapes of at least three women who were familiar to residents of Darshan Gaon, as well as of other attempted rapes or violent attacks against women.

Despite the uncertainties over the exact numbers involved, we do know that violence occurred across major urban areas, most notably Suva, Nausori, and Labasa, small towns including Korovou and Rakiraki, and rural farming areas such as Vunidawa, Muaniweni, and Dreketi, at a scale previously unseen in postindependence Fiji.

A Short-lived Peace

Finally, on July 9, the military's lobbying efforts paid off. The Muanikau Accord was signed by Speight and Commodore Bainimarama. In return for amnesty, Speight agreed to support the installment of an interim civilian administration whose members would be selected by the GCC. Four days later, Prime Minister Chaudhry and the remaining hostages were released.

The jubilation was, however, short lived as the violence continued. Allowed to go free, Speight's rebels set parts of the Parliament Complex on fire before moving to the outskirts of Suva where they took over a school and commenced to terrorize nearby villagers for food and other provisions. On July 26, the military finally arrested Speight, charging him with treason and detaining many of his supporters. But the rebel uprisings only intensified, and it took another month before the military seemed to have fulfilled its promise of restoring law and order.

A civilian government, led by Prime Minister Qarase, had been put into place following the signing of the Muanikau Accord. Its fate remained insecure, however, and throughout October, rumors circulated among members of the general public that a "second coup" was imminent. By this time people's desire for the military's promised, but as yet unfulfilled, return to "normalcy" was so strong that many were eager for a second coup to take place so that a decisive leader would take control and finally return life back to normal. After months of unrest, many Indo-Fijians hoped that former president Mara or even Rabuka, despite his well-known prejudices against Indo-Fijians, would once more take over the reins of power and return stability to the country.

Another attempt to overthrow the government was indeed still to come. As many had suspected, Commodore Bainimarama had continuing trouble keeping control not just of the nation, but of his own troops. On November 2, 2000, forty soldiers attempted mutiny against him. Breakaway soldiers and the military engaged in intensive assaults across Suva, during which eight soldiers were killed, twenty soldiers were wounded, and six civilians were hit by stray bullets (Robertson and Sutherland 2001). Bainimarama, however, held his ground, and with his backing, the interim civilian administration retained its leadership of the government.

In the end, then, the military prevailed. But it was only after months of utter political chaos during which the country had been plunged into widespread violence and terror.

Racial Rhetoric

In addition to the pervasive lack of law and order, anti-Indian violence was encouraged by a second factor: the widespread popularity of racist, anti-Indian rhetoric. While business and political interests as well as regional divisions, rather than "race," were the motivating factors behind the coup, it is also clear that the coup was undertaken in the *name* of purported racial solidarity among Fijians and racial prejudice against Indians. Much of Speight's rhetoric portrayed irreconcilable racial differences as the core of Fiji's political turmoil. A number of Speight's claims about "indigenous rights" were furthermore echoed by other parties to the political crisis, including spokespeople for the military and the interim civilian government, both parties that represented themselves as opposed to the rebels.

From his first day in front of the cameras, Speight's explanation for his takeover of Parliament was that "the indigenous people of this country have expressed a desire which we have acted upon and which over the next few days and weeks will result in policy changes, legal foundation and framework changes with regard to the affairs of this country which will see them return to their rightful position of self-determination of Fiji" (as quoted in *The Fiji Times*, May 20, 2000, 2). On another occasion Speight stated that "our request is that the government be civilian and be Fijian particularly in view of the fact that one of its principal task [sic] is to develop a constitution that will *look after the interests of Fijians once and for all*" (as quoted in *The Fiji Times*, June 6, 2000, 3, my emphasis).

SAS veteran and CRW major Ilisoni Ligairi, who was one of Speight's closest allies and was sometimes referred to as the brains behind the takeover, described the coup as directly resulting from the necessity of removing an Indian prime minister from office because his "race" made him unsuitable to lead Fiji. "We waited and the last 12 months has proved to us that you just can't trust them," Ligairi stated. "We always knew this and it was naïve for our Fijian leaders to think otherwise. But then again the 1997 Constitution could be a blessing in disguise in that it allowed for us to see what it's like to have an Indian as PM. In that short time Chaudhry was trampling on everything Fijian. . . . We want to make sure they do not get another opportunity to make us fear for our future in our own country" (as quoted in *The Fiji Times*, June 28, 2000, 3).

The language of indigenous Fijian ethnic unity was used by Speight not only to justify his overthrow of the People's Coalition government, but also as a means of deflecting attempts, particularly by Fijians, to remove him from power. Throughout, Speight's forces played up their Fijian identity as a means of leverage against the military. When the first few scuffles between Speight's supporters and the military occurred outside of Parliament, Speight's deputy prime minister, Timoci Silatolu, questioned how far the military was willing to go against the rebels. "Are they [the military forces] willing to pitch their boys against our boys, Fijian against Fijian?" he asked (as quoted in *The Fiji Times*, June 4, 2000, 1). As violent skirmishes between Speight's supporters and the military later proved, they were.

The Politics of Indigeneity: Taukei versus Vulagi

Speight's rhetoric was in many ways a reiteration of what Fijian anthropologist, politician, and taukei sympathizer Asesela Ravuvu has encapsulated in his description of relations in Fiji as characterized by two opposing groups: taukei versus vulagi, or natives versus foreigners. According to this characterization, indigenous Fijians are the taukei, or "owners" of Fiji, both in terms of their ownership of land and their right to govern the nation (Abramson 2000; Tomlinson 2002a). Despite Indians' assertions of their own emotional interconnections with the land of Fiji (Trnka 2005c, 1999), according to the taukei, Indians and other nonindigenous Fijians are vulagi, or foreigners, who are welcomed guests but whose stay is always at the mercy of the taukei's hospitality (cf. Leavitt 2002; Norton 2000a; Rutz 1995).

Ravuvu's depiction of this relationship in his book *The Façade of Democracy* is worth quoting at length. In a chapter devoted to a justification of the 1987 coups, Ravuvu writes,

> Well before the Europeans and other foreigners arrived in Fiji and up till now, Fijians have always categorized the population or inhabitants of the country, or of any locality or village, into two main divisions. A person is either a *taukei* (indigenous or owner) or *vulagi* (visitor or foreigner) in any place.
>
> . . . Traditional protocol requires the *vulagi* to be humble and know well his role and position in the context which he or his ancestors have not been original settlers or *taukei* . . . The *vulagi* are generally the work-horses of the physical and social settings in which they are established. They generally provide their best in order to be acceptable to the *taukei*. It is prudent, however, not to boast or publicly claim honor for their contributions in support of the *taukei* cause, for such contributions and support are expected elements of

cooperation if the *vulagi* are to be acceptable and accommodated in the *taukei* community. It is for the *taukei* to give recognition to the *vulagi* for the contributions and cooperation rendered.

. . . The best analogy to this *taukei* and *vulagi* relationship is that of the host and guest. The host is the *taukei* and the guest is the *vulagi*. Each must play fair and be honest with each other and understand well each one's obligations to the other. The host is generally in command, and the guest must comply with the host's requirements if he is to be accepted and accommodated. If the guest does not comply to the host's expectations then he may very well leave before he is thrown out of the house. (1991, 58–60)

According to Ravuvu's depiction, the taukei is the original, autochthonous occupier of the land and as such has ultimate rights to land-ownership as well as the right to make certain demands—demands for labor and for respect—from the vulagi. In return, the taukei has an obligation to take care of the vulagi, much as a host has the obligation to provide for the needs of his or her guest. Should, however, the relationship break down, the ultimate power always resides with the taukei who can decide to expel the vulagi from his or her territory.

Writing in 1991, Ravuvu invoked the taukei-vulagi relationship to justify what he depicted as a just, ethnically unified indigenous Fijian takeover of government in 1987. He was not alone in doing so. As Henry Rutz has powerfully demonstrated, by 1987 the concept of taukei, which had originally delineated local groups' ties to specific land areas, had been extended by Fijian nationalists to encompass the ethnic unity of *all* Fijians in relation to their ownership of Fiji, in opposition to Indian outsiders, or vulagi (Rutz 1995; see also Leckie 2002a; Tomlinson 2002a).[10]

Frequently, assertions of the rights of the taukei refer not only to exclusive Fijian ownership of land but also to notions of the political "paramountcy" of indigenous Fijians. Taukei leader Tora, for example, gave a speech following the deposition of Prime Minister Timoci Bavadra in which he rallied popular support for the 1987 coup by claiming that all indigenous Fijians have unique and "paramount" political rights in Fiji by nature of being taukei. According to Tora,

We are not a wealthy community but we have shared our only asset, the land, generously with others. . . . Our generosity has been used to slap us in our

10. The close link between land rights and indigenous Fijian social organization, as reflected in Ravuvu's extended discussion of taukei, is also evident in his examination of other indigenous Fijian concepts such as the mataqali (familial land-owning unit) and the *vanua* (chiefdom or locality). See Ravuvu 1991; also Tomlinson 2002a.

faces . . . to deprive us the paramountcy which the Deed of Cession guaranteed and which the fathers of the present constitution undertook to protect for all *taukei* forever. . . . This sacred covenant is now broken . . . upon us is imposed a new colonialism from within our own country by those who arrived here with no rights and were given full rights by us the *taukei*. . . . We cannot remain silent as our traditions are endangered, as the leadership of our turaga [chiefs] is spurned, as our land, our only asset and the source of our security, is put in the control of others. . . . We cannot become strangers in our own land. (quoted in Norton 1990, 137)

In a similar vein, in its 1996 recommendations to the Fijian Constitutional Review Commission, the predominantly indigenous Fijian Soqosoqo ni Vakavulewa ni taukei (SVT) Party, then a leading political party headed by former prime minister Rabuka, asserted that the paramountcy of Fijian interests must be constitutionally protected and that there is nothing wrong with the "interests of the dominant race or culture" being given a privileged place in government. To explain why Fijian interests must be given precedence against all others, the SVT argued that "the Fijian claim of supremacy and political control are also based on the understanding of his role and his status as taukei and his perception of what an immigrant, a visitor or a guest is" (as reprinted in B. Lal 1998, 149). The SVT then went on to quote Ravuvu's depiction of taukei-vulagi to illustrate this relationship (ibid., 149).

The exact formulation of what "Fijian paramountcy" entails has been kept strategically vague since the concept was first utilized in the 1920s by the British to counter demands by Indo-Fijians for increased political power (B. Lal 2002c). But by 1964, paramountcy had clearly come to mean "political paramountcy" and at that time encompassed such goals as "greater internal self-government" in response to British colonial rule and increased land rights (ibid., 154). In the context of postcolonial political debates, particularly following the 1987 and 2000 coups, "Fijian paramountcy" has come to encompass not only a notion of Fijian "rights" to land-ownership and to ethnically based affirmative action but also to keeping political power in the hands of ethnic Fijians (ibid.).

In a particularly revealing passage intended as a rebuttal to Western critics, the SVT in its recommendations to the Constitutional Review Commission justified the need for Fijian political paramountcy thus:

these Western-influenced critics are usually blind to the inadequacies, weaknesses and failures of the systems of government of those very countries that they belong to. In these countries assimilation, which is another term for domination and annihilation of indigenous peoples' culture, had been the official ideology and practice of the dominant communities. They criticize the concept of paramountcy of Fijian interests (a concept that the British colonists introduced) as unfair, anti-democratic and an ideology for ethnic dominance and oppression, quite forgetting that in the advanced democratic countries (New Zealand, Australia, United Kingdom, USA and India), there are also operating paramountcy of the interests of the dominant race or culture. It is just that they accept such paramountcy in their own countries but not in Fiji. It is the paramountcy of either the Anglo Saxon culture or the Indian Hindu culture. (reprinted in B. Lal 1998, 148).

As demonstrated in the statements by the SVT, Tora, and Ravuvu, the closely intertwined assertions of the unique rights of the taukei and "Fijian paramountcy" in politics are key facets of indigenous Fijian nationalist discourse. Together, they are utilized to support the claim that indigenous Fijians have a unique, moral right to rule Fiji.

Nor do they stand alone. Alongside the notions of taukei rights and Fijian paramountcy there is yet a third pillar of indigenous Fijian nationalist politics: Christianity.

Christianity in Fijian Politics

Christian missionaries have been active in Fiji since 1835. While there were some early setbacks, including the infamous murder and cannibalistic consumption of Reverend Thomas Baker in 1867, Christianity, and in particular Wesleyan Methodism, was quickly adopted throughout most of Fiji. The speedy acceptance of Methodism was facilitated by the 1854 conversion of Ratu Seru Cakobau, the *vunivalu*, or warlord, of Bau, leading to the widespread conversion of his many followers (Toren 1988). By 1856, one Wesleyan missionary claimed that fully one-third of indigenous Fijians had converted to Methodism (ibid., 698).

Today, Christianity is widespread and almost all indigenous Fijians are Christians. Methodism continues to be the most popular denomination in Fiji, but as a number of contemporary ethnographers have pointed out, many Fijians practice a unique style of Methodist worship, drawing together European Methodism and pre-Christian Fijian polytheism (Belshaw 1964; Tomlinson 2004; Toren 1988). A small number of Fijians belong to other Christian denominations such as the Roman Catholic Church, the Anglican Church, and the Seventh Day Adventists, and in more recent years, the Church of Latter Day Saints and some of the evangelical churches such as the Assemblies of God.

While Christianity has been incorporated into Fijian culture, so much so that it is considered *vakavanua,* or part of traditional Fijian custom, literally "the way of the land" (Kaplan 1990), only a small proportion (6 percent) of Indo-Fijians are Christians (Fiji Islands Bureau of Statistics, 1996). Alongside the many churches, Fiji's landscape is dotted with a number of Hindu temples, Sikh gurudwaras, and Muslim mosques.

Christianity has also had a privileged place in Fiji's political life. Though there have notable dissenters among its Methodist leaders, since the 1980s the Methodist Church has frequently lent its support to the Fijian nationalist cause (B. Lal 2003b, 275). In 1987, when Lieutenant Colonel Rabuka, who was a lay Methodist preacher, executed his two political coups, he did so not only in the name of indigenous Fijian rights but also out of a desire to enhance the position of Christianity in Fiji (Rabuka 2000). Through measures such as the short-lived Sunday Ban, which required Sunday to be a day of rest, outlawing work and non-church-related social activities on the Sabbath, Rabuka's government transformed Fiji into a Christian state in which all citizens, regardless of their religion, had to abide by certain Christian precepts. The Sunday Ban was later repealed, but as part of the buildup to the 2000 coup, there were renewed calls for Christians to rise up against the "Satanism" that some Christians saw as embodied by the non-Christian prime minister (L. Thomas 2002).[11] While the Methodist Church, Fiji's leading Christian denomination, publicly condemned the 2000 coup, some of its representatives openly met with and counseled Speight and his men during the takeover of Parliament. Furthermore, many of the taukei's followers were inspired by rhetoric that described the coup as a Christian act, and especially by the rebels' calls for Fiji to return to its status as a Christian state. Speight held regular Christian prayer sessions with his followers in Parliament. His followers also sang Christian hymns when about eighty of them marched through Suva on their way to demolish the country's only television station (due to what they considered to be its anti-rebel bias) and caused the coup's first two deaths in the process. Even many indigenous Fijian Christians who did not support the coup struggled with the interpretation that Speight's actions were just because they had been inspired by God (Trnka 2002b).

Invocations of Fijian Unity in 2000

Whether voiced in the terms of taukei versus vulagi, Fijian paramountcy, or the need for a Christian state, the image of a pan-Fijian unity defending itself

11. For more on the role of Christianity in the 2000 coup, see Tomlinson 2002b.

against a unified Indian threat was commonly employed by many of the parties who were involved in the power struggle that the 2000 coup unleashed.

Speight was one of the primary proponents of this point of view. While his methods were criticized by Fijians and Indo-Fijians alike, Speight had great success with his argument that the overthrow of an Indian prime minister was necessary because the rights of the indigenous Fijian people could only be protected by "one of their own." His statements regarding the need for indigenous Fijian paramountcy echoed concerns that had been voiced by indigenous Fijians around the country since Chaudhry's election (and were themselves echoes of the taukei rhetoric that had followed the 1987 election) and further galvanized such racial prejudices. The result was that many of the political actors who attempted to wrest control away from Speight utilized similar arguments. As Lal foresaw as early as June 2000, "George Speight himself might not find a place in the civilian administration although his supporters and most certainly his vision will" (2000c, 292).[12]

In 2000, members of the military and the interim civilian government echoed Speight's terminology in their press releases and public statements. The military in particular repeatedly expressed its agreement with Speight's aims, if not with his methods. Various spokespeople for the military reiterated Speight's demand for a new constitution that would better safeguard indigenous Fijian rights. Lieutenant Colonel Tarakinikini explained the need for a new constitution on the grounds that the coup had been caused by the previous government's negligence of the needs of indigenous Fijians. In an interview with *The Fiji Times*, Tarakinikini declared, "The indigenous concerns [sic] is the root of the problem we are facing. The fact is that we cannot really ignore the interest of the indigenous Fijian. They are the ones whose agitation led to the uprising and the coup. So we have to start off with that and then beyond that take into consideration the interest of the wider Fijian community" (June 19, 2000, 3).

The interim civilian government, many of whose members later made up the elected government of Prime Minister Qarase, likewise asserted that among the government's first tasks was the restoration of indigenous Fijians to the place of national paramountcy. As the new president Ratu Josefa Iloilo stated in his national address a few days following his swearing-in, "We now have Fijian leadership. I am your president. I will appoint a Fijian prime minister. *The paramountcy of Fijian interests will always be a guiding principle of governance in this country*" (Iloilo 2000, my emphasis).

---

12. Similar analyses have been made by Field, Baba, and Nabobo-Baba 2005; Kelly and Kaplan 2001b; B. Lal 2002b; Leavitt 2002.

In doing so, the government implicitly agreed with Speight's assertions that it was "race" and "racial difference," rather than class or regional divisions or the fanaticism of a small faction who did not represent the interests of the wider populace, that led to the coup. Ratu Kubuabola, the interim government's minster of information, put it bluntly when he declared that the coup had been motivated by a Fijian community unified against the Chaudhry government. Kubuabola stated, "The 1997 Constitution had proved a failure; it was effective for 12 months, when it was overthrown, unleashing a *widespread Fijian uprising*" (*The Fiji Times*, August 11, 2000, 2, my emphasis).

Interim prime minister Qarase likewise contended that discontent among indigenous Fijians was to blame for the nationwide instability. The first policies the Qarase government proposed were thus focused on ensuring calm among indigenous Fijians through increased expenditure on ethnically targeted programs. In early August, following a plea for national unity in his radio address, Qarase promised that he was going to improve the living conditions of indigenous Fijians by reinstating a $1.5 million grant to the Fijian Affairs Board to assist development in the provinces, altering the 1997 Constitution to better ensure indigenous Fijian rights, and restructuring land leases to improve the rights of indigenous Fijian landholding units. He also said that he would bring back restrictions on development loans from the Fiji Development Bank so that they would only be granted to indigenous Fijians and Rotumans.

In his defense of his *Blueprint for Fijian and Rotuman Development*, a government proposal for protecting indigenous Fijian rights through changes in the administration of land policies, business taxes, and other measures, Qarase further argued that it was necessary to privilege the enhancement of indigenous Fijians' living standards because "when Fijians and Rotumans are satisfied and happy with their well-being and welfare, it makes it easier to ensure peace and order for the whole of Fiji" ("Government Response . . .", August 13, 2000).

When criticism was quickly leveled against the blueprint for limiting the rights of Indo-Fijians and other nonindigenous citizens of Fiji, Qarase publicly stated that the plan was "not racist" and that by ensuring indigenous rights, he was (in the words of *The Fiji Times*) "not forgetting Indians and others who make up 48 percent of the population." But, Qarase continued, "I strongly believe that if the indigenous Fijians are at peace with themselves and with all communities in Fiji, there will be long term peace and stability in our country. So we, as a nation, need to invest more resources to ensure that Fijians in their development, through their own hard work, are keeping pace with the rest of society" (*The Fiji Times*, August 26, 2000, 10). Qarase furthermore announced plans to initiate the Constitution Review Commission to rewrite the constitution and publicly stated that only indigenous Fijians should be allowed to hold the offices of prime minister and president. By capitulating to the demands of the taukei, Qarase thus promoted the view that the coup was the result of racial differences that could be addressed through a series of measures focused on improving the rights and quality of life of indigenous Fijians.

Like the members of the interim government, former coup maker and prime minister Rabuka, who declared himself a mediator in the 2000 crisis, did not hesitate to use racially charged language in his discussions of the troubles facing the country. In an interview with the Australian Associated Press that was also run in the *Daily Post*, Rabuka was described as stating that a categorical animosity exists between Indians and Fijians. "Many indigenous Fijians hate Fiji's ethnic Indians because of perceptions that they are greedy and unwilling to understand the country's original inhabitants, according to former Prime Minister Sitiveni Rabuka," the article reported ("Why Fijians . . ." 2000, 3). Relations could be improved if indigenous Fijians retain national leadership, Rabuka suggested, explaining that "discontent over Indian power was one factor behind the May 19 coup" (ibid.). Rabuka furthermore stated that he did not believe Indians genuinely wanted to get along with Fijians or to understand them "because they don't have to understand us" (ibid.). He summed up his thoughts on Fijian politics with the assertion that "I think everybody in Fiji, or most of us, would like to bring the two races closer together—as long as the leadership [of the country] remains in our hands" (ibid.). These statements were in line with interviews Rabuka gave as part of his second biography in which he suggested that while he supported the recognition of Fiji as a multiethnic, multicultural nation, he also hoped that "circumstances-driven migration" would lead Indians to voluntarily leave Fiji so that the numbers of Indians in the country would be at a "manageable level" that would not cross the "the tolerance threshold of the Fijians" (as quoted in Sharpham 2000, 316–17; see also Trnka 2005c). Rabuka's sentiments were further compounded by the *Daily Post* interview being run under the provocative headline, "Why Fijians Hate Indians," the newspaper effectively insinuating that Rabuka's remarks were an accurate portrayal of the sentiments of *all* indigenous Fijians.[13]

13. Each of Fiji's newspapers has its own biases. Of the three major English-language dailies, the *Daily Post* was the only government-owned newspaper in operation during the coup. It was also, according to journalist and media academic David Robie who conducted an

Opposing Voices

Racially divisive sentiments such as Speight's, Qarase's, and Rabuka's dominated the public sphere during the coup. The first public articulation of a counterpoint to such rhetoric from someone directly involved in attempting to resolve the 2000 crisis (i.e., from within the interim government, the military, the GCC, or among the mediators of the crisis) came only years later, from Commodore Bainimarama. Indeed, part of Bainimarama's explicit justification for overtaking the Qarase government in 2006 was to put a stop to the Qarase government's promotion of racially divisive, anti-Indian policies. Not only did Bainimarama refuse to stand behind the banner of "indigenous Fijian rights," but he also alienated his government from two key indigenous Fijian institutions: the GCC and the Methodist Church. None of this could, however, have been foretold by Bainimarama's actions in 2000. During the period that Bainimarama led the military response to Speight, he shied away from publicizing his own view of the nation of Fiji, leaving this role to various military spokespeople.

In 2000, those who opposed *both* Speight's overthrow *and* the capitulation of the military, the interim government, and the GCC to the demands of the taukei were largely silent during the crisis. In part this was because some of the most vocal critics of the taukei were the members of the People's Coalition who were being held hostage and then recovering from their ordeal. Chaudhry later embarked on a world tour to bring attention to the damage the coup had wreaked on Fiji's citizenry, but his and other MPs' voices were missing from the public sphere during the height of the crisis.

Prior to being taken hostage the FLP ministers had publicly promoted themselves as standing for interethnic harmony. Rather than declaring the paramountcy of any one ethnic group's interests, both indigenous Fijian

---

extensive analysis of local media coverage of the coup, the only paper to set up guidelines for its journalists in order to prevent them from granting Speight's rebels an air of legitimacy (2001). Journalists were instructed, for instance, to refer to Speight as "the leader of either the kidnappers, the gunmen or the hostage takers, but never as 'coup leader' to avoid giving him legitimacy in the minds of indigenous Fijians" (Robie 2001, 156). But as the headline "Why Fijians Hate Indians" indicates, the *Daily Post* was not always blameless for stirring up communal sentiment.

Nor was *The Fiji Times*. It is the most influential paper in Fiji, with sales of about 32,000 on usual weekdays, but up to 55,000 during the coup (Robie 2001, 15). (In comparison, both the *Daily Post* and the *Fiji Sun* were estimated as selling about 6,000 copies a day (Robie 2001, 15). Part of the Rupert Murdoch media empire, *The Fiji Times* was strongly criticized for its anti-Chaudhry bias. In fact, Robie and other media analysts suggest that *The Fiji Times'* negative coverage of the FLP's first year in office, along with its continued focus on communalism and communal sentiment, may have helped galvanize supporters of the coup (Field, Baba, and Nabobo-Baba 2005; Robie 2001).

and Indo-Fijian members of the FLP had publicly claimed to have a mandate from "the people" of Fiji and to represent the needs of "the people," as the name of "the People's Coalition" suggests. This was in spite of the fact that the FLP is commonly referred to in the media and elsewhere as being an "Indian party," given the high number of its supporters who are Indo-Fijian. However, rather than proclaiming that its mandate stemmed out of the needs or rights of Indo-Fijians, the FLP and the coalition government it formed made the much broader claim of speaking for "the people." In part, this was because a cross-section of voters from various ethnic, class, and regional backgrounds swept the FLP into office, which Chaudhry made sure was not forgotten.

A number of NGOs were similarly focused on representing what they saw as the needs of the general populace, regardless of ethnic background. Composed of a multiethnic membership, organizations such as the Citizens Constitutional Forum; the Fiji Women's Rights Movement; the Women's Crisis Centre; the Ecumenical Centre for Research, Education, and Advocacy; and the Blue Day Committee, among others, oriented themselves toward an ethnically inclusive vision of citizenship in Fiji. None of these groups, however, held the same political clout during the coup as Speight's rebel forces, the interim government, the military, or the GCC.

There were also small stirrings of public protest. In June 2000 Indo-Fijian sugarcane farmers in western Viti Levu raised the possibility of a sugarcane strike. A day of national prayers for peace was held in early August 2000, drawing participation from indigenous Fijians and Indo-Fijians alike. Another protest occurred on "Fiji Day" in October 2000 when critics of the military-installed regime wore the color blue.

In the months following May 19 there were also numerous critical letters sent in to local newspapers and heated political discussions on radio talk shows. Repeated calls for a general strike did not, however, materialize, and many people I spoke with expressed fear over losing even more of their wages by striking when the country was already entering a financial crisis. For reasons of personal safety, the level of overt public demonstration against the political situation was nowhere near that displayed by predominantly Indo-Fijian protestors in Australia, New Zealand, and the United States who took to the streets demanding the return of the democratically elected government.

In Fiji, it was only after the civilian government was firmly in place that the voices of the opposition began to make a political impact. During the months of political turmoil, their views remained largely muted.

The result was that public discourse about the coup, as voiced by Speight, the military, the interim government, mediators in the crisis, and members of the GCC, widely promoted the interpretation that ethnic, or in local terms "racial," conflict was the source of the crisis. Despite widespread awareness and public discussion of the other forms of social, political, and economic cleavage that contributed to the coup and despite the fact that armed skirmishes took place between indigenous Fijians—as rebels and as members of the military and the police—Speight's invocation of indigenous rights and the support he received from a range of people ready to march to Parliament, join the rebel forces, or take part in brutalities against the Indo-Fijian populace, led to the perception that the crisis was, at heart, caused by the competing interests of indigenous Fijians versus Indo-Fijians.

The depth of these sentiments was such that they continued to shape public opinion well into the coup of 2006. As in 2000, the political struggle that took place in 2006 was indisputably between competing indigenous Fijian interests, with Prime Minister Qarase on one side and Commodore Bainimarama on the other. However, Bainimarama's criticism of Qarase's ethnically divisive policies along with the appointment of Chaudhry as Bainimarama's finance minister resulted in a number of members of the public referring to 2006 as Fiji's first "Indian coup."

It is, moreover, likely that future confrontations will similarly be painted in racial terms. Bainimarama has tried to stay away from such rhetoric, attempting to portray his actions as benefiting the general public, regardless of ethnicity. Bainimarama is also a vocal critic of the taukei. But some political analysts speculate that this will only further entrench support for policies intended to promote "indigenous rights" once there is return to parliamentary democracy and elections are again allowed to take place (e.g., Madraiwiwi 2007).

Police and Military Collusion in Anti-Indian Violence

In 2000, the crisis in political legitimacy, widespread lack of law and order, the political sidelining of the needs of Indo-Fijians, as well as public debates surrounding the coup that often framed issues in ethnic terms, such as "Why Fijians Hate Indians," contributed to the opening up of a terrain of anti-Indian violence. But there was yet another factor at play that we should not overlook, which was how those responsible for ensuring citizens' safety turned a blind eye to many of the assaults, thefts, and other acts of violence against Indo-Fijians.

Throughout the 2000 crisis the military and the police, both of which are largely composed of indigenous Fijians, were subject to factional disputes and in danger of fragmenting, thus reducing their ability to maintain law and order throughout the country. But just as many of their spokespeople publicly expressed sympathy for the demands of the taukei, there were cases in which the military and the police were directly implicated in aiding, and in some cases actively taking part, in anti-Indian violence.

In the vast majority of the cases that we know of, Indo-Fijians who were subject to civilian violence responded by fleeing from violent areas rather than fighting back.[14] Partly this was due to the relative attractiveness of other options for those with the means to relocate. It was also due to Indo-Fijians' assessments of the dangers of confronting not only the bands of youths who were harassing them, but also the military and the police who were perceived as frequently acting in the interests of Fijians rather than in the interests of all of Fiji's citizens.

One of the Indo-Fijian community leaders I interviewed told me that the refusal to fight back was a conscious strategy employed by Indo-Fijians to stop the escalation of violence. Responding to my questions as to why Indo-Fijian youths did not feel compelled to rise up in response to the violence against them, their families, and community members, he replied, "They are not doing anything because we are not letting them. . . . Because if we did fight back then the Fijians would use it against us." He, like many others I spoke to, were critical of the police and military inaction in protecting Indo-Fijians, though they shied away from making such statements in public lest they lead to further confrontation.

We have already noted the military's unwillingness to act against Speight and the rebel forces as well as speculations that the military continued to supply arms to the rebels after the hostage taking, all of which promoted violence. It has also been widely reported that members of the police actively took part in crimes against Indo-Fijians. According to Fiji TV news and other media outlets, in early June 2000 members of the police were seen transporting cows that had been forcibly removed from Indian farmers and delivering them to Parliament to help feed Speight's supporters. Indo-Fijian accounts of the police and military's responses to violence also indicate that individuals were forced to strike up deals with the police and military through bribes and offerings of food and other goods in order to secure their protection. By January 2006, according to Andrew Hughes,

14. The same was also true in previous conflicts (as noted by Kelly 1998). But see chapter 6 for accounts of attacks in which Indo-Fijians physically defended themselves and others.

who was the commissioner of police at the time, twenty-five members of the police force had either been charged or were under investigation for complicity in criminal activities relating to the 2000 coup (The Republic of Fiji Islands Fiji Police Force 2006).

Finally, there were cases in which the political accommodation of the rebels and their supporters led directly to police inaction. One illustration was the application of the Muanikau Accord. The purpose of the accord was to resolve the crisis by granting Speight's supporters amnesty for the acts they had committed, in return for the release of the hostages and the return of weapons that had been confiscated from the military. The amnesty agreement stipulated that all "political acts" from May 19, 2000, until July 13, 2000, were accorded amnesty. The purpose of this clause was to assure not only the hostage takers but also their supporters that they would not be prosecuted for the crimes they had committed since the takeover of Parliament.

As, however, the accord was signed on July 10, 2000, it opened the door for a variety of offences to take place in the following three days, all of which would be protected by the amnesty as long as they could be justified as "political acts." In practice the amnesty agreement was furthermore applied to a variety of acts, including assaults against Indo-Fijians. The mugging and harassment of the Indo-Fijian wedding guests in Korovou Town with which this chapter opened is an example of how a criminal act was interpreted by the police as an excusable "political act," protected by the amnesty accord.

In the Korovou case, the mugging and assault were considered "political acts" because they were committed by indigenous Fijians against Indians. If we take taukei rhetoric to its extremes—and while many don't, some taukei supporters do—then all Indo-Fijians are akin to foreign guests who are welcome in Fiji only at their hosts' discretion. If it appears to the hosts, who, as Ravuvu describes, have a right to expect respect from their guests, that the vulagi are overstepping the line by, for example, taking possession of things, such as land, which don't really belong to them, then it is up to the hosts to set things straight. Such reasoning, buffered by widespread support of "Fijian paramountcy" and a belief in the superiority of Christians over Hindus, suggests that indigenous Fijians have the right to reclaim what Indians have taken away from them. For many taukei supporters and sympathizers, this means they have the right to reclaim land, which is why moments of political turbulence such as the 2000 coup result in silently simmering resentments over land rights bubbling up into the open. But others interpret this much more broadly and "take back" a variety of goods, as they consider *all* of Indians' material wealth as fundamentally based on Indians' exploitation of land that should actually be in the hands of the taukei. Unlawful acts such as mugging and assault were thus interpreted not as criminal violence but as forms of political action intended to reclaim what the taukei has lost.

While we do not have to agree with this logic, we now have a better sense of why perhaps the police responded as they did. Their own political leanings may have already biased them toward the assailants rather than the victims of the crime. The police were furthermore caught up in a situation where rebel forces had taken a number of police within Korovou Town hostage, and it was likely that they did not want to draw attention to themselves by protecting the rights of Indo-Fijians in the face of the rebels' demands for taukei paramountcy. Finally, faced with an incident that could be interpreted as part of the taukei struggle to reclaim what has been wrongfully taken away from them, the police chose to view the muggers' actions as legitimated by the military through its signing of the accord.

In sum then, the events of May 19 created a crisis in political legitimacy that continued for months after Speight's storming of Parliament. Despite a general awareness of the multiple factors that were behind the 2000 coup, the most prevalent opinion voiced in the public sphere was that the coup resulted from ethnic antagonism. In a space of political confusion and open contestation over political power in which the coup was explained in terms of "Why Fijians Hate Indians" and the forces responsible for protecting Indo-Fijians' safety were absent because of internal divisions and their own political sympathies, violence against Indo-Fijians intensified and was interpreted by some parties as an integral part of the political struggle.

3 Living in Fantastic Times

"We live in unusual times, almost like Alice in Wonderland, where things are seldom what they seem or are claimed to be," stated newspaper columnist and legal scholar Sir Vijay Singh in the midst of the chaos of the 2000 coup (2000b, 7). Indeed, the events following George Speight's overtaking of Parliament opened up a time unlike any other in the nation's history. Across many parts of Fiji, the crisis that began that day stripped away the familiarity and comprehensibility of daily life, plunging people into a space in which it was difficult to differentiate between rumors and reality, where real life often seemed more like something out of a fantasy novel or a Bollywood movie. Singh's statement neatly encapsulated the feelings of many who found themselves living through events that they had previously reconciled to the domain of fiction.

Throughout the months of turmoil, Indo-Fijians across the country struggled to comprehend and articulate what had become of their lives as well as to probe the boundaries of the crisis. In the process, three forms of expression proliferated amongst them: evocations of despair; rumors; and jokes. Each of these was evident from the first days of the coup, and although they had radically different emotional tenors, each was employed to bear witness to the fantastical nature of the crisis.

Premature Premonitions

One year before the 2000 coup, the announcement in May 1999 that Mahendra Pal Chaudhry would be Fiji's next prime minister had sent a tremor across Fiji. Once the election results were made public, expectations of

violence were rife and rumors of imminent civil uprisings swept through
Suva. On May 19, 1999, the day of Chaudhry's swearing into office, academics at the University of the South Pacific warned me that I better have
my bags packed and a plane ticket in hand in case of violence. Elsewhere,
some had already mistaken the national election itself as the inevitable first
step to a violent, governmental overthrow. Anthropologist Matthew Tomlinson reported that on Kadavu on the eve of the 1999 elections, he asked a
teenage boy, "What begins in Fiji tomorrow?" and the youth immediately
answered, "Ku! [Coup!]" (2002b, 13).

Such expectations of trouble were, however, premature. The first month
of Chaudhry's leadership was marked by high levels of anxiety, but the
widespread speculations of an impending governmental overthrow quickly
subsided. Political speculation soon dissipated, giving way to the necessities
and interests of daily life.

In Darshan Gaon, a village located in the Suva-Nausori corridor where
violence broke out immediately following Speight's storming of Parliament, no one had given the impression of living in the shadows of a loom-
ing political emergency. Even if they had, they could not have predicted the
intense social turmoil it would entail. In late April 2000, an increase in political activity by taukei, or nationalist indigenous Fijian, activists began to
stir up fears of possible political turbulence. Still, however, there was little
indication of the events that would so radically rearrange both the political
landscape and people's everyday lives.

It was well known that another taukei rally was scheduled to take place in
Suva on May 19, 2000, but most of the people I spoke to in Darshan Gaon
said that the two previous taukei demonstrations, which had taken place
the month before, had been peaceful and so there was no reason to expect
that this one was going to be any different. They predicted that the rally
would involve nothing more than the waving of placards and the chanting
of racist, anti-Indian slogans. Most Indo-Fijians and Fijians went to work
on May 19, 2000, expecting little from the day's political events.

By that evening, however, the country was in complete disarray.

First Reactions

The first reactions to the news of Speight's takeover were confusion and
panic. Within an hour of news of the coup being broadcast over the radio,
Nausori Town was shut down. By noon, the town's schools, medical center,
and market were deserted. Retailers had hurriedly boarded up the shops
along the main street, while the few remaining customers were frantically

Nausori Town, the nearest urban center to Darshan Gaon. Photo by John M. Correll.

buying up groceries from the supermarkets before they too closed their doors. And then the looting began.

In Suva, the destruction was already well under way. Earlier that morning crowds that had taken part in the taukei rally ransacked the downtown, looting and destroying shops and businesses. By midday, the flood of people desperately trying to get out of the city and off the streets had gridlocked traffic. Frantic Fijian and Indo-Fijian parents rushed to local schools. Already concerned about the safety of their children, they told me they were horrified to find that some of the teachers and principals had abandoned their students, fleeing the premises to get back to the safety of their own homes.

Fears of ethnically motivated attacks were at the forefront of many Indo-Fijians' concerns. For the first few days following May 19, many Indo-Fijians in Suva and Nausori did not leave their homes but remained indoors, closely observing the news on television and radio.

Although many indigenous Fijians also despaired over the chaos in Parliament and urged an end to the violence, a few others (wrongly) assumed that this was the worst things were going to get and decided to make the most of

Indigenous Fijian women selling produce at the Nausori Town market. Photo by John M. Correll.

the unexpected holiday. One day after the takeover, on May 20, 2000, I took a quick drive from Darshan Gaon to Nausori Town. While the streets of Darshan Gaon were deserted, in Nausori Town I found the public areas thronged with people, all of them Fijian. In the public park, a group of young Fijian men played rugby while Fijian spectators milled around on the sidelines. Unlike the shops, which were still boarded up, the market was open, but with two exceptions the only vendors were Fijian, as were their customers.

It was hard to believe that more than 50 percent of the residents of Nausori Town and the surrounding area are Indo-Fijian.[1] Due to the near invisibility of the town's largest ethnic group, I grew quite excited when I saw a car with Indo-Fijian occupants driving into town only to watch them pull up at the local police station, presumably to ask for help or to report a crime. Indo-Fijian residents from Darshan Gaon, most of whom were too

1. According to the most recent census data, Nausori Town has a population of 5,744 people out of whom 2,201 (38.3 percent) are indigenous Fijian, 3,167 (55.2 percent) are Indian, and 376 (6.5 percent) are "Other." In the wider Nausori area, the population breakdown is approximately 66 percent Indian, 30 percent Fijian, and 4 percent "Other" (Fiji Islands Bureau of Statistics 1996).

terrified to leave their houses, much less the neighborhood, later questioned me as to the state of Nausori Town. Who was on the street? Exactly which shops had been looted in the violence the day before?

Incomprehensibility and Terror

While most people avidly listened to the latest news, the information coming from the media did little to calm them. Speight was initially introduced on the TV news as the new head of state with live coverage of his announcement that he had selected Timoci Silatolu as the new "interim prime minister." A little while later, a confused-looking Fiji TV news reader blurted out that the Fiji military had rung up the TV station demanding that they stop calling Silatolu the "interim prime minister." From now on, he announced, Silatolu was going to be referred to as "the so-called interim prime minister." Local residents' fear and incredulity over the political situation only increased in the coming days as the media ran photos of Speight's supporters reveling and hanging out their laundry in their encampment in the middle of the Parliament grounds, at the same time as it was reported that Prime Minister Chaudhry had been physically brutalized and dragged out onto the Parliament lawn with a gun pointed against his head.

In an effort to keep up with a political situation that fluctuated hour-by-hour, most families kept their radios and televisions running all day and on low volume throughout the night. It was not unusual to see people buying not one but two or all three of the different daily newspapers to get the most up-to-date news. This time the coup was televised, so that even in areas where there was no violence, television viewers would tune in hourly to see new images of the chaos. On one occasion, I visited a middle-aged Indo-Fijian woman who was attempting to listen to the TV news with one ear while holding a transistor radio, tuned to the hourly news update, up to the other.

A great deal of time and energy was devoted to obtaining every available scrap of information on the political events that were reshaping their nation and their lives. But other than repeating what they had heard from their friends and relatives or on the latest news broadcast, most Fijians and Indo-Fijians in Darshan Gaon admitted that they had little idea what was going on. Some suggested that Fiji's political situation could only be understood in terms of fantastical fables such as children's fairy tales or popular TV and film plot lines. Suddenly, the anthropologist was not the only one running around asking, "What is the meaning of all of this?"

By a shaking of the head or by wordless and uncontrollable laughter Indo-Fijian villagers conveyed in its simplest form the incomprehensibility of current events. A week into the coup, a group of Indo-Fijian men assembled in front of the local corner shop read out loud to one another a newspaper report of how members of the military who supported Speight were being allowed free access in and out of Parliament, thus potentially creating a pipeline for information, arms, and other goods necessary to the hostage takers. Their only response was to break out into laugher. On another occasion, when I asked a group of people about a nearby school that had been set alight the night before, they only shook their heads and laughed. In many cases, people's inability to put their sentiments into words was a reflection of the profound sense of confusion and despair they felt about not only their immediate daily lives but also their prospects for the future.

The pace of events, both in terms of the political maneuvering taking place and the spread of violence, was often hard for people to keep up with. The most common remark about how the crisis might play out, in either the short or long term, was "ne sako jāno," or "it cannot be known." Almost as often, however, people remarked that the instability could not possibly carry on much longer and that soon the situation must come back to normal, with a return to their regular routines of community prayer, children going to school, and adults going to work. No one could, however, say how or when such a return to stability would be achieved.

Many people compared the coup to narratives of the fantastic, noting that incidents of violence were more like something they would expect from the movies than from real life. Parvati, my fifty-year-old neighbor, told me how a group of Fijians had broken into her relative's house in the interior of the island and demanded that the family give them all their valuables or else they would kidnap their daughter. "It's just like in a film!" she exclaimed and laughed.[2] Another village resident, twenty-six-year-old Elizabeth, believed a widespread rumor that deposed President Ratu Sir Kamisese Mara and other members of Parliament were Freemasons who had retained political power by praying to the Fijian *vu* (gods) and consuming human blood. Trying to explain how this could be so, she recounted that it all made sense to her once she likened Ratu Mara and the MPs to the "council of the bad gods" on her favorite television show *Hercules*. Parvati and Elizabeth's comparisons of the coup to fantasy sto-

2. Subramani (1997) has masterfully captured the ways in which the violence of the 1987 coups was similarly interpreted as mirroring the plot lines of popular films. In his short story "Captive in Liberated Bush," he depicts the torture of an Indo-Fijian academic suspected of political subversion: "He would probably end up in the trunk of a car, like the young man in the movie. For a moment he was amused by the thought that he and his captors had watched the same movie, sitting next to each other at the Regal on a Saturday afternoon" (1997, 246–47).

ries were widely shared and echoed Sir Vijay Singh's assertion that life was now like a tale from *Alice's Adventures in Wonderland.*

Weariness and Despair

While there were plenty of events that generated fear and excitement, within a few weeks many Indo-Fijians in Darshan Gaon expressed a growing sense of weariness. People began to openly complain of boredom and to despair over the overturning of normal social relations, expectations, and daily routine. Fear had transformed a village in which visiting and socializing between neighbors had been the norm to a place where the houses now looked unapproachable, their curtains drawn, the front doors locked, and the front gates padlocked all day long. Indo-Fijian men continued to frequent the kava-drinking circle outside of the corner store, some more so now that there were so many days on which it wasn't safe to go to work. But for Indo-Fijian women the complete halt of communitywide religious gatherings often meant an end to socializing beyond the members of their households or their immediate neighbors, leading them to rely on the telephone for their only other form of social contact. Their resentment was sometimes voiced in racial terms. Reflecting on the lack of work due to the continuation of school closures in early June, Ganesha, a middle-aged Indo-Fijian schoolteacher, remarked to me that the situation was now "boring." "We can't leave the house, we can't do anything," she said. "But Fijians," she added, "can move about and are enjoying themselves." When I asked her how long she thought the situation would last and what sort of government might come out if it, she shook her head as if to dismiss these questions and said, "We just want to go back to work."

It was also increasingly common to find people sleeping through the day. Many Indo-Fijians said that they had trouble sleeping at night because they feared they or their homes might be attacked under the cover of darkness. One family told me that they regularly locked everyone into a single bedroom at night so that if someone broke into their house, they could help themselves to their belongings without assaulting them. Others found it increasingly necessary to remove themselves, however briefly, from the crisis by sleeping the day away rather than facing up to the violence and their progressively precarious economic situations.

Other villagers tried to unsuccessfully return to their old routines. One evening, Parvati's husband Rajesh told me he was tired of watching the news and following all this "drama" so he was going to ignore it all and devote some time to making necessary repairs to his house. But when the evening

In the weeks that followed the 2000 coup, numerous checkpoints were set up by the military to enforce the curfew. Photo by John M. Correll.

news came on, he was the first to call everyone to sit down in front of the television. Given the ever-changing security situation, he, like many others, felt continually pressured to keep track of the latest political developments.

Rumors or Reality?

As the violence increased in July and August 2000, the bouts of boredom and frustration gave way to ever increasing stress. The most serious threat against the security of Darshan Gaon occurred on the night of July 21, 2000, when four armed Fijian men tested the resolve of the military checkpoint at the nearby Rewa Bridge. The official version broadcast by the media was that four men had driven a car across the bridge, breaking the curfew and refusing to stop at the military checkpoint. The soldiers on duty had responded by firing warning shots. The men then abandoned their car, hijacked a passing vehicle, and drove off in the direction of Suva.

That night numerous phone calls across the village and the surrounding area spread the story that the four men were actually a much larger mobilization by Speight and his supporters and that the village's small Hindu school, which backed against the house that I was renting from Rajesh, was going to be the site of the next rebel encampment. The news sent many into a panic. Rajesh telephoned our home in the middle of the night to inform us of the shooting and advise us that all the women in the village, including his wife and me, must immediately flee. He told us that "four hundred to five hundred men" carrying burning torches were marching up the street toward the village, most likely with the intention of setting some of the houses on fire. He also asked my husband to stay behind to help him protect his property.

Nothing of this story eventuated, and as far as I am aware, everyone in the village stayed in their homes that night. The next day Rajesh seemed confused and embarrassed. His first words when I saw him were accompanied with laughter. "Last night I thought they might burn all this," he said and laughed as he gestured toward his house, "and [my] shop in town!" He then told us how he had spent the night before desperately searching his home for his and his wife's passports, which in his nervousness, he could not find.

"He wanted to take the next plane to Australia this morning!" Parvati laughed. "But instead, he went to work."

It is still unclear what elements of truth there were to the story of a possible mob intent on marching into Darshan Gaon. A few weeks after this incident an indigenous Fijian friend, Billy, informed me that according to Fijian-language radio reports, which often differed in content from English-language and Hindi-language radio, on the same evening close to four hundred rebels and Speight supporters had been preparing to quit their camp at Kalabu Fijian School (where they were in fact arrested a few days later) and were looking for a school to take over in Nausori. I was not, however, able to confirm this report with any other sources. But whether the plans for rebels to take over land in Darshan Gaon were true or not, the possibility that it might occur was probable enough and the events of that evening reflected the acute uncertainty and fear under which all of the village's residents were now living.

Circulating Stories—Oral Transmissions of News and Rumor

The confusion over what was and was not actually happening manifested itself in the increasingly panicked circulation of both official news and rumors, by which I mean carefully crafted accounts of unverified, and often unverifiable, events. Villagers were constantly relating to one another what they had heard on the news and what they thought it *really* meant. Alongside this, they traded various stories and unofficial accounts, some of which were circulating locally through the village, others that were being shared across Fiji.

Like other forms of word-of-mouth communication, coup-related news and rumors traveled through criss-crossing networks of kin, neighbors, workmates, and friends. In Darshan Gaon, this meant that most people got their information from residents of the same ethnic group. Just as gossip and community news were passed from one Indo-Fijian household to another, so were analyses of the crises.

The lack of communication between Fijian and Indo-Fijian households reflected the generalized alienation between neighbors of different ethnic groups. While every Indo-Fijian family in the village claimed to be acquainted with and to have some knowledge of all the other Indo-Fijian residents, many lacked basic facts about their Fijian neighbors such as where they came from or their household composition. Sometimes this extended to not knowing the gender of the Fijian children in the village. In a particularly revealing example, a Fijian family in the village had a two-year-old son they called "Benny Boy" but because of the boy's long hair, many of his Indo-Fijian neighbors mistook him for a girl. It was clear that the family had hardly ever spoken with their Indo-Fijian neighbors, despite a number of years of living only a few yards away from each other. The tremendous fearfulness created by this divide was portrayed by one of the fantastical rumors that swept through Darshan Gaon following the coup. According to a few Indo-Fijian residents, "all the Fijians" in the Suva-Nausori area had been warned about the coup before it happened. "They all told each other beforehand," one middle-aged schoolteacher explained to me, "that's how they all knew to stay home." In fact, many indigenous Fijians were caught out by the violence, just as Indo-Fijians were.

In the space of radical uncertainty, there were also, however, moments when anyone and everyone who might be able to provide the missing pieces of the puzzle was given a hearing. People were not immune to getting political updates from strangers at the bus stop or in the grocery store line. There was also evidence in Darshan Gaon of Indo-Fijian families attempting to cultivate ties with their indigenous Fijian neighbors, discussing, for example, whether or not it would be wise to pay a visit to Fijian residents with whom they had little social contact before in order to open up new pathways of acquiring news. In some cases the coup did in fact inspire Indo-Fijian villagers to take steps to foster further goodwill between themselves and their Fijian neighbors. This included taking part in ad hoc cooperative endeavors to protect the village as a whole. As fellow property owners, for example, the Indo-Fijian and Fijian men in Darshan Gaon formed a neighborhood patrol to guard their homes against violence.

Some of these efforts were successful, but others were marred by years, or even decades, of lack of communication. Linguistic difficulties also proved challenging. Many middle-aged and older Indo-Fijian women who had been raised in the interior had limited schooling and thus little competency in English. As they also didn't speak Fijian, this made communication with non-Hindi speakers almost impossible. In one case, an Indo-Fijian woman in her mid-forties who spoke only Fiji Hindi telephoned me in tears, explaining that the Fijian woman who lived next door to her "had spent all day" trying to warn her of something, but she couldn't understand what she was saying.

Fantastical Accounts

People's willingness to gather information from a variety of sources, some of which they understood better than others, resulted in them passing along a mixture of official news, their own or their friends' accounts of current events, and fantastical rumors that they themselves weren't sure whether they believed or not. Cobbling together bits and pieces of various accounts, many people attempted to put together a narrative through which they could, however momentarily, provide a sense of order and rationality to the events unfolding around them. In some cases, however, the circulation of these explanatory narratives only increased people's confusion and alarm. It is important to note, however, that people's reception of unofficial news was similar in this respect to their responses to the official news on the media—both were avidly consumed because they provided at least a partial framework for explaining events, and both incited further panic.

In addition to widespread rumors of impending violence, such as Rajesh's warning of the oncoming mob, there was a plethora of rumors explaining the origins of the crisis. Some of these focused on the supposed inevitability of the coup, suggesting reasons why the former government *had* to be removed from power. One of the most provocative rumors, widely popular among Indo-Fijian Christians and Fijians, described how former president Ratu Mara held onto power by consuming human blood. A prominent and respected high chief, Mara had been deposed during the first week of the 2000 coup and unceremoniously sent back to his home island in the Lau Province. Various popular explanations sprang up as to why it had been morally necessary for the military to force Mara to step down, many of them denouncing both Mara's provincial allegiances and his respectability as a Christian.

A particularly vivid version was related to me by an indigenous Fijian schoolteacher named Sera, who asserted that the narrative was an accurate accounting of events. Sera's story went something like this:

Former president Mara, his wife Lady Mara, and a number of prominent members of Parliament were members of the Freemasons and as such had fueled their long-lived political careers by practicing magic rituals, including the worship of pagan gods and the drinking of human blood. The blood was supplied to them by the director of the nation's leading hospital, Mary Schramm. (Here, Sera explained that she knew this was true because she had heard a woman caller to a radio station explaining that after giving birth in the hospital a few years ago, she had been walking toward the toilet in the middle of the night when she saw a European man in another room drinking blood. The woman had been so frightened that she urinated on the spot).

As the hospital's director, Schramm was able to smuggle blood out of the hospital and over to the Freemasons. The Freemasons then consumed the blood in a room on the tenth floor of the Ro Lalabalavu Building, a prominent structure in the heart of Suva's downtown, named after a well-known woman from Lau, which is also Mara's home province. Sera didn't mention this, but the tenth floor of the Ro Lalabalavu building is also where the Ministry of Finance has some of its offices. Hidden inside the wall of this room, Sera told me, is a book that looks like the Bible but it "does not have the word of God in it." Instead it is full of "bad words" (which she did not specify), the names of the Fijian *vu* (gods), and a list of the names of the members of the Freemasons, among which appeared Ratu Mara, Lady Mara, and Ro Lalabalavu.

These facts were unearthed when Schramm was (literally) stripped of her disguise as a reputable hospital director. According to Sera, Schramm had tried to visit the rebels inside Parliament but was required to undertake a strip search after she was caught trying to smuggle in poison, cleverly disguised as makeup. The strip search was even more revealing as it turned out that Schramm is actually a man, a fact that Sera asked me, because of some of my work conducting observations in a local medical clinic, to confirm for her.

Sera's account has all the classic features of a fantastical rumor. It tantalizes listeners by offering not only an explanation for the coup, but also an assertion of its moral inevitability (Mara *had* to be forced to step down, given his immoral practices), while provoking them to question its genuineness. It recounts improbable events but asserts their veracity by amassing a huge amount of detail, including the exact locations where the blood was consumed and the eyewitness account of someone so frightened they lost control and urinated on themselves in public. It is also clear, however, from Sera's request for confirmation of Schramm's gender that she too had some doubts about whether or not the story that she recounted was completely true.

The narrative gathers further force by invoking local social tensions. On the political level, it reflects provincial alignments by placing Launs, namely Ratu Mara, Lady Mara, and Ro Lalabalavu, on the "wrong" side of Christian morality. Sera herself hails from Bau, the chiefly island within the Caukodrove Province, and was often scathingly critical of Lau's political domination, which would make the story even more appealing to her. The fact that the blood was consumed at the site of the Ministry of Finance also suggests a reference to criticisms of how the previous government had managed the country's finances—a topic that frequently stirred up public controversy.

Finally, the narrative engages listeners by depicting a range of what many would consider shocking inversions of locally acknowledged truths. Instead of Fijians having once engaged in cannibalism, cannibalism is now depicted as being practiced by "Europeans," such as Mary Schramm and the man in the hospital, the very people who, as the bearers of Christianity, were responsible for abolishing this practice. The hospital is described as not just a place where people go for medical treatment and where women (including Sera herself) go to give birth, but as a site of the grotesque consumption of the human body. The Bible is no longer the "word of God" but is full of "bad words" and the names of pagan gods. Makeup can actually be poison; Mary Schramm is really a man; and respected community leaders such as Ratu Mara are vampires in disguise.

One of the reasons why this narrative proved so popular was because these inversions resonated with a social world which appeared to many, including Sera, to have been turned upside-down by the events of the coup. While the story of President Ratu Mara drinking human blood struck many as farfetched, to others it mirrored the incredulity they felt when they heard that the military was allowing guns to flow into Parliament and into the hands of the rebel leaders. Such fantastical rumors, believed by some, discounted by others, and leaving many more uncertain what to believe, provided a metaphor for real-life events that were no less extraordinary.

As noted in another context by historian Luise White, the fantastic elements of such rumors and the disbelief they engender are part of the reason why they are recounted. Fantastical rumors are not *meant* to be credible

but rather, by recounting things that appear to be bizarre, they compel listeners to engage in a "reassessment of everyday experience" (White 2000,
43). In this case, rumors that many found persuasive yet also unbelievable
forced them to face up to how they might distinguish between what is and
is not beyond the bounds of credulity. To some, this particular rumor of
President Mara's blood-drinking proclivities was beyond the pale. For others, it articulated and channeled their outrage, so much so that a mob was
inspired to torch the Masonic lodge in Levuka, Ovalua, in July 2000.

The Prevalence of Rumor

In and amongst the fantastical rumors, there were other, less dramatic,
but nonetheless unverified accounts. At one stage during the coup, villagers
in Darshan Gaon were terrified to go to a local grocery store in Nausori
Town because they had been told that Indian shoppers were being attacked
when they exited the shop. I asked one man who was spreading this news
why this had not been reported on the radio and he told me that the media
was shying away from reporting such events in case it inspired similar attacks. It was a very plausible explanation. But was it true? Just as with
Rajesh's panic that Darshan Gaon might be the next site of Speight's rebel
encampment, I could never determine with any certainty if this event had
happened. Given, however, that there *were* numerous occasions when violent events took place but were *not* officially reported, it was difficult for
everyone to judge which information they should act on and what they
should dismiss as "mere rumor." Certainly there were incidents that were
not reported in the media, but it was easy for anyone looking for it to find
physical evidence of them. On the evening of May 19, 2000, for example,
half of one of the local Nausori schools was burned down. I saw it the next
day, when many of the classrooms were still smoldering. But it was days before *The Fiji Times* ran a story reporting the fire. Around Nausori I also
documented a number of small Hindu shrines which had been burned
down almost beyond recognition, with all of their *murti,* or religious idols,
irreparably damaged. As far as I am aware, none of these were reported in
the official media.

Such omissions added further force to news and rumor that traveled by
word of mouth. As Tamotsu Shibutani has noted, in times of intense crisis
the shortage of news coupled with the need for speedy transmission of ur-
gent information results in widespread "spontaneous improvisation" and
transmission of unofficial accounts, only some of which are later validated
(1966, 23). Such was the case in Fiji where some of the seemingly incredulous rumors that were first circulated by word of mouth were later verified

A Christian school run by Indo-Fijians that was burned during the May 19, 2000, riots. Photo by John M. Correll.

while others appear to have been developed out of panicked and overeager imaginations.

Regardless of the veracity of particular rumors, and in some cases regardless of their content (Bhabha 1994), it has been well documented that the act of passing on rumors draws people together into an affective coalition, be it one of panic, fear, or hatred (e.g., Lienhardt 1975). This is one reason why rumors sometimes mobilize groups into violent action (see Das 2007, 1998; Guha 1999; Shibutani 1966). But rumors can also provide comfort and ease psychological tension by giving order to events that otherwise appear confused and meaningless, often fitting in with people's existing conceptions of social behavior (Allport and Postman 1947, 155).

In contexts where there is a preexisting need to rely on unofficial sources for news, the credibility of rumor is compounded as people are already accustomed to passing along news that is never officially reported (Kapferer 1990). This was the case among Indo-Fijians who are used to exchanging news that is locally very significant, but that never makes it into the newspaper or onto the radio. Such exchanges of local news and gossip are,

A Hindu temple that was smashed and set alight during the first days of the 2000 coup. Photo by John M. Correll.

moreover, often carried indirectly and anonymously. Through what Brenneis (1978) has called the "coy reference "—a pun on the English "coy" and the Hindi "koi," which means *someone* or *anyone*—Indo-Fijian gossip and storytelling is often characterized by a purposeful indirectness about who said what about whom in order to preserve local decorum. Much like rumor, such signatureless exchanges provide a way of talking about people without necessarily owning up to one's statements or sentiments (Brenneis 1984, 491). This common practice of spreading innocuous, and sometimes not so innocuous, anonymous gossip is an activity that is considered crucial for being in the know about ordinary village comings and goings (Brenneis 1984, 1978). It is thus not surprising that it became even more intensified during the crisis.

The result was that oral accounts of official media reports, unofficial news that was later verified by the media, as well as stories that were never verified, traveled side by side along the same pathways, spreading throughout the village and along other social networks. The concurrency of these exchanges made it more difficult to distinguish real events from fantasies, promoting further disbelief and panic. By the same token, official news reports were often so incredible that they had a similar effect. Whether or not they came from official media outlets, stories and rumors were tantalizing in their promise of giving people a foothold on how to interpret events and ascribe meaning to the chaos. Through such exchanges, audiences and narrators found a means of expressing their tumultuous emotions and crafting possible explanations, some more outlandish than others, but each tempered with the realization that they could never truly capture the radically changing social world in which they lived.

Laughing in the Face of Fear

If the general atmosphere following the coup was one of fear and confusion, there were also moments of overwhelming hilarity. Much of the laughter was intentionally provoked, inspired by a flurry of jokes that Indo-Fijians made in the months that followed May 19. These included jokes about George Speight, racist jokes about Fijians in general, and jokes directly focusing on the violence.

In an influential analysis of rumor published at the end of World War II, American psychologists Gordon Allport and Leo Postman (1947) briefly noted the concurrence of rumors and jokes and suggested that both provide emotional relief in times of stress.[3] If, however, we look closely at how rumors and jokes were deployed during the coup, we shall see that the two forms of discourse had divergent emotional and cognitive effects.

Rumors, like news reports, were fueled by a panicked incitement to share the latest piece of news and were thus speedily passed along from one person to another. In contrast, jokes were much more spontaneous. The kinds of jokes told during the coup did not appear to be circulated from one group to another but were spur of the moment creations, fashioned in response to specific stimuli. Jokes also differed from rumors in that they were not used to explain the crisis. Instead of asserting a purportedly logical explanation of events, they did quite the opposite, making the crisis appear completely ridiculous. In doing so, they succeeded in puncturing the

3. American concerns over "rumor mongering" during World War II provided the impetus for a number of studies on the relationship between stress and rumor, including Allport and Postman (1947) and Shibutani (1966), who includes among his case studies his own research on Japanese and Japanese-American responses to the Second World War.

atmosphere and allowing for a different kind of sensibility—pleasure—to momentarily displace people's feelings of confusion and terror.

Just as important, jokes suggested a limit to the chaos. While fantastical rumors acted to expand the possibilities of violence into the realm of the bizarre, jokes indicated that some things were not to be taken seriously but could indeed still be laughed at. By *purposefully playing* with people's credulity, jokes enabled individuals to point out the absurdity of what was already occurring and to assert that there were still things that were indeed incredulous. In times of acute uncertainty, the production of humor thus imparted to those who partook in it a sense of orderliness and "normality" that was otherwise in question.

George Speight and Other Jokes

Joking among Indo-Fijians was not uncommon before the coup, especially when used to diffuse tension or as a means of regulating behavior, such as prodding an errant child back into line. But joke-telling positively proliferated during the political turmoil as a flurry of jokes began on May 19 and showed no sign of waning over the next four months.[4]

Thematically, the jokes told during the coup were focused entirely on current events. Many of the jokes poked fun at coup-leader George Speight. One popular target of humor was Speight's baldness, a notable physical characteristic that set him apart from most Fijians. For example, an Indo-Fijian man said to a Fijian business acquaintance who sported a rather large hairstyle, "Shouldn't you cut your hair now to look like Speight?" The Fijian acquaintance responded by laughing and commenting that not everyone supports Speight. Another woman joked with me that she hadn't seen many Fijians who were bald like Speight. Both of these quips not only downplayed Speight's importance by making him the butt of their laughter, but also playfully suggested that by lacking a physical characteristic shared by so many Fijians, Speight may not be as representative of indigenous Fijians as he made himself out to be.

Other jokes expressed the absurdity felt by Darshan Gaon's residents as they were repeatedly faced with things that were beyond their understanding. As mentioned, on the first day of the coup, Speight declared that Silatolu was the rebel government's new prime minister. (This decision was

---

4. Indigenous Fijians likewise responded to aspects of the crisis through joking, and although there has been little anthropological analysis of Indo-Fijian humor, there is a growing literature on the place of joking among indigenous Fijians (e.g., Arno 1993) and Rotumans (e.g., Hereniko 1995), some of which focuses directly on indigenous Fijian joking in response to political tension (e.g., Toren 2005).

reversed the very next day when Speight himself took on the role of prime minister). At this point, the television news was still accepting Speight's terminology and had introduced Silatolu to its viewers as the nation's new "interim Prime Minister." Silatolu then gave his first speech as "prime minister" entirely in Fijian, a striking departure from the standard use of English in most official governmental forums. I sat alongside Meena, a middle-aged Indo-Fijian woman, who moved close up to the television screen and watched Silatolu as if she was mesmerized by him. A few minutes into his speech, I asked her to tell me what Silatolu was saying, assuming that she must understand Fijian from the intensity with which she was following his remarks. But she shook her head and said she didn't know Fijian at all. At the end of Silatolu's speech, Meena turned to her husband and asked, "Who was that man?" But Vijay didn't know either. "We've never heard of him," she explained to me and began to laugh. "And he can't even speak English!" she added, turning Silatolu's conscious tactic to alienate half the nation's citizenry by addressing them in Fijian into a hilarious shortcoming in the nation's new "prime minister."

Other humorous expressions of the outlandishness of current events focused directly on the violence that was occurring. Just as the news spread that Indo-Fijian homes in the interior were being burned down by gangs of indigenous Fijian youths, one of my Indo-Fijian neighbors was putting the finishing touches on a house he had just built. He planned to sell it, but because of the violence there weren't going to be many buyers now. I asked him what he was going to do with it. "What am I going to do with it?" he joked. "I am going to take a match and burn it!" Both he and the men working alongside him laughed uproariously.

On another occasion, Devi, my closest confidant in the village, made a similar assertion of the absurdity of the violence after she had a particularly distressing phone call from her elderly mother who lived in Vunidawa, an area in the interior of Viti Levu that had been hardest hit by ethnically targeted violence. Directly after hanging up the phone, Devi declared that her mother had just told her that all the Fijians in the area were having a meeting. "My mother thinks they are discussing how to kill all the Indians," she said and then burst out laughing. A few moments later she seemed confused about whether to take her mother's fears seriously or to continue making light of them.

In addition to humor focused on the rebels and on the violence, another mainstay during the period of unrest was racist jokes about "the Fijians." These jokes tended to cluster around three broad themes: thievery, ineptitude, and primitiveness and dangerousness.

During the height of the looting of downtown Suva, there were a number of racist jokes about Fijians stealing commercial property. As the images of shops being ransacked and torn apart by crowds of indigenous Fijians were broadcast on television, an Indo-Fijian woman I was watching TV with laughed and began to joke, "It's cashier-less shopping!" and a little while later, "It must be a rebate sale!" When asked what would happen to his business after the coup, a small business owner similarly responded with a laugh, "Let the Fijians have it!" All of these jokes emphasized the widespread perception that rather than working for a living, Fijians are more than happy to undermine the rules of commercial trade through theft.

A second set of racist images revolved around Fijians' supposed lack of intelligence. During the riots, most of the schools that were targeted by the mobs were Hindu or Muslim schools, but close to Darshan Gaon a Christian school run by Indo-Fijians had also been burned down. I asked an Indo-Fijian woman why this was so. She laughed and replied, "They must've missed part of the sign. They just read the [Indian name of school] in the title and missed the word Methodist!"

Another Indo-Fijian owner of a small business, the bulk of whose customers were Fijian, was having his company van repainted. The phone number of the company was being painted onto the van in very small numbers and my husband suggested he make them larger so his customers could see them better. "[But] they don't know how to read numbers," the man quipped. "They only know how to burn houses."

These jokes not only underscored perceptions of Fijian ineptitude but also the supposed "dangerousness" of Fijians. They suggested that it is not only a matter of Fijians not knowing how to read, but of knowing very well how to terrorize others. The same theme is evident in a joke told by two teenage boys about an hour after the TV news announced that an Australian journalist had been shot in a skirmish between Speight's supporters and the military. One boy recounted to the other that the journalist must have seen a *jungli* (i.e., an indigenous Fijian) and said "hello mate" and then got shot. The punch line here was a reference to the number of foreign reporters who either resided in Parliament or made daily visits there as guests of George Speight during the hostage crisis, seemingly oblivious to the danger they were putting themselves in. In this case the joke suggested that it was the foreign journalists who were inept; thinking the *jungli* should be treated politely, they warmly greeted him only to be attacked in response.

But the jokes that perhaps best capture the theme of purported "dangerousness" of Fijians were those that invoked Fijians' historical association with cannibalism. Following the kidnapping of two white Air Fiji pilots from New Zealand by Fijian nationalists in Savusavu, one Indo-Fijian woman expressed concern to me over how "white people" [*gorā log*] such as myself might be targeted by Fijians. She said that I should not forget that "before they made shoe soup out of white people" and laughed heartily. She was referring here to the Wesleyan Methodist missionary Reverend Thomas Baker who was killed and consumed by Fijians in the Nausori Highlands (often confused with Nausori Town) near the Sigatoka River in 1867. A popular version of the story relates that Fijians had never seen shoes before. Thinking that his shoes must be a part of Baker's body, they boiled them and attempted to eat them as "soup."

Another cannibalism joke was made in October, after the worst of the violence had died down, by twenty-five-year-old Sunita as she and her mother Virmati prepared supper together. Virmati had told me that the future looks "bleak" for Indians in Fiji for at least the next ten years. What do you think will happen in ten years? I asked. Sunita responded, "We will be roasting in the ovens in ten years!"

Theories of Humor

Much of this humor lends itself to the Freudian-inspired analysis of racist jokes promoted by anthropologist and folklorist Alan Dundes. In his examination of a range of racist and other "sick" joke cycles, such as jokes about Auschwitz, Dundes has suggested that the motivation behind racist jokes is the expression of taboo states, in particular anxiety or aggression toward the ethnic Other (see Dundes 1987; also Dundes and Abrahams 1987; Dundes and Hauschild 1987). When voiced by disempowered groups, such forms of humor coincide, moreover, with John Burma's analysis of humor as a "conflict device" used by oppressed minorities (1990 [1946]). The examples of African-American jokes that Burma documents indicate that these forms of humor are used to assert one's superiority over a dominant group as well as to reflect cognizance of one's positioning in society.[5] Similar analyses of humor as a mode of resistance used by oppressed minorities are also suggested by James Scott (1985) and by Donna Goldstein (2003).

As we have seen, there was an abundance of racist jokes that circulated among Indo-Fijians during the coup, many of which focused on alleged negative character traits of indigenous Fijians and afforded Indo-Fijians a fleeting sense of superiority in a situation in which they felt they had little

---

5. Dundes's and Burma's explanations of racist jokes thus draw from Hobbes's theory of humor as a means of attaining a sense of superiority over others.

or no control. But such an analysis cannot adequately account for the impetus behind joke-telling during the coup. Not all of the jokes generated during the coup targeted indigenous Fijians. Many of the jokes focused less on the ethnic Other than on the social and political chaos generated by the turmoil. Indeed, much of the humor generated during the coup emerged out of a conscious or partially conscious recognition of the intense social disorder and emphasized the confusion of a world turned upside-down by incomprehensible political and social events rather than fears of domination by members of an antagonistic ethnic group.

It is thus more useful to look beyond analyses of ethnic jokes per se and consider more comprehensive explanations of humor. Many of these suggest that in general, humor develops out of situations of disjuncture. Laughter, a number of scholars propose, is a means of giving voice to a situation that strikes one as radically irregular. Philosopher John Morreall, for example, asserts that for humor to occur, "we must be caught off guard by the changes [in our cognitive or affective state] so that we cannot smoothly adjust to what we are experiencing" (1987, 133). Many of the jokes generated during the coup appear to have emerged out of recognition of such discordance as people struggled to comprehend the tumultuous events they were living through.

But while these explanations suggest how social upheaval makes fine fodder for humorists, they leave unanswered the question of why people feel compelled to voice these incongruities through humor rather than through other modes of expression. As we have seen, many people also articulated such feelings of intense upheaval through evocations of despair or through the telling of fantastical rumors. In fact, many of the same people who loudly lamented the effects of the coup and partook in recounting fantastical rumors also made jokes about it. If all of these expressions were stimulated by being plunged into an atmosphere of discordance, what distinguished one from the other?

One way to answer this question is to consider the emotional effect produced by jokes. Rather than looking back at the cognitive or affective context out of which jokes originate, it is crucial to look at the results of humor, for the production of jokes is not only the reflection of discordance but the active creation of it. Moreover, and just as important, it is the production of a certain kind of discordance, a discordance that is pleasurable.

We can take a further cue here from Sigmund Freud. In his interpretation of gallows humor, or galgenhumor, Freud outlines how such humor provides an alternative outlet for pain and distress and suggests that "humour is a means of obtaining pleasure in spite of the distressing affects that interfere with it; it acts as a substitute for the generation of these affects, it puts itself in their place" (1963 [1905], 228).

Inspired by Freud, a number of anthropologists have pointed out how humor, regardless of its content, acts as a release from social convention and transports one into a fleeting moment of pleasure. According to Mary Douglas, humor produces "an exhilarating sense of freedom from form . . . attack[ing] sense and hierarchy" (1968, 365, 170). In his analysis of clowning in the Pacific, William Mitchell likewise asserts that "humorous laughter is a time-out or out-of-time covering response for savoring the disruptive event until cognitive order and speech returns. It is a rather strange pleasure with a touch of thrill—even ecstasy at times—that is spontaneous and, even when anticipated, unmannered" (1992, 26).

Such analyses offer us insight into one aspect of the motivation behind making jokes during times of violence. They show us how, through the perlocutionary effect of a joke, people were able to transform, however momentarily, the sensibility of panic and fear into one of pleasure. Telling a joke thus allowed for a feeling of momentary mastery over a situation that was otherwise experienced as beyond one's control. For one moment, the narrators of jokes were authors of a situation, in the sense of being the authors of an emotional sensibility that replaced their, and others', fear.

There is, however, a second aspect to the power of joke-telling, particularly evident in times of social crisis. Douglas and Mitchell, as well as Freud, are concerned with how laughing in response to a joke acts as a moment of liberation and disordering, but they tell us little about what happens at the conclusion of the joke when there is a return to a sense of orderliness. I would like to suggest that if we are to appreciate the power of humor in times of crisis, then we need to consider not only the disruptive nature of humor but also how jokes indicate a sense of everyday regularity and order through the very act of briefly overturning it.

In times of acute social disorder, making jokes not only forces us to think beyond our social norms but also implicitly suggests that there are indeed social norms to think beyond. During the coup, one way that people expressed their uncertainty and the acute discomfort that it caused them was to push ideas to their extreme by telling jokes. By briefly extending the boundaries of what was imagined as possible and creating a momentary sense of discordance, jokes suggested that there was indeed still a realm of impossibility. Depicting even more absurd situations than those of the current course of events, jokes indicated that there were limits to what could occur. Life is after all *not* so absurd that people will burn down their own houses, it is *not* so absurd that Indo-Fijians will be roasting in ovens in ten years time.

Like fantastical rumors, jokes thus pushed the boundaries of credibility. They did so, however, not by incrementally stacking up evidence to convince listeners of their veracity, thus expanding the limits of the possible while simultaneously requiring a review of the credibility of everyday life, but by jolting listeners out of one cognitive and/or affective state into another and then back again. The production of this abrupt discordance produced a fleeting moment of confusion and disbelief following which there was just as quick a return to the sensibility of "orderliness." In contrast to evocations of despair that lamented the confusion of everyday life or fantastical rumors that extended credulity and questioned life's limits, jokes asserted the unreal in order to reanchor listeners in their perceived reality.

The effects of the joke were, however, only momentary. They punctured the space of terror, broke up people's fear, and afforded a fleeting sense of respite. They did not, however, resolve the questions of how far the violence might go. Nor did they settle people's concerns over what the future might be. As one form of wrestling with the disorientation that the 2000 coup inspired, humor, like fantastical rumors and expressions of despair, gave voice to the intensity of the chaos but could not provide a sense of resolution to the crisis.

As the days slipped into weeks and the weeks into months, it became clear that the crisis was going to be much more severe and last a lot longer than anyone had initially anticipated. Each day's news brought fresh fodder for public speculation, humor, and panic. But some events captured the public's imagination more than others. We turn now to one of the moments that evoked widespread public condemnation, in many cases more than the hostage taking or the overthrowing of the government: the looting of downtown Suva.

4 Looting, Labor, and the Politics of Pain

On the same morning that George Speight and his gunmen broke into Parliament, crowds of indigenous Fijians broke into Suva's shops and restaurants. In the capital city and later in nearby Nausori Town, the looters began to help themselves to a variety of merchandise. Along with a handful of Nausori businesses, it is estimated that 167 businesses in downtown Suva, most of which were owned by Gujaratis, Indo-Fijians, and foreign firms, were looted that day.

The looters were Fijians of all ages. They included youths, elderly women, middle-age men, and women carrying infants. Some of them were violent, leaving behind smashed windows, broken glass, and burned-out buildings. But others, from the TV news footage shown later that night, appeared calmly walking into shops and simply pocketing whatever consumer goods were available. Not that everything that was stolen could be pocketed. People staggered off carrying large kitchen appliances or drove away in pickup trucks loaded with stolen TVs. A Fijian taxi driver told me that a number of looters had offered him a portion of their takings, ranging from jewelry to one of a dozen frozen chickens, in exchange for a ride.

The looting continued for hours. A garment factory owner later remarked to me that he let his employees off after the storming of Parliament, thinking they would collect their children and hurry home, but instead many of them they flocked downtown to take part in the pillaging. The police and military presence were almost negligible, and when present, did not actually do much to stop the looters. Police Commissioner Isikia Savua, who was investigated but cleared for alleged collusion in the coup, was shown on the TV news standing alongside police officers in the middle of the street, forlornly watching as shops were broken into, literally shaking his head in a show of disbelief and despair. Footage of looting from earlier in the day revealed his unarmed officers idly standing by as people walked off with stolen merchandise. By evening the police had acquired golf clubs, allegedly taken from a sports store that was among the many businesses that had been broken into (Field, Baba, and Nabobo-Baba 2005, 97, 103).

The event of the looting of downtown Suva is of interest for two reasons. First, it is a moment of violence that captured a place in the public imagination unlike any other event of the coup, attracting attention and debate among Indo-Fijians and Fijians alike. In fact, as I discuss here, the looting became for many Indo-Fijians the defining event of the early weeks of the coup, more so than the hostage taking or the destruction of Indo-Fijian homes, schools, or sites of religious worship.

Second, Indo-Fijian responses to the looting encapsulated their fears over their place in the Fijian nation. Talk of looting among Indo-Fijians became a space for assertions of their rights to citizenship as based on their intense physical labor, bodily and economic discipline, and bearing of the physical pain such efforts incur. Many Indo-Fijians responded to the events of the coup, particularly the looting, by emphasizing these characteristics as not only an integral part of Indian identity but as determining their role as the harbingers of the modern capitalist economy in Fiji. As part of this representation, the Indian body, because of the physical exertions it has been subjected to both during and after girmit, was depicted as directly linked to the economic development and transformation of Fiji. The vision of a national identity that linked Indians' physical labor and bodily suffering to national progress was moreover endowed with further moral weight through its evocation of Hindu ideals of labor as a selfless sacrifice to God. The legacies of indenture, current economic and labor practices, as well as Hindu religious values, were thus brought together to craft a sense of an enduring past against which the events of the 2000 coup could be made meaningful.

It is important to note that the particular characteristics that were emphasized in this manner were not arbitrary but linked to a colonial and postcolonial history in which Indo-Fijians and indigenous Fijians were categorized as "racial groups" with different relationships to labor and the capitalist market. This is not, however, to suggest that the selection of these attributes as emblematic of Indo-Fijian identity was somehow predetermined. Indo-Fijians had at their disposal a multiplicity of ways of imagining and making sense of their pasts (cf. Brenneis 1991; Kelly 1988b). The political contingencies of 2000, compounded by similar, ongoing political tensions in recent decades, made these ways of imagining and articulating Indo-Fijian history, tradition, and identity more salient than others. Taking the crafting of tradition, or as Bauman suggests "traditionalization," as the "active construction of connections that link the present with a meaningful past" (Bauman 1992, 136) and recognizing the politically contingent nature of the production of such meanings (N. Thomas 1992), we can trace how these characteristics came to be imbued with the status of being emblematic of an ethnic group.

But let us start off with the event that was perceived as a direct threat to Indo-Fijian labor and all it had accomplished—the looting of downtown Suva.

Looting, Labor, and Ethnic Difference

From the first moments of the coup, looting came to occupy a privileged place in the concerns of Indian residents in Darshan Gaon, as well as in Suva and other areas of Nausori. In fact, many described it as the most devastating moment of the political crisis. Given everything else that was going on in the country, such as the hostage taking, the destruction of Hindu temples and schools, and the burning and stoning of Indo-Fijian homes, why did so many Indo-Fijians focus their despair on looting? And what can the fear and anger elicited by the looting tell us about Indo-Fijian perceptions of what was at stake in the crisis? To answer these questions, let us look in more detail at how Indo-Fijians reacted to the destruction of downtown Suva.

By late June 2000, some six weeks after the May 19 looting, the violence that had descended on central Suva had been quelled (for the time being at least) and most shops and businesses in the Suva downtown were open again for business. I had spent the afternoon conducting observations in one of the city's outer lying medical clinics. At the end of a long day, I walked out of the clinic accompanied by Dr. Singh, an Indo-Fijian doctor in her mid-thirties. Before we parted, Dr. Singh turned to me and said in a very tired voice tinged with anger, "I am beginning to hate this race."

"Who?" I asked, not quite sure where this conversation was heading.

"Fijians," she replied. "Because of what they did to Suva."

Assuming she was referring either to the hostage taking or the rebel encampment in Parliament, I suggested, "because of the hostages—"

"That too, but the looting!" she exclaimed. "The shops! Some of my favorite shops are gone. Like Boomerang [the name of a downtown shop]. We used to go there."

One of many Indo-Fijian establishments in Suva that was looted, ransacked, or set on fire during the May 19, 2000, riots. Photo by John M. Correll.

Her remarks might seem flippant but they encapsulated a deep-seated concern shared by many Indo-Fijians over the future of Fiji as a modern, capitalist state. Dr. Singh was hardly alone in her sentiments. For weeks after the looting on May 19, when visiting neighbors, running into people at the market, or chatting with strangers at the bus stop, conversation inevitably turned to the horrors of the looting. Many people expressed distress over shopkeepers' loss of goods and money and over insurance companies' refusals to cover them. There was also great concern over the physical damage done to business establishments and how long it might take to rebuild the downtown.

Although the majority of shops in Fiji are owned by local Indo-Fijians, Gujaratis, and foreign multinationals, it was not only shop owners and those with close ties to business who were visibly affected by the destruction. Even Indo-Fijians whose primary relationships to business enterprises were as customers spoke of the looting as if it constituted a personal attack. Likewise, many indigenous Fijians expressed their great despair over the destruction of Suva's shopping district. In both cases, their concern was not over the actual destruction of the shops and businesses per se (Dr. Singh's love for Boomerang notwithstanding) but over what these assaults on commercial establishments and commodities represented for the nation of Fiji.

For many indigenous Fijians, the looting symbolized an utter disregard for biblical values and the kind of conduct deemed appropriate for Christians. One of the first public statements regarding the looting came from the indigenous Fijian political leader Adi Kuini Speed, the Coalition Government's deputy prime minister. Expressing shock and deep dismay over the behavior of the looters, Speed gave a radio statement in which she depicted looting as a moral breach of the rules of Christian society. She said that she grew up thinking that to be Fijian was to be caring, generous, and kind, but that the actions of the looters and rioters were flagrantly "unchristian" (FM 96, May 20, 2000).

Other indigenous Fijian community leaders echoed her concern. Former prime minister Sitiveni Rabuka stated that the looting and other events of May 19 were setting the country "back to even before the Christian missionaries came" (as quoted in *The Fiji Times*, May 22, 2000, 7). The secretary of the Christian Citizenship Social Services of the Methodist Church, Paula Sotutu, remarked that the image of Fiji as embodying the characteristics of Christianity had evaporated and that "as you have already heard on the radio, read on e-mail, and seen on television, governments abroad are advising their people not to come here. . . . We have been dubbed unruly and uncivilized because of the way government was taken over, the lack of crowd-control that resulted in the break-in and looting of shops, and burning of a number of properties" (as quoted in *The Fiji Times*, June 4, 2000, 9).

Sotutu's comment about the reactions of foreign governments, which was repeated by indigenous Fijians I spoke to, indicate that his concern was over both the loss of Christian values and the economic damage that the appearance of this loss would cause to Fiji's tourism and other industries (see also Teaiwa 2000). Sera, an indigenous Fijian primary school teacher I knew well, told me, for example, that in addition to her concerns over what the looting suggested about how Christianity was practiced in Fiji, it promoted an international image of Fiji as a dangerous place, which would have serious consequences for tourism and trade. In particular, she was worried about "what must you Europeans be thinking about Fijians now."[1]

For many Indo-Fijians, the economic implications of the looting were similarly critical. Indeed, many asserted that the looting was the ultimate

---

1. The term *European* is widely used in Fiji for Australians, New Zealanders, Americans, and the British. Together they make up the bulk of the tourist industry, and along with Asians, are major investors in foreign-owned businesses.

attack on capitalism and the economic development of Fiji. As weeks passed and they continued to talk about the looting, I sometimes suggested that the shopping district would recover and that perhaps the continued political standoff, the fact that many members of Parliament were still being held hostage, the continuing loss of income from tourism, or the possibility of a currency devaluation (as had occurred following the 1987 coups) might be even more damaging to the country's future. They would often respond to me in surprise. "But the looting was horrible [kharāb]!" they replied.

Prompted for further explanation, they focused on what the looting symbolized for Fiji's economic future and on what it said to them about ethnic difference. For many, looting had become a way of talking about the broader issue of Indians' and Fijians' differing relations to labor and physical and economic discipline. Not only were Fijians blamed for carrying out the looting, but they were generally posited as incapable of undertaking the rigorous physical labor and economic discipline that had built up Fiji's economic structure in the first place.

In conversations I had with Indo-Fijians in Darshan Gaon, in Suva, and around the nation, they invoked their pride in how Indo-Fijians had *single-handedly* developed Fiji's economy. Relating to me how her family had first come to live in Darshan Gaon, Devi gestured around the village and stated, "When Fijians were here, it was only jungle. Then Indians came and cleared it [sāf kiya]." During a discussion of the local history of the village, Ram told me, "Indians are the ones who developed this country. They did the hard work." In contrast, Fijians were often portrayed as undisciplined and incapable of the kind of sustained, systematic labor necessary for national development.

We will return to examine in greater detail how Fijians were depicted in this discourse, but for now I want to focus on the other half of this equation, looking more closely at what responses to the looting reveal about Indo-Fijian conceptions of themselves.

Seva and the Religious Underpinnings of Labor

Whereas Fijian responses to the looting, and to the crisis more generally, were explicitly focused on both its economic implications as well as what it meant to them in terms of Christian morality, many Indo-Fijians were vehement that the crisis had nothing to do with religion but was, they told me, all about labor, economics, and "race." In part, downplaying religious differences may have been an attempt to deflect Fijian assertions that Christians should not need to live among "pagans" (i.e., Hindus), much less have one as their prime minister. But the language of economic moral-ity that many Indo-Fijians invoked to explain the crisis was in fact imbued with religious imagery, in particular, through their repeated emphasis on the importance of physical labor as acts of service to God.

Anthropologist John D. Kelly has extensively analyzed how Indo-Fijian Hindus conceptualize the spiritual value of labor as part of a devotionalism that was evident during indenture and later popularized as the central form of Hindu worship in Fiji by followers of Mahatma Gandhi in the 1930s (1992, see also 1991a, 1988a). Much of my discussion here is informed by his work.

Archival and interview materials collected by Kelly and historians of in-denture (especially Lal 2004b, 2000b; and Ali 1980a, 1980b, 1979) show that on their arrival in Fiji, the girmitiyas engaged in various forms of reli-gious worship, often drawing Muslims and Hindus together in observances of Holi and Tazia. On some plantations, Hindus regularly gathered to read the Tulsi Das *Ramayana*, finding strength and solace in the story of the ex-iled god Ram whose suffering eventually results in his triumph over evil. As Kelly has noted, the *Ramayana* provided many on the plantation lines with models for struggle and survival, offering them a sense of dignity, moral worth, and hope (2001, 323).

Caste had all but been done away with during indenture due to the in-termixing, and in many cases intermarriage, of girmitiyas from a variety of caste backgrounds. It was quickly replaced by a postplantation politics that emphasized egalitarianism rather than hierarchy, at least between men (Brenneis 1983, 65; see also Kelly 1988a). As part of this spirit of egalitari-anism, *bhakti* was adopted as a form of Hinduism that would allow all of Fiji's Hindus an opportunity to develop a relationship with God through prayer, devotion, and labor.

Given the shortage of religious and community leaders among the initial migrants, requests were sent back to India for religious missionaries, teach-ers, barristers, and other community leaders. The first to respond were the Arya Samajis who sent a number of missionaries and teachers to Fiji in the 1920s. As part of their vision of reforming Hinduism into a more "pure" Vedic faith, the Arya Samajis promoted the centrality of religious knowl-edge (rather than devotion) and the worship of a formless and impersonal divinity (Kelly 2001). While a minority of the original girmitiyas identified as Samajis, most did not and the missionaries' proposals provoked contro-versy among the newly "freed" Indian community and the colonial author-ities alike (Kelly 2001).

By the early 1930s the Arya Samajis had been joined by another group of Indian missionaries who advocated what they called a more "traditional" and "orthodox" form of Hinduism based on bhakti devotionalism and linked to Gandhi's nationalist movement. This latter group referred to their religious practices as Sanatan Dharm or the "eternal religion." Promoting devotion over knowledge, emphasizing the centrality of the Tulsi Das *Ramayana* in local worship, and lending support and religious credence to the informally organized groups of former girmitiyas who were already coming together to read the *Ramayana*, the Sanatani preachers proved popular. The impact of their efforts is apparent in Fiji's current religious makeup. Of the 77 percent of Indo-Fijians who presently identify as Hindus, approximately 74 percent identify as Sanatani as compared to less than 4 percent who identify as Arya Samaji (Fiji Bureau of Statistics 1996).

Some of the missionaries promoting Sanatan Dharm portrayed themselves as directly following in the footsteps of Gandhi, who had similarly referred to himself as a "sanatani Hindu" (Jordens 1998, 82). Gandhi was highly respected in the Indo-Fijian community both as a religious leader and for his political lobbying on behalf of the rights of Indian indentured laborers in the colonies. He first became directly involved in Fijian politics when he made the abolition of indenture the goal of one of his *satyagraha,* or civil disobedience campaigns, sending his friend, Reverend C. F. Andrews to Fiji to collect damming evidence of the brutal conditions of plantation life. Later, having won the battle against indenture, Gandhi responded to further calls for assistance from Indo-Fijians in the 1920s by sending barristers, some of whom became central figures in Fiji's union movement, to provide legal assistance and political support.[2] One of the barristers Gandhi sent to Fiji was A. D. Patel who dedicated the next forty years to advocating the rights of the Indo-Fijian community, up until his death on the eve of Fiji's independence.

Gandhi's direct engagement with the needs of the Fiji Hindu community lent additional salience to bhakti devotionalism and other aspects of the Sanatani mission. One strand of Gandhi's vision that has had enduring effect is his emphasis on the importance of labor and of seva. As developed in Gandhi's philosophy, seva is an act of service that is enacted on the interpersonal level but has much wider religious and political effects. Gandhi regarded seva as an integral element to the struggle for political freedom.

---

2. Indenture was officially abolished in Fiji in 1920, but the importation of indentured laborers from India had been suspended in 1916 due to the need to employ British ships toward the war effort. While Fiji's colonial government was keen to reinstate the importation of Indian laborers following the war, the lobbying efforts of C. F. Andrews and many others resulted in widespread condemnation in India of the exploitation of indentured laborers, especially women, and forced the colonial authorities there to put a halt to the practice (see Kelly 1993).

Gandhi's approach to labor as both an act of devotion and part of political struggle reverberates through the concepts of work and physical exertion that are voiced by many contemporary Fiji Hindus. In particular, labor is seen as a crucial means of cultivating the relationship between the devotee and God (Kelly 1992, 97, 108). Through the conceptualization of "labor as a divine service," Sanatan Hinduism has promoted the interrelationship of labor, religious duty, and "an etiquette of selfless service" as a pathway to the divine (Kelly 1992, 108, 110). Gandhi's vision moreover incorporated a wide range of labor activities, including wage labor within the capitalist system (Jordens 1998; Kelly 1992). Again we can see a reflection of this in the perspectives of Fiji's Hindus among whom labor, as Kelly argues, is not only "necessary to self-development" but "labor in a capitalist enterprise is labor in service to community and God" (1992, 113).

Though many Indo-Fijians may not consciously recognize Gandhi's influence on their religious practices, much less support the contemporary politics of Fiji's union movement that Gandhi helped found, the perspective they hold of the intertwined moral and political value of labor is nonetheless deeply indebted to the impact that Gandhi and his followers made on Fiji.

Local Conceptions of Labor

The spiritual value of work is sometimes explicitly asserted by Fiji Hindus. A few months after the 2000 coup, for example, Devi explained to me that "Hindu people do a lot of work, and sweat, and God blesses them."

I asked her to tell me more. "They are blessed?" I questioned.

"Yes, Hindu people are blessed because they are very hard working, so they grow, always gaining, generation after generation is blessed." She gestured in a circular fashion to show the cycle of one blessed generation after another, and then continued, "Fijian people pray a lot but God does not listen because they do not work, they do not sweat. God blesses the Hindus. It is a payback."

At this point, I interjected that many Fijians work very hard. "What about Fijian women working at home?" I asked her, knowing that she had Fijian neighbors. Since Devi spent most of her time at home, I thought she must see the Fijian women next door doing their household chores.

Devi grudgingly admitted that *some* Fijians work. She pointed across the fence that separated her from a neighboring Fijian household. "Mereia over there is a nurse and works hard, but in general," she shrugged, "those people are lazy."

The ethnic differentiation explicit in these and many other such comments will be examined in the next chapter. What is important for our purposes here is how such statements indicate the religious underpinnings of labor.

In a number of conversations we had about the importance of work, Indo-Fijians asserted the widespread sentiment that working hard today will produce an economically comfortable tomorrow. But in addition to its productive value they also emphasized the moral value of men's and women's labor. Labor, they suggested, is beneficial not only for the material good it does for one's family, but also for what it means in terms of one's relationship to their community and to God.[3]

The emphasis in this discourse is furthermore not only on what one achieves through work but also on the physical investment they put into their labor. Both Fijians and Indians are judged according to their physical capacity to work, rather than according to their mental capabilities or their innate talents. But value is accorded not only on how much one can do but also on the amount of effort they expend. While Fijians are sometimes appreciatively noted for their brute strength, more often they are criticized for what is perceived as their lack of discipline. In contrast, Indo-Fijians take pride in how industrious they consider themselves to be. When it comes to gardening, for example, much attention is paid to how much a gardener sweats and toils over the land, rather than to the bounty that his or her garden produces. What is valued is bodily discipline and the effort put into physical work rather than innate characteristics such as strength or cleverness.

In devotional terms, work, and in particular the sweat or physical exertion of physical labor, become as much of an offering as the incense, flowers, and *prasād* that form the Sanatan *pūjā*.[4] Working hard is thus respected, almost regardless of the specific outcome that it produces. In turn, evidence of hard work, such as the shops and businesses built up by Indo-Fijian toil, is regarded not only in terms of its practical value but also as an indexical link to labor.

While the particularly vociferous articulation of this view was striking during the 2000 coup, the values it expressed did not arise out of thin air. Indeed, both its purchase in making sense of violence and its emotive force stem from its use in the construction of sociality in times of relative political stability. Long before anyone knew who George Speight was, the moral

---

3. While the discourse through which these sentiments is evoked is specific to Sanatan Hinduism, a comparative case is Weber's analysis of the Protestant work ethic, as discussed by Kelly (1991a).

4. *Prasād* is the food offering made to the gods and is a central part of a *pūjā*, or act of devotional worship.

value of physical labor and the physical suffering it produces, and as we shall see in the following chapter, the transformative abilities of labor to turn "the jungle" into a cultivated space, were central themes in the everyday makings of Indo-Fijian sociality. That there were collective attempts to utilize the same values that governed social life prior to the crisis in order to attribute meaning to violence goes far in explaining the force of such imagery.

Let us continue our examination of these themes by considering two sites in which physical labor, along with the physical pain it produces, are key points in the construction of collective identity. The first site is the everyday interactions of village life in which both Indo-Fijian men's and women's labor are crucial for creating a sense of shared community, but where women are often left to draw attention to their physical suffering in a bid for recognition for their labor contributions. The second is the national, political stage on which generations of Indo-Fijian politicians, historians, and community leaders have commemorated the suffering and toil of the girmitiyas as part of their attempt to ensure Indo-Fijians' citizenship rights.

The Moral Meanings of Labor

Industriousness and diligence are generally accorded great value in everyday Indo-Fijian community life. While it is very common for both men and women to frequently comment about how busy they are and how much they have to do, the same people would later complain of being "bored" when they found themselves temporarily without anything to do. Rather than welcoming a reduction of their workload, it seemed that being busy and visibly *appearing* busy were akin to wearing a badge of honor.

But while these activities are highly valued, in daily life the worth attributed to these acts, and to labor in general, often goes unstated. There are a few important exceptions. Children, for example, are actively taught the importance of diligence and hard work. In addition to being exposed to the examples of their perennially hardworking parents, aunts and uncles, older siblings and older cousins, children are exhorted to look to members of the animal kingdom as models for industriousness. A short story in the widely used Class Five Hindi reader, for example, expounds on the gloriously hardworking nature of ants and holds up the insects as appropriate models that children would do well to learn from. "Ants are very intelligent and hardworking," the uncle narrating the story tells his rapt niece and nephews, "look [and learn] children . . . for they teach us that work yields a sweet outcome" (Ministry of Education 1990, 42, my translation).

The importance of work is likewise continually stressed in religious sermons. During one wedding, the Brahmin pandit who performed the ceremony drew on yet another example from the pantheon of hardworking animals, urging the bride and groom to take heed of the "honey fly" (or honey bee) who distinguishes itself from the other flies by working hard to produce a substance as beneficial as honey. Perhaps, he implied, if they applied themselves, their own diligence could produce something as useful?

In comparison to the moral didactics of school books and religious sermons, until the turbulence of the 2000 coup when the importance of work, how one works, and what one does with the fruits of one's labor came to dominate community conversation, women and men did not commonly reflect in everyday conversation on why it was important to work. Women spoke of working in the garden, of taking care of children, and of cooking for the temple as things that were at times physically difficult to do, but that were *good* to do without explaining why this was so. In mentioning the challenges faced by women employed outside of their homes, some women commented to me on the importance of women's domestic and outside labor in maintaining family life. Men likewise emphasized the importance of staying busy, but in general, they assigned to these activities a moral worth that did not require further elaboration. While there was much talk in Darshan Gaon about the specific tasks that needed to be done for a particular occasion or activity to take place, villagers' everyday conversations indulged in very little conscious reflection on the morality of work.

A series of formal interviews I held toward the end of my fieldwork shed a bit more light on the moral value accorded to labor. When I specifically asked women about the importance of their labor, many of them phrased their responses through the value of *khushī*, which means happiness and is one of the most desirable states to have within a family. It is closely allied with another highly desirable state, that of *shānti*, or peace. Through their religious endeavors, many Hindus consciously aspire to greater khushī and shānti, considering both states to be achievable through discipline, dedication, and labor.

Numerous observers have remarked on shānti as one of the central values of Indo-Fijian ontology. Kelly has noted that shānti is considered "one of the highly desirable results of clean living, hard work, and closeness to god" (1998, 183). Gill similarly remarks on the importance ascribed by Indo-Fijians to cultivating "contentment with one's station in life, and concordance in social relationships" as well as the centrality of women's roles in preserving shānti in the domestic sphere (1988, 91, 198–199). Shānti is moreover not always an end-in-itself but is also considered a precursor for

Hindu religious ceremonies like this one are a focal point of community life. Photo by John M. Correll.

further activity. "Out of peace [shānti], all of your work/activities will be completed," one pandit instructed his audience. Another pandit advised a professional couple that they needed to set aside a few minutes each day for prayer and the cultivation of shānti or all of their industriousness would be for naught.

My observations revealed that alongside shānti, many Hindus also spoke of khushī as an auspicious state realizable through labor. In sermons particularly directed at women, they are exhorted to work toward promoting both khushī and shānti in their family through such domestic endeavors as cooking nurturing meals or speaking only out of love to their children.

Significant religious practices such as hosting a *Ramayana* reading, taking part in a pūjā, or singing devotional songs as part of a religious ceremony are all considered to spread both khushī and shānti throughout the religious community. Of great importance when hosting a *Ramayana* reading, Devi once explained to me, is that you make everyone who comes to

Hindu devotees taking part in a religious ceremony in the waters off of Suva Point. Photo by John M. Correll.

your home *khush,* or happy. There should therefore be no "bad words" spoken in the house, she instructed, the food you cook should be particularly pleasing to your guests, and the atmosphere should be generally conducive to promoting happiness.

Indeed, most prayer meetings, whether small-scale prayers involving extended family or larger communitywide celebrations were marked with an air of enthusiasm and joviality. While they were often serious occasions, there was also a palpable sense of enjoyment, generosity of spirit, and goodwill spread among the assembled men, women, and children. Such social harmony was not accidental but was seen by many as having been consciously cultivated through their endeavors.[5]

Further insights into the moral dimension of labor can also be gleaned by responses to those who were seen as not upholding their religious responsibilities. In Darshan Gaon there was one Hindu family who were viewed by others as particularly hardworking but were also frequently subject to derogatory comments due to their perceived self-interest. By local standards, the Lals were wealthy but were also on the margins of village society. When my husband or I would socialize with them, we were often

---

5. Semantically, as Brenneis has noted, khushī is a state that happens to one, as opposed to a state that is made by one such as *tamashabhaw,* or playfulness/fun (1995, 246). But I have found that the way that women speak about khushī is similar to what Brenneis records men as saying about the creation of tamashabhaw; both emphasize the need to actively participate in socially cultivating these states.

chided and told that the Lals did not partake in community activities and were for this reason to be avoided. As one of their neighbors explained, "When there is a funeral in the village, Lal does not bring anything, or even attend. There is little you can do [when someone dies], but you go [to their house] and bring some food since the family is not allowed to cook. But the Lals don't do that." As this neighbor and others in Darshan Gaon expressed it, the willingness to try to alleviate a neighbor's suffering during a death is a necessary component of community life. One's efforts might not to add up to much ("There is little you can do"), but the moral obligation of showing respect and goodwill to others remains.

Even though popular sentiment, as well as the academic literature on Fiji, highlights how Fijians engage in cooperative labor for the benefit of their village, extended kin, and church, while Indo-Fijians are said to focus purely on their familial needs,[6] the examples I've highlighted demonstrate how Indo-Fijians do not value work solely as a means of meeting the material needs of one's family but also emphasize the importance of labor in creating a peaceful, harmonious, and respectful community life.

Gender and the Cultivation of a Community Ethos

While selfless service and the promotion of peace and happiness are desirable acts for both Indo-Fijian men and women, how they go about enacting them differs according to gender. Both men and women share similar respect for physical labor, industriousness, and the importance of taking part in familial and communal work. The value of men's work and the products of their labor are, however, highly regarded, while women's work tends to be publicly accorded lower status.

Men's Labor

Whether they are working in an office or as part of a gang cutting sugarcane in a cane field, sweating over a friend's car, or running the local school committee, men's labor dominates public space. Particularly in rural areas where many Indian women are restricted from freely inhabiting public space (Adinkrah 1999; Lateef 1990; Trnka 2005d), men and their work are more publicly visible than women. On a Saturday evening in Darshan Gaon, it wasn't uncommon to see my neighbor Vijay relaxing with a beer on his front porch accompanied by a friend or two who had just spent the

6. Such scholarly analysis is exemplified by Ravuvu 1991. For examinations of popular sentiment, see N. Thomas 1992; and Trnka 2002b, 2002c.

entire day helping him renovate his house. Another weekend I might find Vijay down the street with a group of friends huddled over someone's old car, tools strewn across the driveway. Vijay's wife Meena usually spent her Saturdays inside the house cooking and cleaning, or hidden away in the back garden, hanging up the family washing.

The male residents of Darshan Gaon take part in many kinds of labor. Some are employed in the public sector or in large-scale commercial enterprises, while others work as part of a small, family business. As male householders, they are effectively in charge of these small-scale family enterprises, though they often call on their spouse, sons, and daughters for assistance. As sons, men are expected to have a long-term commitment to assisting in the family business, unlike their sisters who will depart from the family and the family business once they are married.

Men also undertake a range of domestic responsibilities, which often involve the exchange or cooperative pooling of work with men outside of their household. Whenever possible, most men would rather rely on friends or kin to repair their truck or help build a new addition to their house than to pay outside laborers to do the job. The result is the creation of informal networks of labor exchange. In this way, men's labor creates visible links between individual men and their families throughout the village.

Many men in Darshan Gaon are also active members of local religious committees. Only Brahmin men can act as priests but non-Brahmin men often hold prestigious positions on the mandali (neighborhood prayer group) organizational committees, positions that are not available to women. Some men are also active on school committees that oversee the running of local schools. A few men from Darshan Gaon have also gone into politics and run for public office, though none have been successful in recent years. In these and other areas, there are opportunities for men to occupy positions of power and public prestige and make their participation in community events known in ways that are unavailable to women.

Men's visibility in creating a sense of shared social identity is such that one ethnographer of Indo-Fijian life has suggested that the social bonds that link individual Indo-Fijian households and create villagewide amity are cultivated primarily through men. According to anthropologist Donald Brenneis, the religious activities that are essential to cultivating social amity in Indo-Fijian village life are "by and large, restricted to males" (1990b, 121). Other ethnographers, in indicating the centrality of women's roles within the domestic sphere, have likewise implied that it is primarily women's roles to preserve peace in the domestic rather than the public sphere (Lateef 1990). Such observations, however, overlook the crucial role played by women in creating community cohesiveness. While it would be foolish to devalue the prominence of men's roles in creating social cohesiveness, it is also clear that women make an effort to promote khushī and shānti between village households through the work they undertake.

Women's Work

In urban and rural areas alike, Indo-Fijian women engage in a number of different kinds of physical labor. Many take part in formal paid labor, as well as having a variety of domestic responsibilities. Collectively, they partake in exchanges of labor, including caring for ill neighbors, exchanging food with other households (particularly in cases of death or illness), and swapping child care.

Women also fulfill a number of religious responsibilities such as cleaning the temple or cooking for religious functions. While men form the organizing committees of the mandalis, women are expected to contribute to the mandalis' larger functions. Many women also take part in neighborhood associations called "*kirtan* clubs." Ostensibly the purpose of these clubs is to provide sites for religious instruction as well as to organize women into neighborhood kirtan, or devotional singing, groups. But the clubs also act as labor units for the various village mandalis, their members working together to complete the majority of the shopping, cooking, and cleaning necessary for large-scale prayer ceremonies. During major festivals such as Ram Naumi or Diwali, this can mean hosting up to one hundred people. Groups of women from various households pick flowers, string *māliyā*, or flower garlands, prepare the prasād, or food offering, for the gods, and at major festivals, prepare meals for all of the devotees.

Women also assist one another with the labor necessary for family-sponsored religious functions, such as funerals, weddings, or household *Ramayana* readings. Some of these events require huge outlays of labor. Funerals, for example, require feasts of dozens of dishes for dozens of people.

As with men, many of these endeavors rely on informal networks of labor, drawing together women from various households. Their collective efforts, however, usually remain behind the scenes.[7]

But if the "sweet outcomes" of their labor are not as readily acknowledged, another way that women can draw attention to their industriousness, and in particular to how strenuously they work, is to highlight the

7. For comparisons with other cultures in which women's domestic labor is seen as "natural" and similarly does not draw much public attention see Heitlinger and Trnka 1999, 1997; Oakley 1974; Romero 1992; and Trnka 1993.

very visible effects such labor has on their bodies through frequent articulations of physical pain.

Pain as an Idiom for Labor

Many Indo-Fijian women share with one another the locations and intensity of their bodily aches and pains on a daily basis. Often, when women over the age of twenty-five or so ask one another how they are ("Kaisai hain?"), they will respond with a standardized reply followed by a statement expressing their physical pain, as in "I'm fine [but] my legs hurt" ("Thīk hain. Mere gor piraye"). The most common complaints are of muscular pain in their backs, arms, legs, or along the side of the body or of headaches. Usually such statements are made without any further elaboration. But in the rare cases where the etiology of pain is contextualized, the context most often has to do with women's labor. More precisely, the activities to which pain is attributed are generally related to physically strenuous effort women undertook for the benefit of others.

Many women are particularly resistant to other kinds of explanations. When women visit medical clinics, physicians will sometimes suggest to them other etiologies of their pain, such as pain caused by cold weather or due to family stress. Women tend to dismiss these explanations and very rarely invoke them themselves when they speak about their own pain with other women.[8] Nor do women openly discuss physical pain that results from their efforts toward physical self-improvement such as exercise or dieting. Rather, physical pain is generally expressed as being about the relation of the self to others for whom one has labored. As such it becomes the public manifestation of self-sacrifice.

In Darshan Gaon, it is infrequent for women to openly complain of the work that lies ahead of them or to give any indication of attempting to reduce the amount of their workload. They do, however, make retrospective comments as to the amount of labor they have completed and link it to the suffering incurred on their bodies. Many women, for example, point out that the month preceding Diwali is a particularly busy time for them as they must clean their house from top to bottom, host a *Ramayana* reading for their extended family and for other community members (if they are financially able to do so), and cook a Diwali dinner for their non-Hindu neighbors. On Diwali day, a number of women expressed exhaustion and

8. For more on pain and Indo-Fijian women's interactions with medical practitioners, see Trnka 2007, 2005b.

relief that the festivities were almost over. At the height of the celebrations, one woman complained to a sympathetic friend how much her back hurt, and then commented, "It is good that Diwali is ending, [because] I've been cleaning the house the last two weeks!" Another woman gestured to her arms and shoulders and said to me quite simply, "I worked and [now] everything hurts." Such direct reflections on women's workloads are, however, uncommon and usually voiced in special contexts such as the end of a particularly hectic month of celebration.

All of this occurs in a context in which it is otherwise very unusual for women to actively focus attention on themselves. Just as Brenneis has noted of talk among Indo-Fijian men, it is similarly infrequent for Indo-Fijian women to explicitly invoke the personal.[9] Indeed, assertions of physical pain are one of the rare discursive forms by which Hindu women in Fiji actively focus attention on themselves.

They do so, however, primarily to spotlight their relationships to others.[10] Because it is considered appropriate that women direct their industriousness outward, toward the needs of their families and religious communities, the statement, "I am in pain," or more precisely, "my legs/arms/etc. are paining," acts as an indirect commentary that initially draws attention to the woman herself, but also makes a powerful assertion about the woman's relationship to her family and community. Invoking women's contributions to family and community, this "talk of the self" suggests not the alienation of the person-in-pain (Scarry 1985) but their active involvement in addressing the needs of others. By using expressions of pain to indicate their industriousness, women emphasize that they are not only participating in community life but are straining themselves to the point of injury in order to cultivate khushī and shānti in their households and communities.[11]

---

9. Writing of his field site in rural Vanua Levu, Brenneis remarks, "However they may actually perceive their world, Bhatgaon villagers rarely talk about it in terms of a personal self" (1990a, 217).

10. For a comparative case of how indigenous Fijian women not only conceptualize but actively experience their bodies as interconnected with those of other women, see Becker 1995.

11. Both Veena Das (1996a, 1996b, 1990b) and Arthur Kleinman (1992) have demonstrated some of the communicative uses of expressions of pain. Kleinman, in particular, has suggested we consider how expressions of pain can act as an "idiom of distress" or as part of a "rhetoric of complaint" (1992, 170, 175). I am suggesting that in order to understand Hindu women's discourses of pain, we must further expand the range of meanings expressed by such communications. See also Trnka 2007, 2005b.

Indo-Fijian men repairing a truck laden with sugarcane. Sugar has remained at the core of Fiji's economy since the days of indenture. Photo by the author.

Industriousness, Sacrifice, and the Figure of the Indian Laborer

While they might not receive the same public recognition for their work, many Indo-Fijian men and women are intensely proud of their labor. Members of both sexes take part in discourses that emphasize the importance of physical labor as a fundamental part of one's relationship to their family, their religious community, and more broadly, to the nation of Fiji.

The image of the Indian forever toiling to produce "the sweet outcome" is in fact one of the most common stereotypes of Indo-Fijians in Fiji and it is worthwhile considering what this widespread representation of the "hardworking Indian" tells us about how Indians have been typecast by themselves and by others. A fruitful place to start is with the entry of Indians into Fiji during the indenture period, as one of the most prevalent ways this discourse is represented on the national level is through the image of the suffering indentured Indian laborer. The majority of these contemporary representations are of men, though amidst the wealth of portrayals, examples of female indentured laborers can also be found.[12]

The girmitiyas, or indentured laborers, spent the first five years of their residence in Fiji tending sugarcane on colonial plantations. Thought of by the British as, in Hugh Tinker's words, "units of production" the forefathers and foremothers of many contemporary Indo-Fijians were brought over to Fiji precisely because of their perceived capacity for physical labor (1974, 38). While the colonial authorities attempted to reduce indentured laborers into workhorses, or "coolies," as they were commonly called, the girmitiyas themselves had other ideas and responded to their new surroundings by fostering the development of new kinds of familial, religious, and other forms of social life (Kelly 1993).

Indo-Fijian participation in the sugar industry, and Indo-Fijian labor more generally, were of central importance in the establishment of Fiji's capitalist economy. And while there has been much shame associated with the brutality associated with plantation life (B. Lal 2004b, 3), the legacy of indenture remains a source of pride in many personal family histories, as well as in academic histories and in Indo-Fijian political discourses today.

When I arrived in Fiji in 1999 and was initially introducing myself to a range of Indo-Fijian families from different economic, educational, and religious backgrounds, some of the first stories they commonly told me were about their ancestors' hardship and struggles during indenture. All of their stories were of men. A twenty-year-old woman named Sita devoted one of her first conversations with me to the tribulations that faced her great-grandfather when he arrived in what he thought would be the land of plenty. Instead, she told me, he was plunged into deep despair when he discovered the deprivations and physical brutalities of the indenture lines. Many others likewise told me of their fathers', grandfathers', or great-grandfathers' struggles, and their eventual successes, in eking out a living following indenture. The recurrent image was that of a life characterized by appalling conditions, pain, and hard labor that finally paid off.

The former girmitiyas themselves have contributed to this portrait of their lives. One former indentured laborer, choosing to speak of the indenture

12. Depictions of female indentured laborers in Fiji, particularly of the abuse they suffered, received a great deal of international attention in the early twentieth century; some scholars suggest that outrage in India over the sexual abuse of indentured women in Fiji led to the abolishment of Fiji's system of indentured labor (see Kelly 1991a). Today representations of female indentured laborers are not, however, so prevalent in popular discourse as are those of their male counterparts.

experience in the second person, recounted, "You spent your *girmit* days . . . with great difficulty, but after obtaining your freedom you worked extremely hard and are now a rich and prosperous cane farmer" (as quoted in Mishra 1979, 7).

This particular laborer's narrative was recorded by Indo-Fijian historian Ahmed Ali and appeared in one of four anthologies that commemorated the one hundredth anniversary of Indian settlement in Fiji in 1979, Vijay Mishra's *Rama's Banishment: A Centenary Tribute to the Fiji Indians.*[13] These publications and the events surrounding them have done much to keep the legacy of the girmitiyas alive and well in public consciousness. Indeed, historian Brij V. Lal has observed that the 1979 commemorations reintroduced the word *girmit* into popular speech (B. Lal 2004b, 3).

The Pain and Brutality of Plantation Life

Particularly emphasized are the numerous hardships that the girmitiyas went through. Songs and memorials recounting those who died in passage as well as memoirs and historical and fictional accounts of the brutal conditions of plantation life keep the girmitiyas' pain and suffering alive in popular memory. The most succinct descriptions were of plantation life as "hell," characterized by one form of extreme hardship followed by another (Ali 1979; see also Kelly 1991b).

From what we know of the plantation lines, the conditions that most girmitiyas encountered were indeed atrocious. They were housed in cramped, often filthy, quarters, given little to eat, and subject to harsh discipline. The result was high rates of suicide, disease, and malnutrition. Women laborers had an additional burden, frequently finding themselves subject to rape and sexual abuse by plantation overseers.

As Lal has noted, workers were paid according to tasks completed but overtasking (i.e., setting the level of tasks too high) was common, particularly in the early days of indenture. Workers who were unable to complete the labor allocated to them found themselves caught up in a vicious cycle. According to Lal, "In the early years the tasks were excessive and were rarely completed on time. Nor did labourers always achieve the minimum statutory wage. Underpaid workers lived on inadequate diets, which caused sickness, which led to absence from work, which in turn led to reduced pay" (2004b, 11).

13. Three other commemorative anthologies are Subramani's *The Indo-Fijian Experience* (1979); Ahmed Ali's *Plantation to Politics* (1980b); and the Ministry of Information's official souvenir of the celebrations, *Girmit: A Centenary Anthology 1879–1979* (Reddy 1980).

We can get a further sense of the suffering they endured by looking at the words of former girmitiyas themselves. An indentured laborer who arrived in Fiji in 1911 described the first days he and his fellow travelers spent in Fiji thus: "When we arrived in Fiji, we were herded into a punt like pigs. . . . We were given rice that was full of worms. We were kept and fed like animals" (as quoted in Ali 1980b, 6). Another recounted some of the hardships faced by women, relating the example of Narayani, an indentured woman whose baby died at birth. Three days later, "an overseer said that she should go to work, even though, according to the government law, a woman is not able to go to work for three months after giving birth to a child. But why should a white overseer attend to these rules? Narayani said, 'My child is dead. I will not go to work.' At this the overseer beat her so much that she became unconscious and fell" (Sanadhya 1991a, 44).

A longer account, this one collected from one of the girmitiyas interviewed by Ahmed Ali, further illustrates some of the difficulties the laborers had in achieving their allotted tasks and the depths of fear and despair that the plantation regime incurred upon them:

> If one were given the task of loading a truck with cane, one had to do so until one had completed it, even if it meant working into the evening. If the truck fell because of bad loading then one had to re-start and complete the task. Once I loaded and loaded the truck thinking that the more I put in it the better remunerated I would be, but I was warned that this would wreck the truck and made to distribute the load into other trucks. By the time I had completed my work it was nearly 1 a.m. and when I got home and had cooked and eaten, it was 4 a.m. And at 5 a.m. I was to go back to work for another day. That day I felt bad. And by the time I went to bed it was morning again. I locked my room and went off to sleep. I slept until four that afternoon. But when I woke up I was frightened. I thought I would be punished because I had stayed away without permission. . . . [Another day] the overseer gave us a task of 24 chains and he told us that we had to finish this otherwise he would whip us and that he would come and check at three to see how much of the work we had done. When he returned at three o'clock and found that some people had not completed the task, he whipped them as he had promised. Except for three of us in our gang everyone was beaten. . . . It was just as well that indenture lasted only five years. Had it been for six years I would have preferred to be dead, even perhaps by my own hands. During the five years I counted the days each day to find out how many were left. The five years were five years of hell. (as quoted in Ali 1979, 9–11)

The Emphasis on Hard Work

Many accounts of girmit portray indenture as the defining event in Indo-Fijian history not only because it was the reason for Indian migration to Fiji and because of the intense suffering it entailed, but also because it is credited as being the moment when the Indo-Fijian work ethic was born. These accounts link the characteristic of industriousness with the experience of forced labor during indenture. Fiji's Indians, we are told, learnt through the brutality of indenture that work was their lot, and that through diligence and perseverance, they could work their way up to, if not prosperity, then at least an honorable living.

Ali, in particular, stresses girmit's transformative characteristics. In his own commemorative anthology, *Plantation to Politics*, Ali argues (1980b, 12),

> for Indians *girmit* provided a lesson and ethos: to survive one had to make sacrifices and live a life of industry in an intensely competitive capitalist system. *Girmit* taught them the lesson that they must survive and subsist first and foremost in this world or else all was naught. It provided them with the incentive, determination, orientation, acquisitiveness and individualism for success in the capitalist system.

In another commemorative forum, Ali describes girmit as the "crucible" through which Indians learned that "industry and individualism were prerequisites for success in the new world they had journeyed to explore and make their own" (1980a, 11). Even following the conclusion of their five-year contract, he adds, the work did not relent, as the former girmitiyas "toiled without ceasing to retrieve their izzat," or pride and self-respect (Ali 1980a, 11).

Although girmit has certainly left its imprint on Indo-Fijian culture, it is dangerous to argue that it has indelibly stamped the characteristic of "hard work" onto Indo-Fijians in a way that permanently differentiates them from other groups in Fiji. Not only does this ignore other aspects of Indo-Fijian responses to girmit and to capitalist labor more generally, such as resistance, but it also overshadows alternative ways that labor, diligence, and industriousness are conceptualized by Indo-Fijians.

Kelly (1988a) has masterfully countered Ali's assertions with an account that locates the roots of the girmitiyas' work ethic back to religious ideals initially articulated in South Asia, rather than on the indenture plantation. I take this to suggest that a religious ethic of bodily discipline and physical effort accrued differential value according to its political context, taking on new saliency during the historical experience of indenture, in which Indo-Fijians were viewed by plantation managers as "units of production," and later as part of the continuing political struggle over Indo-Fijian rights in a climate where Indo-Fijians have been pigeonholed as exemplars of the capitalist work ethic. These multiple strands of value were drawn together in the making of an Indo-Fijian "tradition" of hard work in the present-day; the result is that work and physical discipline have come to be conceptualized by many Indians as both an ethnic (Indian) and religious (Hindu) trait.

Most important for our purposes here is how all of these popular accounts promote the image of the girmitiya as the hardworking laborer par excellence. Obviously, in order to survive plantation life, the girmitiyas did work—and work hard—but my point here is to note how this single image of the struggling laborer, and in particular the male laborer, as opposed to the girmitiya as a mother caring for her children or as the devoted Hindu or Muslim engaging in religious rituals—has come to dominate the public imagination. There are many other ways to depict life on the indentured lines, but by far the most prevalent in Fiji today is the figure of the "hardworking Indian."

Indo-Fijians are not the only ones popularizing this image. The portrait of the ever-toiling Indian laborer is also commonly depicted in Europeans' and indigenous Fijians' representations of Indian life. From the earliest days that the Indians spent ashore in Fiji, European commentators both welcomed and feared their productive capacities. European missionaries described the girmitiyas as "frugal, industrious and intelligent" and worried that these characteristics might pose a danger to the well being of indigenous Fijians (Kelly 1988a, 412). One Reverend Henry Worral, for instance, declared in 1912 that "the Indian . . . [is] microscopically frugal, unrestingly industrious, and possess a mentality as keen and as ruthless as a sword-blade" and feared what this meant for the future of Fiji now that the Indian "has come to stay, to work out a destiny for himself" (as quoted in Kelly 1988a, 412).

European businessmen had similar stories of the impact of the hardworking Indians as their own competitors in the world of commerce. In a retrospective on the history of land tenure in the popular daily newspaper *The Fiji Times*, former colonial administrator and businessman Sir Edward Buck was described as fearing that Indians in Fiji "once freed would be a danger as a competitor to any white man" ("The Seeds . . ." 1999, 11). Buck was quoted as giving the following anecdote as an illustration: "I took two ordinary agricultural coolies [Indian indentured laborers] working on a sugar plantation after their contract was over, as my shop assistants. They were with me one and half years. Now they are running a shop opposite me and beating my head off" (ibid.).

We can add to this wealth of depictions of hardworking Indians some of the accounts of Indians that are voiced by indigenous Fijians. Perhaps one of the more lucid exposés of cross-racial stereotyping is Pio Manoa's essay "Across the Fence," the closing piece in yet another centenary volume, Sub-ramani's *The Indo-Fijian Experience.* Here Manoa reflects that it is widely believed that "hard work is the preserve of Indians, many Indians think as do some Fijians. . . . The overall impression would probably be that the Indians are able to keep at it, to be constant no matter how meager the product while the Fijian wants to get it all done in one fell swoop, to produce something big in a single effort. . . . They [i.e. Indians] have built themselves up and in the process built up the economic life of this country" (1979, 196). Manoa then goes on to suggest that the Indian emphasis on work needs to be understood as part of their "migrant ethic" (1979, 197).

The image of the hardworking Indian thus looms large not only in Indo-Fijian consciousness but also in the stereotypes of Indians held by Europeans and by indigenous Fijians.

Indenture in Political Rhetoric

This account of the girmitiya acts not only as an "explanation" of purported Indian character traits, but has also become part of Indo-Fijians' bid in the national struggle for political rights and recognition. Historically, the image of the struggling, hardworking Indian has been evoked at times of political contestation as well as commemoration. Ali suggests that following the end of indenture "Indians found that the government which they naively called ma baap (mother and father) was indifferent to their plight. Indians thought they were playing an indispensable part in the growth of Fiji; they argued that their toil and sweat had transformed bush and swamp into lush plantations and growing towns. Others saw them as merely accomplishing tasks assigned to them and enjoying conditions better than they would have had in the land of their ancestors" (1980b, 38).

Two decades later, arguments about Indian productivity and rights were raised during the 1946 Deed of Cession Debate. Initiated by a motion in the Fiji parliament by a European, A. A. Ragg, the stated purpose of the Deed of Cession Debate was to ensure the safeguarding of indigenous Fijian rights as outlined in the 1874 Deed of Cession, which transferred political power to Britain. With this in mind, Ragg suggested a public accounting of the various "contributions" each ethnic group had made to Fiji and by extension "the prescriptive rights to which they are entitled" (as quoted in Kelly and Kaplan 2001a, 169). Ragg's own position was that while Fijians were the original owners of Fiji and Europeans had guided the country's development, Indians were "aliens" who had contributed little other than a "spirit to dominate" (ibid.).

At the forefront of the Indo-Fijian response to Ragg was Gandhi's emissary A. D. Patel who argued that it was "Indians whose labor had saved Fijians from exploitation and whose initiatives had led to the greatest improvements in Fijians' political and economic lives" (ibid., 171). In reply to the representation of Indians as a threat to Fijians, Patel countered that the real threat lay with the Europeans who "gobbled up half a million acres of freehold land from the Fijian owners" (ibid., 169). Patel went on to point out that both indigenous Fijians and Indians were subject to the indignities of colonial rule, arguing that "as far as the brown men of the Colony were concerned life and limbs of the Indians and Fijians had no value at all" (ibid., 171). Moreover, it was Indian labor that liberated indigenous Fijians from the fate of enforced labor that was met by so many of the indigenous peoples in colonies around the world; as Patel put it, "the coming of my people to this country gave the Fijians their honor, their prestige, nay indeed their very soul. Otherwise I have no hesitation in saying the Fijians of this Colony would have met with the same fate that some other indigenous races in parts of Africa met" (ibid.).

The resonance between the position taken by Patel and other Indo-Fijian leaders in the 1946 debates and in the statements made by Indo-Fijian political leaders following the coups in both 1987 and 2000 is striking.

In the run up to the 1987 coups, Indo-Fijian political discourse frequently highlighted the importance of Indian labor in Fiji's development. Through what Kelly calls the "Romance of Development," the devotional values of work and self-sacrifice came to be intimately linked with lobbying efforts to secure a political position for Indo-Fijians in Fiji (1988a, 405). "All the races of Fiji were portrayed as pioneering and Fiji was imagined as a harmonious synthesis of like-minded communities, come together for the same goals: modernization, spiritual and material development, and prosperity," Kelly writes (1988a, 415).

Similar sentiments were broadcast in 2000. Running less than three weeks after the May 19, 2000, coup, a *Fiji Times* article headlined "Slaves of the Economy," was devoted to depicting how strenuously Indians labor and "sweat like buffaloes" for the benefit of Fiji (Sharma 2000, 12). A Fiji Girmit Council representative was quoted as stating that it is "sad that Indians have been questioned about their loyalty to Fiji after toiling and sweating for the last 130 years" (ibid.). Predating the coup by just a few days, in his May 16, 2000, *Fiji Times* column, Sir Vijay Singh likewise recognized the anniversary of the first coming of Indians to Fiji by noting the historically divergent roles that the British envisioned for Indians as indentured laborers and for Fijians as the indigenous peoples of Fiji. Singh wrote, "Had the Indian girmitiyas not arrived to provide the European landowners the labor they needed to convert their lands into profitable plantations, the fate of the Fijians can only be imagined" and concluded that "were Fijians and Indo-Fijians to recognize that the event that began on May 14 almost a century and a quarter ago [when the first indentured laborers arrived] has been hugely beneficial to both communities, there might be, one hopes, a more fraternal, and constructive approach by each to the present day needs and aspirations of the other" (V. Singh 2000a, 17).

These examples from 1946, 1987, and 2000 represent the continuing effort to secure Indo-Fijian rights by emphasizing the contributions that Indo-Fijian labor has made to the nation's development and by asserting national development as an inter-ethnic project. Continually reassessing Indo-Fijians' past history in Fiji, such statements are part of a conscious effort to bring to national awareness and acceptance the role of Indo-Fijian labor in developing Fiji and thus lend credence to Indo-Fijians' continuing struggle to retain their rights within the nation.

Echoes of these sentiments are, moreover, found in the broader culture. We can see them, for instance, in Indo-Fijian poetry. Indo-Fijian writer Raymond Pillai's poem "The Labourer's Lament" (1979, 160) is a perfect example, emphasizing both the pain of girmit and the sacrifices of the girmitiyas whose struggles are portrayed as ultimately benefiting not only themselves but the nation as a whole. Pillai's Indo-Fijian narrator mourns,

> We came in answer to your plea,
> We came to build your land.
> But now that you are strong and free,
> You turn our hopes to sand.
> We, who tilled from dawn to dark,
> Who worked in wind and rain,
> We, who strove to make our mark,
> Now find we toiled in vain.

For a brief time, the valorization of Indo-Fijian labor and its role in the development of Fiji even spilled over into the rhetoric of indigenous Fijian statesmen, if the occasion required it. If we take another look at the 1979 commemorative anthologies, we see that the Fiji government honored the occasion of the hundredth anniversary of Indians in Fiji with a national, two-day celebration (B. Lal 2004b, 1). According to the official souvenir program put out by the Ministry of Information, two highly prominent Fijian statesmen, perhaps the most influential political figures in all of Fijian politics, Ratu Sir Kamisese Mara, who was the prime minister at the time, and Ratu Sir George Cakobau, who was the governor-general, spoke on this occasion and chose to focus their remarks on the positive contributions of Indians as laborers in Fiji.

Speaking of the girmitiyas, Ratu Mara told his audience,

> we have all benefited from the labor and sacrifice of these early pioneers. . . . Not only has the sugar industry in which the descendants of the *Girmit* laborers are so closely involved played an inestimable part in our national economic progress; but the children of these first workers have turned to business and, through sacrifice for education, to the learned professions. And in all these fields they have advanced our country. (Reddy 1980, 9)

Cakobau made similar remarks, stating that

> The people of Fiji should be thankful that the Indians were brought here to work the land because of the indenture system, an unpalatable term as it is, completed the triangular components of Fijian land, European money and Indian labor which molded what Fiji is today. . . . Our Indian friends and their forefathers have worked hard for themselves and for Fiji—they have had a big hand in shaping what we see in this country today. (Reddy 1980, 5)

Cakobau closed his speech with a prayer that Indians "enjoy living in their adopted home and that peace and prosperity will prevail in this country of ours in the next hundred years" (Reddy 1980, 5).

Twenty years and three coups later, in 2000 one would've been hard pressed to find indigenous Fijian statesmen making such unequivocal statements in honor of Indians' contributions to Fiji. In 2004, reflecting back on the hundredth anniversary celebrations, Lal commented that "that kind of gesture, so generous and inclusive and accommodating, would be unthinkable now" (2004b, 1). Since the first coups in 1987, indigenous Fijian statesmen have been more likely to focus on the importance of protecting indigenous Fijian paramountcy from the threats of Indo-Fijian "foreigners" than to hail the contributions of non-indigenous Fijians to

Fiji.[14] In fact, Cakobau and Mara's words resonated with arguments made during the 2000 coup, not by indigenous Fijian statesmen but by Indo-Fijians who were desperate to bolster support for their community on the basis of the sacrifices made by the girmitiyas and their descendants.

These discourses, the cultural, religious, and political values they attribute to physical labor and physical suffering, and the links they make between labor and Indian identity give us some insight into why Indo-Fijians were so distressed by the looting that took place in Suva in May 2000. The shops and other commercial enterprises that were destroyed during the looting were seen by many to embody Indo-Fijian labor and the physical sacrifices that such labor often entailed. They represented generations of suffering that Indo-Fijians had endured in Fiji, first as indentured laborers and later as "free" laborers struggling to make a living. These businesses were perceived as having been built up out of not only economic capitol, but also out of what was viewed as an entire ethnic group's physical and emotional investments of time, physical labor, bodily discipline, physical exertion, and pain. When they were smashed or set alight, their destruction encapsulated for many the physical and emotional devastation of the coup.

But Indo-Fijians' reactions to the looting of Suva cannot be entirely attributed to the economic and symbolic cache of shops and businesses as an index of Indo-Fijian labor. They also represented in the starkest terms Indo-Fijians' fears over what would replace the rubble; a nation built not on Indian toil and sacrifice, but a nation reverting to jungli.

14. For a comparison of the 1979 commemoration with the situation of Indo-Fijians in 2004, on the 125th anniversary of their arrival to Fiji, see the latest commemorative volume, Lal's *Bittersweet* (2004a), particularly his essay "Girmit, History, Memory" (B. Lal 2004b).

5 Fear of a Nation Returning to *Jungli*

While Indo-Fijian political leaders and community spokespeople were busily promoting a vision of the Fijian nation as built on the cooperative and harmonious endeavors of Fijians and Indians alike, for many grassroots Indo-Fijians this image was shot through with racial divisiveness. Most of Indo-Fijians' discussions of local history, national belonging, and national development invoked pride in what Indians have achieved in Fiji, but did so on the basis of making negative comparisons with what they depicted as indigenous Fijians' *inability* to undertake sustained, systematic labor or to discipline their spending. In these discussions, it was Indians *alone* who were portrayed as developing (*develop kare*) or moving the country "forward." Recall Devi's comment that "when Fijians were here, it was only jungle. Then Indians came and cleared it."

In contrast to Indians, indigenous Fijians were depicted in these discourses as "dirty" and "lazy" "spendthrifts" whose desire for money and material goods led them not toward labor, but toward theft. Although there existed important counterdiscourses of inter-ethnic solidarity, many Indo-Fijians reified ethnic distinctions between Fijians and Indians by suggesting that ethnically distinct work ethics, economic practices, and levels of "civilization" were at the heart of the political conflict. With alarming frequency Indo-Fijians derogatively referred to Fijians as "junglis," portraying them as the bearers of "primitivism" and "animality" who, it was feared, would return Fiji itself to the realm of the "uncivilized jungle."

In taking these stereotypes seriously and examining their historical roots as well as their deployment during the 2000 coup, I am aware that my analysis might be misread and used to reify the very racist images that I wish to interrogate. This is a danger inherent in any analysis of racist stereotypes but it is not one that I believe should preclude us from looking at how racism structures identity and experience. Rather, the power of racist images, which leads some scholars to shy away from them, or worse yet, to deny their existence, is what behooves me to examine them here. In doing so, I follow a line of anthropological inquiry that has demonstrated the necessity of examining racism and ethnic stereotyping as part of the constitution of national identity and everyday experience. As Liisa Malkki (1995), Mary Weismantel (2001), and Michael Herzfeld (2005), among others, have argued, a deeper understanding of how national identities are consolidated can be gained by critically examining governmental and popular channels through which ethnic and racial stereotypes are constituted, as well as the political, material, and emotional effects of their deployment.

I find it useful in undertaking this task to return to Fredrik Barth's classic notion of oppositional ethnicity. At the core of Barth's groundbreaking theory was the assertion that ethnic identity develops and is sustained through *interactions* between those who perceive themselves as belonging to different ethnic groups. In an effort to steer research away from the cataloguing of the supposedly "objective" criteria that constitute ethnic groups, such as shared language, customs, and dress, Barth suggested that anthropologists focus on the boundaries between different ethnic groups as sites where ethnic identities undergo continual renegotiation (1969). What I take from Barth is his emphasis on the oppositional nature of ethnic identity. The question thus becomes not only how is ethnic identity constituted, but *against* whom is it constituted. In the case of the reification of "Indian" identity in Fiji, the tensions lie between three groups: Fijians, Indians, and Europeans, none of which are natural or essential categories, but each of which came to be defined based on their interactions with one another. In examining these dynamics, I am particularly interested in how ethnic stereotypes came to be deployed as part of Indo-Fijian responses to the 2000 coup and what they reveal about the constitution of fear, alienation, and hatred—what Das (1998), in another context, has referred to as the "social production of hate"—during times of violence.

Images of Intractable Difference

Some of the most prevalent sentiments of ethnic difference were typified in a conversation I had with Ganesha and Parvati just a few days prior to the May 2000 coup. With the renewal of taukei activism, the violence of the

1987 coups was on their minds. As we prepared dinner, they reflected back on the events of 1987, and Ganesha spoke at length about what she considered to be the main political tension in Fiji.

"It all comes down to land," Ganesha stated, explaining that she thought that the root of the political problems in Fiji was due to Indians wanting to make use of Fijian-owned land. "But what do they [Fijians] want with the land?" she angrily exclaimed. "They don't grow anything!"

"Except dalo and—" I began to reply.

"Dalo and cassava," she agreed, naming two popular root crops, primarily used for subsistence agriculture. "But all the sugarcane [Fiji's primary agricultural export] would turn to jungle!"

Parvati laughed in agreement and added, "They [i.e., Fijians] organize their lives differently."

When I asked how, Ganesha explained, "Fijians don't save money, they share it."

Ganesha and Parvati's remarks are typical of many Indo-Fijians' comparisons. According to widespread stereotypes, while Indians are extremely hardworking, Fijians, regardless of age, class, or gender, are "lazy" and uninterested in disciplined labor. Fijians are depicted as living an "easy life," not willing to work hard but "wanting everything" that Indians produce. Many Indo-Fijians told me that in rural areas, Fijians lie on mats all day instead of working and do not bother to clean their homes or villages. As one elderly woman put it, they just want to "sleep on mats. They work until their bellies are full, and then they sleep." Her remark echoed the widespread assumption that Fijians indulge in momentary pleasures rather than working hard to responsibly secure their and their families' futures.

Moreover, those Fijians who *are* recognized by Indo-Fijians as being gainfully employed are often criticized for not knowing how to treat money. Rather than budgeting and providing for the needs of their immediate family, they are portrayed as "unable" to save money. A common characterization is of Fijians as prone to spending a week's pay in a single day. Brijesh, a young Indo-Fijian clerk, gave me the following example. "I get $100 a week and so does the Fijian man in the office," he said. "I get the money on Thursday and use it all week and save some. He spends all the money by Friday."

In a pointed criticism of Fijian practices of distributing cash and goods to extended family members and fellow villagers, Fijians are also severely rebuked for giving away material goods one day that they sorely need the next. As Ganesha put it, the problem is that "Fijians don't save money, they share it."

But the "problem" goes further than that. On a number of occasions, Brijesh and others told me that when Fijians use up their finances, they approach their Indian colleagues and request more cash. If the cash is not forthcoming, Brij and others claimed that the result is sometimes theft.

The notion that Fijians' desires to reap the rewards of the modern economic system without working hard result in theft was commonplace. It was no surprise then that many Indo-Fijians used a similar logic to explain the May 19 looting, stating that it was because Fijians do not want to work, and even when they do work they do not exercise prudence with their money, that they resort to breaking into shops. I was told that rather than working hard, making money, and buying what they needed or wanted, the looters indulged in "laziness" and later gave in to stealing to get the commercial goods that they desired.

This caricature of indigenous Fijians as lazy, undisciplined, and prone to theft was often summed up through a single racial epithet, namely that Fijians are "jungli."

Of Jungles and Jungli

Repeatedly, Indo-Fijians (and, occasionally, Fijians themselves) explained that the violence that accompanied the coup was all due to the destructive behavior of junglis. "Jungli Fijians" from the interior (i.e., parts of the country most associated with the "bush" or "jungle") were, they said, dangerous, violent, and best avoided.

In both Hindi and English, the word *jungli* (sometimes spelled jungali or jungly) connotes not only "an inhabitant of the jungle," but also, as per the *Oxford English Dictionary*, something "jungle-like," suggesting a wild and uncultivated state that has not been transformed through human endeavor. Historically, the word *jungle* was initially used not for a particular kind of vegetation, but to denote a *lack*, indicating a site that lacked human cultivation. In Hindi, the original meaning of "jungle" was "in strictness only waste, uncultivated ground" (Yule and Burnell 1985 [1886], 470). Only later, in Anglo-Indian usage, did the term *jungle* come to be applied "to forest, or other wild growth, rather than to the fact that it is not cultivated," with more frequent use with respect to land covered with tropical vegetation (Yule and Burnell 1985 [1886], 470; see also the *OED*).

Contemporary Indo-Fijians use jungle for land that, as one woman put it, is "thick with vines and tangled undergrowth," as well as to indicate a space has not been "cleared" (*sāf karna*) and thus transformed into an appropriate site for human habitation. Jungle is moreover negatively compared to more "developed" parts of the country; the *lack* inherent in the jungle may thus refer more broadly to a site that lacks infrastructural development, rather than a place that is not inhabited. The "primitivity" of the jungle is furthermore viewed as potent and unbounded, and fears flourish over jungles as sites from which "wildness" can further disseminate.

The dual connotations of jungle as a site covered with tropical vegetation and as a site lacking in human cultivation are similarly reflected in the term *jungli*. As used in Fiji in both Fiji Hindi and English, jungli indicates someone or something associated with the jungle, as well as a person, thing, or place that is unruly, wild, or disorderly, and by implication, lacking in human cultivation. A person with bad manners or a child who is misbehaving, for example, might be called "jungli." So might a thing or place that is messy or out of order. In popular usage, there is considerable slippage between these various meanings. A reference to a "jungli place" might be used to indicate uncultivated "bush" or merely any place (such as a house) that is messy and out of order. The term is furthermore used by Indo-Fijians and sometimes by indigenous Fijians as a racial epithet referring to indigenous Fijians' supposed "primitivity," by implying that indigenous Fijians live a less "civilized" lifestyle as a result of residing in the "bush" or "jungle."

One telling example of the multiplicity of meanings attached to jungli was a conversation that I documented between a nurse and two doctors in a public medical clinic. Their interchange is worth examining in detail for how it reveals both the innocuous use of jungli and its racist underpinnings.

The exchange took place in the staff tearoom of a medical clinic in which I was conducting interviews and observations with patients and clinic staff. An indigenous Fijian doctor, Dr. George, had been filling out paperwork on the communal staff desk in the middle of the tearoom. A few minutes later, he left the desk to make himself a cup of tea on the other side of the room. Soon after, an Indian nurse named Anita entered the room, looking for a space to work. Clearing away the clutter of papers and books that had piled up on the desk, she began to loudly curse that the desk had been left so messy and "jungli." Dr. George called out from across the room to her, "*Who* are you calling jungli?" his tone suggesting that he had taken the term personally and was reacting to its racist connotations. Anita was visibly taken aback by the possibility of affronting a senior physician and began to quickly explain that it was the *desk*, not the *doctor*, that she was calling jungli. At this point, another Fijian physician in the room, Dr. Samuel, began to laugh. Dr. Samuel pointed at his colleague Dr. George and said that it was true that Dr. George "had grown up in the interior" (i.e., in the interior part of the island which is considerably less developed and thus might be referred to by some as jungli). Anita was getting increasingly upset and repeatedly insisted that she had not called Dr. George jungli. She continued her protestations long after the two doctors, who were still laughing, had left the room, explaining to me that Dr. George had "twisted her words around." Whatever their motivation, and it seemed to me that the doctors were both having a bit of fun at Anita's expense as well as pointedly demonstrating the dangerousness of using such racially laden terms, Dr. George and Dr. Samuel's responses illustrate some of the semantic slide that occurs between categories of "indigenous Fijian," "wild," "uncivilized," "disordered" and "dirty."

Cleaning up the Jungle

Mary Douglas, and other scholars following her lead, have vividly demonstrated how ethnic comparisons that proclaim one's own group as "clean," in comparison to the "dirty" Other, have been utilized as part of a variety of political mobilizations, from the banning of "intermarriages" to full-scale genocide (Douglas 1966; see also Appadurai 2006, 1998; Jackson 2002; Malkki 1995; Mbembe 2003). Colonial powers, in their purported "civilizing" endeavors, have made particular use of ethnicized representations of purity and pollution; be it the "dirty" Irish, Chinese, Indians (a moniker used for South Asians as well as for indigenous people around the globe), Africans, or Fijians, "clean up" campaigns have been part and parcel of colonial consolidations of power in a range of settings.[1] Nor is there a dearth of contemporary invocations of the need to "clean up" undesirable elements. Whether used to justify police brutality against "animalistic" assailants, as in the depiction of African-American Rodney King as a "gorilla" by police (Feldman 1994), or voiced as part of protests against the state, such as in the "Dirty Protests," during which imprisoned members of the IRA transformed themselves into the epitome of the "dirty Irish savage" (Aretxaga 1995), images of the state "cleaning up" savagery continue. In Fiji, in recent years the metaphor of "cleaning up" has been put to use by Fiji's latest coup leader, Colonel Bainimarama, to justify his 2006 takeover of government as a necessary "clean up" of political corruption. Employed by a range of state powers, the rhetoric of "cleaning up" has thus been used in a variety of contexts to garner public support for what is portrayed as a

1. For more details of colonial British sanitation schemes as part of the mission to "civilize" indigenous Fijians, see N. Thomas 1990b.

positive, and necessary, transformation towards order, regularity, and moral purity.

When it comes to images of cleaning up "wild" terrain, we can again draw from an abundance of examples, many of them stemming from times of colonial conquest during which the image of colonialists clearing previously uninhabited or uncultivated land was metonymically associated with a broader process of "taming" and "civilizing" not only lands but also their native inhabitants.

In their extensive analysis of British colonial and missionary discourses in South Africa, Jean and John Comaroff demonstrate how both the African continent and its peoples were portrayed as in need of domestication (1991). Agriculture was viewed as one method of instigating this conversion. The missionaries stationed in South Africa shared a vision of a "countryside . . . [that] would be tilled and planted anew—cultivating the heathen workers as they cultivated the soil" (1991, 80). As the Comaroffs point out, in missionary discourse "the poetic bridge between cultivation and civilization was not coincidental" (1991, 80).

In the Pacific, British settlers in New Zealand and Australia used the term *bush* to indicate areas that needed to be cleared for cultivation as well as the settlers' own sense of "isolation from European civilization" (Birtles 1997, 397). In Queensland, the term *jungle* was commonly used for impassable terrain but carried with it a "sinister meaning" that indicated a space that "harboured many unseen dangers" including possible contamination by diseases, such as dengue fever, which were seen to be spread by "jungle mists" (Birtles 1997, 397–98). In his analysis of how European settlers viewed the Australian landscape, Terry Birtles points out that the term *myall* was initially used to describe a common species of the indigenous wattle plant but was later applied to the Aborigines, linking together dangers perceived as inherent in the wild terrain and in its inhabitants. According to Birtles, the dual use of the term indicated that the native inhabitants were perceived to be as wild and uncivilized as the myall-covered lands in which they lived (1997, 398).[2]

Similar sentiments were expressed by early travelers and British settlers in Fiji. Many early travelers lauded the beauty, fertility, and "unchecked luxuriance" of the Fijian landscape (T. Williams 1982 [1858], 6; see also

2. The British voiced comparable views about a range of settings including India, where inhabitants of the Chotanagpur Plain were referred to by British tea planters as "junglis" because of their association with "primitive" jungles (Chatterjee 2001), and in Colombia where British rubber traders envisaged the Indians of Putumayo as embodying the "wildness" and magical power of the jungles they inhabited (Taussig 1987).

Burton 1910; Thurston 1924) but also asserted the need for British hands
to make it flourish. Consider the words of Edward Schramm Smith, a soli-
citor who arrived in Fiji in 1871. Advocating the incorporation of Fiji into
the British Empire, Smith proclaimed,

> should we now succeed in establishing a government, the prosperity of these
> islands will be assured, and we shall gradually extend our dominion over the
> countless islands, whose useless luxuriance is awaiting the advent of our race,
> to be converted into beneficial fertility, and whose savage inhabitants we
> shall teach the divine religion of work. (as quoted in Young 1984, 25)

Those actually allocated the task of laying down Fiji's agricultural infrastructure did not always paint this situation so positively. Early European
settlers' attempts to harness the local labor force proved difficult and the
focus of reform efforts shifted from inculcating "the divine religion of
work" to fostering religious conversion via religious instruction by the
Methodist Church (Kaplan 1995). Following a period of "blackbirding" labor from other parts of the Pacific, Indians, who were thought by the
British to be from a more "civilized" and "advanced" society, were brought
in from India (Kaplan 1995, 73). The assumption was that their constitution was suited for the rigors of the tropical climate (Kelly 1992, 107), they
could be kept in line, and in the infamous words of Fiji's governor J. B.
Thurston, they would be "a working population and nothing more" (as
quoted by Scarr 1980, 88).

While some British colonial authorities viewed the indentured Indians as
merely units of labor (Tinker 1974), colonists and colonial officials also simultaneously categorized Indians as belonging to a distinct "racial" group
whose characteristics were superior to those of indigenous Fijians. As Governor Arthur Gordon, who masterminded the indenture scheme, proclaimed to the Royal Colonial Institute in 1879, "No one would dream of
placing on one level the acute and cultivated Hindoo or Cingalese and the
wandering and naked savage of the Australian bush. The Fijian resembles
neither; but he has more affinity with the former than the latter" (as quoted
in Kaplan 1995, 73).

But what were the effects of this opposition on Indian indentured laborers? How did the girmitiyas view indigenous Fijians?

British accounts suggest fear and hostility between the two groups as well
as enough of an incipient solidarity to make the colonial authorities worried. The Stipendiary Magistrate of Rewa noted in a report written in 1884
that:

In all the colonies where the coolies have been introduced, I think I am near the truth when I say that in landing they found the land destitute or practically so of any coloured race with whom they are likely to be brought into contact. Here on the contrary a very different state of affairs exists. Here they find a proud and arrogant race professing to be owners of the soil, regarding all others as on sufferance, merely as *vulagis*. The Fijians and Indians regard each other with unconcealed contempt and disgust. The Indians never by any chance speak of the Fijians other than as *"jungalis,"* the meaning of which is understood and deeply resented by them all to a man. (from the Colonial Secretary's Office File 84/2140, National Archives of Fiji, as quoted in B. Lal 2004b, 25)

But despite the colonial administration's emphasis on the racial *chasm* between Indians and Fijians, colonial records also attest to occasions on which there was enough of a cooperative spirit between Indians and Fijians that the authorities felt compelled to intervene. There are accounts of colonial authorities forcing Indians found living in Fijian koros to leave, including some who had married Fijian women (B. Lal 2004b, 25). In one case, an Indian ex-indentured laborer who was married to a Fijian woman, had lived in a koro for many years, and had the support of local indigenous Fijian authorities, requested that he be reclassified by the government as a Fijian. Following some debate among colonial officials, his request was denied (Kelly 1995c). Even Indians who wished to engage in commercial enterprises in Fijian areas were seen as a threat to colonial order. Historian Brij V. Lal notes that in 1895 an Indian storekeeper was refused a license to set up shop on the Rewa delta on the grounds that, in the words of the Stipendiary Magistrate, "These Indians speak good Fijian and are very undesirable persons to be thrown into the society of the natives inland and I wish they could be kept out entirely" (as quoted in B. Lal 2004b, 25).

In addition to the efforts of the colonial administration, there was another factor that kept the two groups apart. As Lal has pointed out, many of the first indentured laborers responded with "ignorance and prejudice" toward Fijians (2004b, 25). Similarly, historian Ahmed Ali who interviewed former indentured laborers in the 1970s, suggests that "Indians originally regarded Fijians as *rashaks* or *hoos* or *jungalees*, terms describing people lacking refinement and this bias prevailed for some time" (1979, xxix).

But if we actually look at the transcripts from Ali's interviews, which were conducted more than half a century after the abolition of indenture, we find a more nuanced range of perspectives. Some former girmitiyas did indeed speak of their fear when first encountering "cannibalistic devils." One man recounts, "When I came to Fiji Fijians used to wear a loin-cloth of *masi* or a mat of leaves. They did not appear to know how to use shirts and singlets. When we used to go anywhere we used to go in a group of seven or eight with a stick because we were frightened of Fijians."

Others expressed more ambivalent attitudes, emphasizing their discomfort over cultural differences but also suggesting possibilities for solidarity. One man stated, "When we first saw Fijians we were scared. We were worried that we might become like them when we saw their hair. On our estate we were told that these were the natives of the country. Their disposition towards us was quite good." Another similarly recounted, "Fijians did not fight with us in those days. They used to bring a bunch of bananas and exchange it for a couple of our *rotis*. They gave us shelter in their villages when we ran away from the estate. They appeared as devils to us, because they were all naked except for a few pieces of banana leaves tied around their waist."

And some were generally positive. "Fijians . . . were very amicable; if you went into their *koro* they received you very hospitably," one man declared. But the most positive statement came from the former girmitiya who asserted, "There was no conflict with Fijians in those days. If you gave them something they reciprocated. During indenture days some Indians used to run away from work and go to a Fijian village, they were often given shelter there, as well as provided with food. If one took yagona into a village then all there would share what they had with you" (all quotes from Ali 1979).

The most full-fledged narrative we have of girmit as experienced by an indentured laborer comes from Totaram Sanadhya. Initially brought to Fiji as an indentured laborer in 1893, Sanadhya spent twenty-one years in Fiji, first on the plantation lines and later working as a "free Indian," before returning to India where his memoirs were published (1991a). Sanadhya also wrote fiction and his short story, "The Story of the Haunted Line" (1991b), gives a vivid portrayal of the possibility of Indian and Fijian friendship during girmit.

The narrator in "The Story of the Haunted Line" is a newly arrived Indian indentured laborer who, due to a shortage of housing on the plantation, is made to live alone in the abandoned quarters that had once housed the plantation's Fijian workers. He soon learns that following the deaths of eight Fijian workers due to an unknown illness, all of the remaining Fijian workers ran away from the plantation and the line in which he has been placed was abandoned up until this time. In his isolation, he struggles to adjust to the regimes of plantation life. After using up his weekly rations to host some passing visitors, he finds himself without anything to eat. Due to strict plantation regulations prohibiting the sharing of food, he is unable get any food from his fellow girmitiyas and begins to slowly starve.

One night, the narrator reaches his bleakest moment. He prepares to hang himself when he suddenly hears a mysterious voice calling from outside his quarters, "Open the door, quickly open the door" (Sanadhya 1991b, 124). He opens his door to find four indigenous Fijians who had long ago lived in the same line, one of whom, Sam, could speak a bit of Hindi. The Fijians request food from him, and following his protestations that he has none, they magically find a few remaining bits of cooked rice in his unwashed cooking pots. They consume the rice and depart, but promise to return, with Sam stating, "You fed us, from today you are my friend" (Sanadhya 1991b, 126). Sure enough the following day they return with bags of food from which they prepare a meal for him. As they prepare to depart again, Sam sees the noose with which the narrator had intended to hang himself. Explaining that he needs it to tie up his boat, Sam pulls the noose down from the rafters and carries it away with him. The story concludes with the narrator, his hunger now abated, embracing the new beginning to his life.

Sanadhya's short story was published in 1922 and is one of the earliest Indian depictions of life on the lines. While Sanadhya's writing is often noted for detailing the brutal hardships of plantation life, what is remarkable about this tale is its portrayal of Indian and Fijian understanding, compassion, and friendship. If we read it together with the accounts of the girmitiyas interviewed by Ali, they suggest that while many Indians viewed Fijians as strikingly different, and in some cases as "frightening" due to their physical appearance and cultural practices, there were moments of intercultural solidarity against the hardships of plantation life. Emphasis was placed on the exchange of goods and assistance, particularly in terms of food and shelter, when indentured laborers fled the conditions of the plantation lines, or in the case of Sanadhya's narrator, when the Fijians rescued him from impending starvation.

Rather than signs of indigenous Fijians' "primitivity," in this context exchanges in kind were seen as forging goodwill and even, as with Sanadhya's narrator, friendship. We will come back to this issue in terms of contemporary inter-ethnic friendships, some of which are similarly created through such exchanges. For now, it is important to note that the role of exchange relations in creating valued friendships, both during indenture and in the present day, is significant in suggesting that the discomfort that many contemporary Indo-Fijians express over indigenous Fijian exchange practices is not a blanket condemnation of nonmarket exchange but a concern over how emphasis *primarily* on nonmarket exchange might result in the erosion of the monetary system. Particularly during the early colonial period, when there was an increasing division between the nonmarket sphere into which indigenous Fijians were relegated and Fiji's nascent plantation economy (which was, moreover, experienced by many girmitiyas as extremely exploitative), the girmitiyas did not view exchanges in kind as a threat to "progress" as much as an amelioration of their suffering.

Most such early attempts to foster bonds between Indians and indigenous Fijians were, however, stifled by fear, cultural differences, and the actions of a colonial regime bent on keeping the two "races" apart through the promotion of separate settlements, education systems, and ways of life.

In a political context where indigenous Fijian culture was to be codified and "preserved" while Indians were viewed as a "threat" to the colonial order (McMillan 1929), the girmitiyas and their descendants defended their right to remain in Fiji by embracing representations of an "Indian" identity that promoted their role in national development. In doing so, many ended up promoting Indian contributions against those of all others, portraying Fijians as "junglis" in need of their "civilizing" endeavors.

Ironically, many aspects of contemporary Indo-Fijian portrayals of their contributions to Fiji echo early colonial British accounts in which agricultural cultivation was viewed as part of the colonial endeavor of "civilizing" "primitive" peoples and lands. By, however, erasing the role that the British (as well as Fijians) played in developing Fiji, these accounts promote an interpretation of Fijian history in which Indians, and Indians alone, transformed Fiji from uncultivated jungle or bush into a developing nation on the road to economic prosperity. So much so that some 125 years after the first Indian indentured laborers arrived in Fiji, within much of contemporary popular Indo-Fijian discourse, the role of the British in developing Fiji's economic infrastructure is almost absent. As Devi summed it up, "When Fijians were here, it was only jungle. Then Indians came and cleared it." In these representations, the British have disappeared, and the figure of the civilized Indian comes to be pitted against that of the jungli Fijian.

Such sentiments are furthermore heightened by the emphasis placed in contemporary Hindu communities on regulating and maintaining spiritual "cleanliness" and "purity." Despite having lost their caste status during indenture, Fiji's Hindus retain an intricate cultural and religious sensibility of the importance of spiritual purity. Fears of breaking pollution taboos regulate and in many cases limit certain forms of interaction between Hindus and non-Hindus. Many Hindus are, for example, wary of engaging with Fijians in exchanges of cooked food, out of fear that they might be exposed to polluting substances. As one Hindu woman explained, "You don't know what they are doing with your dishes after you give them food. They could use them to serve beef, before returning them back to you." Unlike Sanadhya's narrator's desperation to acquire food, regardless of its source, rules of appropriate commensality are strictly observed by many contemporary Hindus. At least some of their references to "dirty Fijians" articulate concerns over spiritual as well as physical pollution that act to reinforce Hindus' perceptions of the advisability of keeping their distance from the junglis.

Escalating Dangers—A Nation at Risk of Reverting to Jungle

As we have seen, the racist stereotypes of civilized Indians versus jungli Fijians have a long history in Fiji. Since the Rewa Magistrate's report of 1884, a wealth of government officials and ethnographers of Fiji have documented variations on these sentiments.[3]

The events of the 2000 coup, however, altered many Indo-Fijians' perceptions of how far such jungliness might disseminate. What was at stake now, many feared, was not just differences or even tensions between "hardworking Indians" and "jungli Fijians," not small-scale conflict or even one-on-one inter-ethnic violence, but the danger of a whole nation reverting to jungli.

Fears of a jungli nation resonate on many levels. One widespread concern was over Indo-Fijians' loss of access to agricultural land. If land rental was restructured so that increasing numbers of Indian tenant farmers were driven off of agricultural land, it was widely feared that such land, much of which had been used for growing sugarcane, would be left uncultivated, literally reverting to "jungle" and no longer contributing to the national economy. (In fact, some of the land returned due to the expiry of land leases is indeed no longer being used for sugar production [Reddy and Lal 2002]). There was also the broader fear of the profoundly negative impact the coup was having on other areas of Fiji's commercial infrastructure, including tourism and investment in the garment industry. And, as the violence intensified, there was increasing concern over the widespread lack of

3. In the 1920s, McMillan (1929, 404) observed Indo-Fijians' use of the term *jungli* as a derogatory term used by Indians to refer to indigenous Fijians' "wildness" and lack of "civilization," but also remarked on their "friendly and cordial" relations. Mayer (1973), whose fieldwork was carried out in the early 1950s, does not discuss the term *jungli* per se, but mentions that in times of conflict Indo-Fijians derided indigenous Fijians for their monetary practices. Gillion (1977), Ravuvu (1991), and Norton (2000a) each note the use of *jungli* as a derogatory reference to indigenous Fijians and their cultural practices. Likewise, I found Indians referring to Fijians as junglis both before and following the 2000 coup (Trnka 2002b, 2002c).

law and order. All of these fears were encapsulated in Indo-Fijians' concerns about the destructive capabilities of junglis.

As noted, such racially loaded language occurred primarily in private discourses as opposed to public ones. After systematically searching through representations of inter-ethnic relations in nearly two years' worth of *The Fiji Times* (January 1999-October 2000), I recorded only one instance in which the imagery of jungli was invoked. This occurred in a National Federation Party (NFP) press release in August 2000. In their "Statement on the Current Political Crisis," the NFP condemned the lack of law and order in the country, stating

> from May 19th members of the Indo-Fijian community have fallen victim to acts of terrorism and thuggery. These unarmed and defenseless citizens have been forced off their homes and farms. Houses have been ransacked, some burnt down, livestock has been slaughtered, and crops have been stolen by criminal elements. *This is the law of the jungle.* (*The Fiji Times*, August 12, 2000, 21, my emphasis)

The NFP statement, however, was careful to make the distinction that the acts were being carried out by "criminal elements" and thus to disassociate itself from the perspective that all Fijians live by "the law of the jungle."

In everyday discourses, such distinctions were rarely made. Not only were "all Fijians" increasingly depicted as lawless, but there was also growing concern over how such lawlessness would strip away the hard-earned "progress" gained by Indo-Fijian labor.

One expression of these fears was the depiction of various events of the coup as moving the country backwards (*piche*) in time, back into a past that Indians had strived to get away from. For example, as we watched a TV news broadcast about some of Speight's political demands, an Indo-Fijian woman exclaimed to me, "Indians have built everything we have. But they want us to go back to being laborers, like during *girmit* [indenture]!"

If we return to the images of looting, we can now see why looting, in particular, became a discursive sign for this regression. Many Indo-Fijians perceived the looting to be a direct assault on Fiji's historical progress as an economically developing nation. When crowds of Fijians of all ages and various walks of life were shown on TV stealing goods, smashing down shops, and frightening away foreign tourists and foreign investment, they were seen as directly attacking Fiji's present and future economic development. Despite the fact that many indigenous Fijians, including well-known political leaders and religious authorities, had forcefully denounced the looting, many

Indo-Fijians continued to considered *all* Fijians as sharing the sentiments of the looters, whether they actually took part in the looting or not. And with Fijians not only making up the majority of the population in Fiji, but also in control of much of political power, what was at issue was no longer Fijians' personal poverty and the threat of small-scale theft and inter-ethnic violence, but the large-scale destruction of Fiji's commercial infrastructure. Writ large, Fijian practices of nonmonetary exchange, and the violence they were perceived as leading to, were deemed a threat to the nation's economic viability. The language many Indo-Fijians used to express this was of inter-ethnic difference, but it is important to note that the perceived target of these attacks was not just Indians, but the country as a whole, as the acts of looting and other forms of violence were seen as directly impacting the future chances of peace, stability, and prosperity of the entire nation.

Some Indo-Fijians went as far as to depict such destructive behavior as nonhuman. "The Fijians are animals," one Indo-Fijian man bluntly told me. "They want everything for free. . . . They look at us going ahead and they want what we have." On another occasion, when an Indo-Fijian market vendor discovered yet another round of theft by Fijian youths, he cursed, "[Those] bastards! They're animals!"

In the midst of the confusion following May 19, such statements were widely circulated in private discourse. They often followed one after another and were voiced by all manner of people in the Indo-Fijian community. The frequency and forcefulness of these exchanges created a tight circle of seemingly never-ending racist commentary, allowing very little space for alternative interpretations. In an atmosphere where rumors were rife, credible explanations were difficult to come by, and people were under intense pressure, these assertions took on a great amount of weight, further promoting people's fear and sense of alienation from those they thought were responsible for the crisis.

The Politics of Financial Redistribution

In addition to their concerns about the destruction of the economic infrastructure, many Indo-Fijians were worried about what would happen to the economic resources that remained. They feared that the impact of Fijians' supposed "inability" to plan for the future would be, or already was, the source of not only the irresponsible spending of individual finances but of those of the nation as well. Many of the negative examples that Indo-Fijians related were of Fijians unable to work for, save, and wisely allocate resources for their family needs. Labor, accumulation, and investment were also, however, recognized as being necessary for furthering national development. The use of land, and in particular agricultural land, was likewise seen as having an effect not just on individual or familial finance, but for the economic viability of the nation as a whole. Cultural practices of labor and economic discipline, as embodied by individuals ("those Fijians next door") were thus of increasing concern in the months following May 19, as they were seen to have implications not only for the living status of indigenous Fijians but for the entire nation.

Some explained the entire May 2000 coup as the overtaking of the country in order to satisfy the taukei's desires for immediate money, status, and power, and their inability to take into account the nation's economic future. When the interim government was installed, many Indo-Fijians angrily complained that the members of the new cabinet were all already "bankrupt" and likely to "spend" away the country's resources, leading the country into certain economic decline.

The suggestion was not only that government ministers were spending the money to line their pockets, but also that they were taking resources that belonged to the nation as a whole and redistributing them to Fijians, not necessarily "stealing" but changing the rules to benefit Fijians rather than Indo-Fijians. As, for example, a group of Indo-Fijian women observed the swearing-in of the interim government on television, a middle-aged woman furiously exclaimed, "What do the Fijians want?" and a teenage girl sitting nearby replied, "They want *everything*, look at their budget" and went on to outline the ways in which government money was going to be channeled to Fijian recipients.

This was not a difficult case to make as the interim government soon made public an explicit outline for redistributing funds toward indigenous Fijians in its *Blueprint for the Protection of Fijian and Rotuman Rights and Interests, and the Advancement of Their Development*. As discussed in chapter 2, the stated objective of the blueprint was the "advancement and acceleration" of indigenous Fijian and Rotuman development. Its directives were wide-ranging and included rewriting the constitution so as to restrict the positions of head of state and head of government to indigenous Fijians; changing land laws in order to strengthen the legal powers of indigenous Fijian landowners over those of tenants; increasing spending on development projects specifically aimed at indigenous Fijians and Rotumans; increasing the number of loans to indigenous Fijian and Rotuman businesses; providing a tax-exemption for indigenous Fijian companies; increasing funds for educational scholarships for indigenous

Fijians; and reserving 50 percent of various business licenses for indigenous Fijians (*Blueprint* 2000).

Indigenous Fijian Perspectives on Labor and Exchange Practices

The interim government's strategies can in part be attributed to the fact that, without the pejorative terminology, Indo-Fijians were not the only ones making these comparisons between Indian and Fijian relations to labor and exchange. In a number of his speeches following the coup, military spokesman Lieutenant Colonel Filipo Tarakinikini also spoke of Fijians' "inability" to incorporate themselves into the capitalist system. Referring to proposed changes to the constitution to better safeguard indigenous Fijian rights, Tarakinikini stated, "Constitution or no constitution, it still does not ensure prosperity for the indigenous. Education is the key. Making sure that indigenous Fijians get a grip of what's called entrepreneurship; you know, being able to save for a rainy day, to be hard on ourselves today in order to guarantee a better tomorrow so to speak. All these things are alien to our culture" (Manueli 2000, 7).

This sentiment was expressed in even starker, and more sarcastic, terms by the popular *Fiji Times* columnist Netani Rika. In a column titled "Get off Your Backside," Rika depicted the majority of Fijians during colonialism as succumbing quietly to the dictates of the British that they "keep to the villages and [to] their communal way of life." Rika wrote,

And the Fijians stayed in their villages and planted a little dalo and bananas.
   Some dabbled in the cane industry and were labeled Indians.
   At night the Fijians drank a little yaqona [kava].
   Some of them drank a little more and couldn't get up in the morning to plant the dalo which would pay for the kids to go to school.
   So the kids didn't go to school, what the heck.
   As long as the villagers had the church, the government and the vanua [land] everything was hunky-dory.
   Meanwhile the Indian kids were going to school and university and becoming doctors and lawyers and climbing the Civil Service ladder.
   . . . Suddenly the Fijians found they were left so far behind.
   . . . Two—make that three—coups later and they're still sitting around drinking yaqona and blaming others for their woes.
   It's no different from 1879.
   We're still sitting on our backsides. (2000, 10)

The statements by Tarakinikini and Rika, individuals from very different social positions, reflect some of the ways in which Fijians make similar ethnic comparisons of disparate practices of labor and economics to those of Indo-Fijians.

A significant number of indigenous Fijians, however, give voice to such notions of cultural variation with a distinctly different set of value judgments, expressing the importance of communal practices of property distribution in comparison to capitalist forms of ownership and exchange. Anthropologist Nicholas Thomas has found that rural Fijians "constantly affirm the moral superiority of the Fijian way to the customs of Indians and those of white foreigners," despite the fact that they also "lament that Fijians are 'poor' " and "often accord the negative side of the equation greater emphasis" (1992, 223).

When Thomas describes visiting Fijian koros, he captures this ethic of generosity precisely:

> Nearly every casual visitor to a Fijian village will be told that the crucial feature of the Fijian way of life is embodied in one's willingness to share. You don't let somebody walk past your house without calling out, 'Come and have a cup of tea', 'come and eat', 'here is your lunch.' (1989, 16)

Other ethnographers of indigenous Fijian society, including Marshall Sahlins and Anne Becker, have described the Fijian practice of *kerekere*, or requests for material goods or labor, as a system in which the concept of private property becomes almost negligible (Becker 1995; Sahlins 1962). As one of Becker's interlocutors explained to her, "There isn't anything that belongs to you that really belongs to you—actually, that belongs to your uncle, to your auntie, to your cousins or anybody" (Becker 1995, 25).[4]

One of the primary debates in scholarly work on exchange economies concerns whether these redistributive practices improve or detract from the material well-being of the majority of participants. Some indigenous Fijian commentators consider kerekere, as well as other aspects of communal ownership, a detriment to indigenous Fijian participation in capitalist

---

4. Not only does such a system utilize bonds of kinship but it also assists in the creation of them. This dynamic is perhaps best expressed by an interchange Marshall Sahlins had with one of his Moalan interlocutors. Sahlins writes:

Early in my investigations of *kerkere* I asked a man the following very naïve question: "Suppose two men, one a relative of yours and one not, had something you needed, which would you go to [to *kerekere*]?" The reply was to this effect: "I would go to my relative of course. If he didn't give it to me, and the other man did, I would know that the other man was really my relative." (1962, 204)

development or as a factor that must be taken into account in tailor-making development programs in response to Fijian traditions (Goneyali 1986; Suguta 1986; and for a non-indigenous perspective see Belshaw 1964). Many others, however, focus on the social advantages of Fijian communal practices in order to critique the exploitation of labor that occurs in the capitalist market. According to anthropologist Robert Norton, the indigenous Fijians he worked among were known to assert "the superiority of a communalistic and hierarchical way of life to the competitive capitalist economy in which most Fijians are so disadvantaged" (1990, 9). Another example comes from the work of indigenous Fijian anthropologist Asesela Ravuvu who compares the "Fijian way" of communalism against market-based economies to conclude that the Fijian system is a more fair and effective way of ensuring comfort and prosperity for all (1991, 57).

Whether critical or complimentary of indigenous Fijian systems of ownership and exchange, there is widespread recognition among indigenous Fijians of the differences between communal systems of exchange and the capitalist market. But these differences often get expressed not as differences between economic systems but as racial differences. Among many indigenous Fijians, Indo-Fijians (and sometimes "Europeans" or all Westerners) are seen as the forces of capitalist domination in Fiji. "The path of money" is often equated with "the ways of Indians and other foreigners" (N. Thomas 1992, 223). Many of the indigenous Fijians I spoke with focused their ire against Indians rather than against problems associated with capitalism or the wage labor market. It was also not unusual to hear the complaint that "all Indians are greedy" or that "all Indians are rich."

Nor were some indigenous Fijian political leaders above expressing similar sentiments. Take, for example, the words of the national secretary of the Fijian Association Party who in 1966 opposed the common roll (or electoral rolls not based on race) on the grounds that it would mean Indian domination. David Toganivalu stated in regards to Indo-Fijians, "It is possible for them, because they have plenty of money, to think only of themselves and to disregard us. That is the way they are used to thinking, unlike we Fijians. In our tradition we always think of others. In general the Indians don't have that quality and they may have no regard for us if they get power" (as quoted in Norton 1990, 90, 162).

Political Rights

Political power was, however, one thing that many Indo-Fijians unequivocally asserted that they did not want. In contrast to their vociferous assertions of their economic rights and their fear that all of Fiji's economic progress would be undone by jungli marauders, many Indo-Fijians stated that their rights to citizenship did not necessarily extend to the right to hold political office. Indeed, following the hostages' release, many Indo-Fijians (including those who had helped to elect the Fiji Labour Party) responded to Chaudhry's violent removal from office with ambivalence. A number of Indo-Fijians told me that having an Indo-Fijian as the head of government had not been necessary, nor even, given Fiji's unstable political climate, particularly wise. In discussing their thoughts on the 2000 crisis and on Indo-Fijian political rights, many of their statements drew on a perception of an inherent relationship between ethnicity and the right to govern that posited Indo-Fijians as illegitimate national leaders.

In mid-August 2000, reflecting back on the origins of the May 19 coup, a middle-aged Indo-Fijian woman named Lakshmi told me that many Indians did not think that Fiji needed an Indo-Fijian prime minister. "It is not our country," Lakshmi said, and then paused. "Well, it is our country but . . . you wouldn't want someone from outside leading your country, why should the Fijians want it?" She then brought up the example of Italian-born Sonya Gandhi's recent failed bid for the position of prime minister in India, saying that the same thing applied to Fiji where only a Fijian should be prime minister.

Likewise, when Chaudhry began his overseas tour to publicize the plight of Indo-Fijians following the 2000 coup, a number of people expressed anger and frustration over what they considered to be his misguided attempt to regain political office. "He is only speaking lies, and in such times of trouble!" an Indo-Fijian woman told me. To speak publicly about the violence was seen to be a pointless and even dangerous exercise that might only lead to its escalation.

Indeed, even before the violence of 2000, among many Indo-Fijians I spoke to there was more fear than pride in having an Indo-Fijian prime minister. Their reactions echo sentiments described by John D. Kelly (1998) who remarked on the effort that many Indo-Fijians put into shunning the political limelight. "There are sensible Indo-Fijians," Kelly noted, "who aspire to minority status, and a minority status as featureless as possible, precisely in order to allay others' fears of democracy and thereby combat a rising tide of violence, both real and threatened" (1998, 177). The views of the many Indo-Fijians I spoke with during the 2000 coup upheld Kelly's claim of Indo-Fijians eschewing political power or even equal political representation. These statements, which consciously distance Indo-Fijians away from the realm of government, must however, as Kelly also pointed out, be understood as occurring in a climate of increasing violence and fear. Many of the Indo-Fijians who endorse exclusive political rights to indigenous Fijians do so because they feel compelled to quell the rising tide of violence. Conceding their political rights is much simpler than imagining that they might one day have to leave Fiji.

Consider two seemingly contradictory statements about Indo-Fijians' political rights, both of which were made by Saraswati, a twenty-two-year-old teacher trainee from Labasa on Vanua Levu.

During the height of the 2000 violence, Saraswati explained to me that Indians in Fiji would never take up arms to fight against Fijians "because it's their [Fijians'] land. They own the land."

"So even though you've lived here all your life and your parents before you, it's not your country?" I questioned her.

"It's our country too," she declared, but then a few moments later she added, "but the country is *Fiji*, the name is *Fiji*, it is for *Fijians*."

Saraswati's statement resonates with Lakshmi's argument that Fiji should not have an Indian prime minister, just as India should not have an Italian one. On the face of it, both assertions seem to adopt the taukei slogan "Fiji for the Fijians." But they also make more general assumptions about what it means to belong to a nation. Lakshmi posited that the country of Fiji belongs to Fijians because Indians (and others) have come from outside. In the same way India belongs to Indians and Italians should stick to governing their "own" country. In contrast, Saraswati based her initial assertion on land-ownership, stating that Fijians own (most of) the land and by implication the basis for economic and political power in Fiji and therefore other groups cannot stand up against them. Following my interjection, Saraswati switched tracks to consider the *country* of Fiji and asserted that because the name of the country is Fiji, "it is for Fijians." Like Lakshmi, she was drawing on widespread conceptions of the "natural" unity that should exist between a single culture, a single nation, and a single geographic unity (cf. Gupta and Ferguson 1992) and ended up implying that Fiji was *not* as much her country as it was Fijians'.

A few days later, however, Saraswati told me that she had come up with a solution to all the political troubles: remove all of the Fijians off of Fiji's second largest island of Vanua Levu and secede the entire island to Indo-Fijians. Vanua Levu, which happened to be Saraswati's birthplace, would then, she said, "be a paradise." This suggestion allowed Saraswati to reconcile the image of a unified culture, nation, and geographic entity with the problem of land ownership. If the country could only be divided in two, she reckoned, each culture could be situated in its own geographic space and, moreover, have exclusive rights to its own area of land. The issue of how to ensure Indo-Fijians access to land on which they could secure their living would thus be solved. And she had no doubt what Indians would do with their island, suggesting they would transform it from jungle into "paradise."

But no one, not even Saraswati, seriously promoted the idea of a Fijian-less Vanua Levu. In a context where Indo-Fijians were subject to increasing violence, dividing the country into two seemed to Saraswati one way of reconciling the appealing, but inherently racist, logic of "one culture, one nation, one country" while preserving a space for Indians in Fiji. Taukei rhetoric was based on a similar view, but unlike Saraswati's flights of imagination, it was backed by the beatings, rapes, muggings, and house burnings that inscribed on Indians' bodies and material belongings the unstable nature of their rights and security in Fiji. Against such a backlash, many had no trouble in giving up political rights and asserting what was of more fundamental concern—their right to stay in Fiji.

Possibilities of Inter-ethnic Solidarity

In July 2000, Devi remarked to me that she was worried about what the continuing political and economic instability would mean not only for Indians but also for Fijians. Looking outside at the rain that had been incessantly falling for what seemed like weeks, she spoke of the difficulties caused by business and school closures and the economic downturn and then remarked, "It is raining all across Fiji, on the Indians and on the Fijians too." On another occasion, Devi asserted that everyone, Fijian, Indian, and European alike, bleeds the same red blood. While such statements might seem to pale in significance when compared to the vociferous discourses of racial difference, they are suggestive of the accounts of inter-ethnic friendship and cooperation that I will consider more closely in the following chapter.

There were, however, very few serious attempts among Darshan Gaon's residents to engage in cross-ethnic class-based or regionally focused interpretations of what was behind the coup or of its impact on Fiji. Even when Indo-Fijians in Darshan Gaon and in surrounding areas realized that the impetus for the coup might lie in part in divisions within indigenous Fijian society and furthermore recognized the likelihood that prominent Indo-Fijian business leaders had financially supported Speight, the most popular explanation of the coup remained that it was caused by differences in Indians' and indigenous Fijians' labor practices and economic discipline.

Many Indo-Fijians in Darshan Gaon, like many Indo-Fijians around the nation, responded to the events following May 19 with an increasingly popular discourse that asserted Indo-Fijian claims to national belonging and the right to live in Fiji on the basis of an ethnic identity characterized by contributions of physical labor, as well as disciplined economic practices, that were seen to have directly resulted in the development of Fiji's economy and status as a "modern" nation. In contrast to what they perceived to be the jungli nature of indigenous Fijians, they described themselves as embracing physical industriousness and economic discipline as valuable and necessary for national development and well-being. They were not, however, doing so in a vacuum. The military, the interim government, and many of the various governments that preceded and followed them were no strangers to this language of racial comparison. Indigenous Fijians likewise used ethnically based comparisons of labor and financial management in their everyday discourses.

It was a rare instance when Elizabeth, an Indo-Fijian university student in her mid-twenties, expressed to me the difficulties of breaking out of such thinking. In an email she sent me in November 2000, just after the violence had abated, she reflected back on her own perceptions of the coup and wrote,

> What I can't understand is the fact that even though the people know that Indo-Fijians financed the damn thing [i.e. the coup]—they still have the racial bias . . . most [of the] time I end up doing it myself and I have to work on myself to forget that it wasn't racial but a class issue. But you really can't help getting affected when you are in the middle of it and actually at the receiving end of the racial things during the crisis.

This demonstrated an unusual moment of self-reflection. In the midst of the violence, Elizabeth had spoken of "jungli Fijians," cannibalistic plots, and a deep rift between Indians and Fijians as at the heart of the troubles. Most people let such contradictions slide—while they were aware that the coup had most likely been financed by Indo-Fijian business leaders, they were similarly certain that the coup was caused by jungli Fijians spreading out of the interior and taking over everything they could. Elizabeth's portrayal of her struggle to get beyond such thinking reveals how deep-rooted such stereotypes are and how powerful they were for ascribing meaning to the violence and expressing the rage and helplessness that many Indo-Fijians felt during the crisis.

While not everyone explicitly reflected on such contradictions in their thinking, in the midst of voicing their fear that the coup spelt doom for all of Fiji, some Indo-Fijians punctuated their pronouncements of ethnic difference with an uncertainty over the salience of the very categories that these discourses enacted. As the violence intensified and, in particular, as Indo-Fijians in the interior began to experience increasing levels of physical brutality, Darshan Gaon's residents not only *feared* more violence but had to cope with the very real violent attacks to which they or their kinfolk were subjected. As we shall see, their responses to these events revealed greater uncertainty over the meanings of Indian and Fijian identity and an awareness that something other than the unleashing of jungli behavior might be going on in the political and social turmoil that followed May 19.

6 Victims and Assailants, Victims and Friends

In mid-July 2000, after spending the morning cooking together, Devi and I sat in her kitchen drinking tea. As it was on most days following the coup, her radio was playing continuously in the background. We were only half-listening until we heard what sounded like a class of Hindi-speaking schoolchildren reciting the final phrase of a chant or poem. "This is our country [*Yeh desh hamārā hai*]," they droned, again and again. When they finished, I repeated the phrase. Devi quickly and firmly corrected me, "This country is *also* ours [*Yeh desh hamārā bhī hai*]."

We quietly finished our tea. Then Devi broke the silence to relate the following story of an attack against her *Bhābhī*, or brother's wife, that took place a few years back.

"About four or five years ago in Vunidawa, during rugby time, my brother was going out to milk the cows. Bhābhī was doing the dishes, when she heard someone in the house. She heard his footsteps and thought it was Brother coming back. But it was a Fijian who knew them, who was Brother's friend. He was wearing something on his head [so that] you could see only his eyes and nose. He came up behind Bhābhī and when she turned he hit her with a piece of firewood, cutting her hand," Devi paused to dramatically gesture between her thumb and pointer finger, and then continued, "She cried out and Brother heard her. When Brother came into the house and saw the man, they began to fight and the stocking on his face was pushed up. He hit Brother and Brother fell to the floor. An uncle heard the commotion and came in. The Fijian ran off into the bush."

"But they knew him, he was their friend?" I asked.

Devi nodded. "They used to exchange dalo and cassava. They did not pay him money. He was their friend. They called the police but they [the police] did not do anything. He [the attacker] ran off into the bush. Bhābhī could have been raped, her hand was cut so." She gestured once more, miming a cutting motion against her hand. "It was about five years ago."

"Why during rugby time?" I asked.

Devi looked at me as if this should be obvious. "Because they [i.e. Fijians] need ticket money, and money to buy things at the game, not just dalo and cassava," she said.

Like many of the sentiments described earlier, Devi's narration of her sister-in-law's attack indicates the widely held Indo-Fijian view that it is Fijians' unwillingness to work hard and earn money, coupled with their desire for commodities—wanting something other than just dalo and cassava—that motivates indigenous Fijians to violence. But Devi's story also evokes a much more complex portrayal of Fijian violence and raises a number of other points worthy of our attention.

First, Devi adds to the motivations of "the Fijian" the possible threat of sexual assault, in the process invoking the contemporary context of violent crimes that followed the May 19 coup. During the time of her narration in mid-July 2000, ethnically targeted brutality against Indo-Fijians, in partic-ular sexual assaults against Indo-Fijian women in the interior of Viti Levu, was driving Indo-Fijians out of their homes, off their leased land, and in some cases, out of Fiji.

At the same time, Devi also highlights a connection between Bhābhī and her attacker, referring to an exchange relationship between Bhābhī's hus-band and "the Fijian" that we are told made them "friends." While this is a story of friendship gone awry, calling the Fijian a "friend" indicates a wider awareness of the possibilities of amicable ties between indigenous Fijians and Indo-Fijians. The narrative thus raises questions about how inter-ethnic friendships are established, what are their limits, and how we can judge their reliability. As we shall see, other violence narratives go further in describing the importance of inter-ethnic friendships and in depicting acts of assistance and cooperation between Fijians and Indians.

Finally, Devi's narrative is also a political commentary. Devi told it in re-sponse to the children's assertion that Fiji belongs to Hindi-speakers (i.e., Indo-Fijians), a politically controversial claim given indigenous Fijian na-tionalists' branding of Indo-Fijians as vulagi, or "foreigners," in Fiji. Devi tempered the children's assertion, stating that Fiji *also* belongs to Indo-Fijians. Her rephrasing of their chant can be understood as a defense against the popular taukei charge that Indians are taking over Fiji. Instead, she stressed that Fiji belongs to Indians *too*. But it is a belonging tinged by violence, as Devi hastened to demonstrate in her vivid story of lost friendship, inter-ethnic assault, and police collusion.

In these ways, Devi's narration of Bhābhī's attack clearly involves more than the perceived dichotomy of "Indian versus Fijian" that dominated talk of urban looting and concerns over the spread of jungliness. It is a story not only about inter-ethnic violence but also about the possibilities and limits of inter-ethnic friendship, about interactions between gendered bodies, and about the roles of the police and state authorities in responding to violence. It exhibits a tension between attributing violence to widely perceived notions of ethnic difference and the need to recount incidents of violence as contextually specific and influenced by factors other than ethnic antagonism. Its style of narration is simultaneously a political critique and an expression of pain.

Devi's story was only one of a number of narratives of past and present violence told by residents of Darshan Gaon. During the months of violent upheaval, Indo-Fijians' articulations of pain and despair and their efforts to give order and ascribe meaning to the tumultuous events in which they found themselves involved the telling and retelling of many such tales. Most of the stories were of current attacks. Darshan Gaon is only a few hours drive from Vunidawa and Muaniweni where anti-Indian violence was widespread; it is close enough that a number of people who fled these areas came to stay with their kinfolk in the village and as these people traveled, so too did their stories. Other accounts, like the story of Bhābhī's attack, were of past violence remembered and retold in a time of escalating attacks against Indo-Fijians.

My focus here is on narratives and fragmentary accounts of physical violence that occurred primarily in rural areas. These accounts were told, and often numerously retold, by victims, their kin, and other interested parties. I call all of those who related these accounts narrators, regardless of how developed or rudimentary their accounts were. I refer to those who listened as members of their audience, despite the fact that many of them had their own stories of violence to tell.

I have two interests in these accounts. One is in how they were related in ways that evoked not only images of ethnic difference but also the importance of inter-ethnic friendships. In their portrayals of Fijians as both friends and foes, accounts of rural violence reflect an important ambivalence. On the one hand, they illustrate the perception, widely voiced among Indo-Fijians during the coup, that all Fijians are dangerous; because of their perceived antagonism toward market-based production and exchange, Fijians are represented as threatening the future of Fiji as a modern, capitalist nation-state. At the same time, however, these accounts invoke personal relations of neighborliness, cooperation, and amicability between Indo-Fijians and Fijians. Furthermore, through their criticisms of the police, they suggest that the state promoted circumstances conducive to violence and was thus in part responsible for these events. The telling of accounts of rural violence thus simultaneously undermined, supported, and added new fodder to preexisting racial imaginaries of irreconcilable Indian and Fijian difference.

The paradigm of local identities transformed by violence into nationalist and/or ethnic ones has been broadly documented (for example, Appadurai 1998; Hayden 1996; Loizos 1988; Sekulíc, Massey, and Hodson 2006; Volkan 2006; R. Williams 2003). I would like to suggest, however, that rather than being indicative of a conversion of local identities into ethnic ones, Indo-Fijian accounts of rural violence demonstrate the multiple kinds of knowledge of the Other that Indo-Fijians used as they endeavored to make meaning out of a society transformed by violence (cf. Das 1996b; Tambiah 1996), a complexity that was notably absent from the responses to urban and state-level violence we considered earlier.

The differences between these accounts were due in part to the nature of the violence. Unlike the mob violence of looting or the assault by unknown rebels on the Parliament, small-scale rural attacks often involved victims, assailants, and third parties such as neighbors and friends who were known to each other. The complexities of their interrelationships were clearly reflected in the ways that narrators struggled to account for how and why the violence had happened or—as was more often the case—was still happening.

Another difference stems from their distinct modes of circulation in terms of when, how, and to whom certain narratives were circulated. Many narratives of rural violence did not make it into the local media, and when they did, they were usually reported long after accounts of the incident had been informally circulated. Unlike incidents of urban looting that a few people witnessed for themselves but most watched on television, stories of rural violence were commonly exchanged word-of-mouth from one person to the next, making it difficult to discern between various incidents (was this the same story with a few altered details or an account of a different event?) as well as between rumors and accounts of events that people had actually experienced.

Often what were passed along were fragments of narratives or lists of violent events which I think of as "inventories of violence." Mirroring short news broadcasts, these accounts were exchanged through avenues of gossip and material goods exchange and in the process were amended by multiple narrators. In Darshan Gaon, most of these stories involved the participation of more than one of the village's residents, as villagers often added or changed details to reflect the most recent news had that traveled from the interior to the village. They are thus reflective of community efforts to pull together some sort of accounting of events that were still unfolding, a process that required continual interpretation and reinterpretation as various narrators attempted to collectively piece together such an account.

The second area of interest that these narratives and fragmentary accounts hold is their affective impact. Some of these accounts were told in ways that made visible the anger, fear, and desperation of their narrators. Many were, however, related in an emotionless monotone, as if being pummeled by wave after wave of extraordinary events had made their narrators unable to feel the impact of the turmoil anymore. The symptoms of shock and profound dislocation evinced by their style of narration reflected how many people appeared momentarily senseless; it was as if they couldn't engage in the surfeit of emotions and had somehow managed to temporarily disassociate themselves from their bodies, their terror, and their pain. And yet it was precisely these emotions and the psychological strain they caused that compelled people to circulate whatever tidbits of news they had at their disposal.

Many people sought out the latest stories of violence in the hope of relieving some of the anxiety of not knowing and not understanding what was happening around them. But, as analysts of narrative and storytelling have shown us, while attempts to map meaning onto events through narrative are common, stories and storytelling can also add to the incoherence of events (Bauman 1986) or lead to the production of fantastical accounts, such as those examined in previous chapters. Moreover, narratives of violence may be told to express a victim's or a narrator's (the two were not always the same person) pain, confusion, distress, or anger, but they can also activate similar emotional effects in audience members.

A number of the accounts that circulated through Darshan Gaon were narrated in ways that resulted in the collective embodiment of terror and pain. Narrators not only recounted but physically reenacted attacks, mapping the brutality on their own bodies. Their audiences responded by cognitively threading together the events of an attack at the same time as they viscerally embodied some of its pain. In such cases, circulations of violence narratives gave people some sense of agency over their situation but also resulted in spreading feelings of terror and helplessness. Rare were the moments when narrators were able to temper some of these emotions by adopting a heroic mode.

By paying attention not only to the content of narratives and inventories of violence but also to how these accounts were put together and the emotional and physical impact of their circulation, we can begin to see how violence and sociality were experienced in this time of intense upheaval.

The Ubiquity of Accounts of Violence

From late May until the end of August 2000, there was an intensification of anti-Indian violence in rural areas. Increasing numbers of people fled from these areas, and their stories began to circulate in public space. Talk of rural violence became a new form of everyday discourse that one could hear while visiting friends or waiting at the bus stop. It also permeated conversations that were not focused on the violence per se so that all manner of community conversations came to be punctuated with stories of violence. I felt this most profoundly during my fieldwork when I found myself unable to escape such talk even during the birth of my daughter in mid-August in a maternity clinic in Suva. Within an hour after I gave birth, an indigenous Fijian nurse just coming onto duty introduced herself as hailing from Labasa, and then entirely unprompted began to tell me about the violence Fijian residents in her village had experienced when the police came in to arrest rebel sympathizers. Later, in the corridors of the maternity ward of the main hospital, I overheard Indo-Fijian visitors in the midst of discussing the health of a newborn baby, relating how they had begun to routinely flee from their homes into the surrounding bush each night in case they were attacked.

Allen Feldman (1991) has noted that violence is not so much a disrupter of an established cultural order but, as culture is it itself processual, a part of the making and remaking of society. In Fiji this was manifest not only in the ways that talk of events that had previously been "extraordinary" became a part of everyday life and discourse, but also in the ways in which the "ordinary" events of daily living became implicated as sites of communication and understanding of political conflict. It was as if there could be no event that was not narrated as in some way a part of the political situation.

As exemplified by the nurse's story, Indo-Fijians were not the only people in Fiji who had stories of victimization to tell. Indo-Fijians were, however, singled out and subject to harassment and assault more than members of any other ethnic group. Furthermore, the vast majority of stories that were known and told in a predominantly Indo-Fijian neighborhood such as Darshan Gaon involved Indo-Fijian victims. For these two reasons, my analysis here is predominantly restricted to violence that targeted this group.

Fragmentary Exchanges

One day when I stopped by Devi's home, the conversation began with her bluntly listing off the latest tragedies she had heard. "In Tailevu, a girl was brutally raped and has killed herself; an old woman, seventy or maybe sixty years old, was beaten up in Tailevu and now lives here in the village; it's going to be very bad now, a lot of people are losing their jobs," she flatly stated.[1] The community news that Devi had always been on top of and that had once consisted primarily of births, deaths, wedding invitations, and pūjās, was now devoted to violence and its repercussions.

The main avenue by which such news and stories of violence traveled was through kin relationships and through geographic proximity. Not surprisingly, the stories that people knew the most about, and that impacted the most on their lives, were those that directly involved themselves or their relatives. When these stories were disseminated in the village, the avenues by which they were circulated were also highly localized. Men would tell stories of violence when they visited one another at home or outside of the corner shop, usually when they congregated there to drink grog (kava) and discuss community events, an activity that was on the increase during the coup when many men were unable to leave the village to go to work because of the curfew in place as well as their fears of attack. Women's circulations of stories were more constricted, as some of their primary sites of news and gossip, such as the village kirtan, or devotional singing, club were suspended during the coup. Women passed stories along on the phone, over the fence with their direct neighbors, and when the situation was stable enough, by visiting nearby friends' homes. What people knew about each other varied according to the sites of news and gossip circulation that they shared in common. When I moved from one side of the village to the other, the stories I heard over the fence involved a different set of families and events than those I was previously party to.

Passed along these pathways, fragmentary accounts of violence were collected, embellished, and when possible, assembled into more-or-less coherent narratives. Great care was paid to getting the information in them as

---

1. The question of whether the woman was seventy or sixty, or if these were indeed *two* older women, became a significant point of debate, as I describe later in this chapter.

"correct" as possible and thus to slowly piece together, from various sources and accounts, narratives of the incident in question.

Piecing Together the Fragments: Shanti's Story

Shanti's account of how she was physically attacked by Fijian youths who surrounded her husband's store in Vunidawa is one such story. I first heard Shanti's story four days after the coup when my husband John and I stopped by the local corner shop. As always, John was invited to drink grog with the men who assembled in the shade of the shop's awning. In Nausori, different groups of men distinguished by ethnicity, socialized outside of different shops. The awning of the corner shop nearest to where I lived was popular with local Indo-Fijian men, while another shop further down the street was frequented by Fijians from Darshan Gaon and other areas. I came to rely on the men outside of the nearest shop, all of whom we knew, as a useful source of information and opinions on the coup and usually stopped by with my husband and daughter on a daily basis. Given that I never once saw a woman sitting with the men, I usually hovered about the entrance to the shop, chatting with the female shopkeeper or "waiting" for John. While the grog and conversation were ostensibly directed at him, the men engaged a question or two from my direction.

On this particular day, Avinash was telling John and me about some of the violence that was occurring in Vunidawa. In the midst of a number of violent events that he briefly recounted, he mentioned that an Indian shop-keeper in Vunidawa had come back from a hunting expedition to find his wife being physically attacked by some Fijian youths inside their shop. Our narrator was, however, quickly interrupted by a second man. "It was not the husband who was out hunting," he told us, "but it was their son who returned home and gave his father his hunting rifle." Corrected, Avinash resumed the story, "the man then shot one of the Fijians in the leg, but there were so many Fijians that they overpowered him and beat him up."

It was a few days later that I met up with Shanti who was seeking refuge in Darshan Gaon. She and her two young daughters, ages ten and eleven, had been taken in by her relatives while her husband, Sunil, stayed behind minding their shop in Vunidawa. It was clear that she was still in shock as she described how a group of Fijian youths had filled drums with kerosene, surrounded her husband's shop and threatened to burn it down.

Sitting with her relatives in my house, Shanti told us that Sunil had organized some of the older Fijian men in the community, about fifty of them, to surround the shop and protect it. Otherwise it would be on fire now, she said.

She paused and I told her that we'd heard about a shooting in that area. "Yes," she nodded, "that was my uncle." She did not say who had been shot or who it was that her uncle had been trying to protect. Instead she told me that her family had had to leave Vunidawa immediately because she was afraid the Fijian youths there might rape her daughters. Most of her account had been given in an emotionless monotone, but at this point, she grew more and more agitated. Suddenly, she repeatedly shouted out, "There was a knife at the throat!" Her relatives hastened to quiet her down. They soon left, with Shanti again exclaiming that her daughters might be raped if they returned to Vunidawa.

Shanti's words about the knife at the throat made very little sense to me until a few days later when her husband telephoned from Vunidawa. Sunil was upset and eager to recount what had happened. He told me that a group of young Fijian men had demanded he open up his shop during curfew. "They wanted booze," he said, "and kerosene and other supplies. They took all of these things and said, 'We will pay you later.' . . . You saw my wife?" He asked.

"Yes," I said.

"They put a knife at her throat," Sunil said.

"Your wife?" I asked in surprise.

"Yes, her and the children. It was on Friday and I was not here. Some Fijians saw that I was on the road so they broke in and they put a knife at her throat and threatened the children."

Sunil didn't say anything more but Shanti's exclamations about the "knife at the throat" and her terror that her children too might be attacked had been put into context.

A few weeks later, Sunil's cousin, Priya, who lived in Darshan Gaon, along with Sunil's aunt, Sangita, who was similarly visiting from Vunidawa in order to have a reprieve from the violence, asked me if I knew what had happened to Shanti. Sangita recounted yet another version of the incident in which a group of Fijian youths were playing pool in the shop when they turned on Shanti. "It's terrible where they are and what happened," the aunt said, grimacing and gesturing with her hands back and forth in a slashing motion along her own throat. Both women then questioned me about my own conversations with Shanti and her husband, asking about the details of what they had said and Shanti's state of mind when I'd spoken to her.

I next met up with Shanti in early August. She had settled in Darshan Gaon by then and she invited me to stop by her house. She told me that Sunil was still up in Vunidawa, and I asked her how the situation looked there. She said it was very bad and gave me a vivid and lengthy description of some of the violence, telling me how "the Fijians take cloths, dip them in kerosene and stuff them under the doors, setting the houses alight, while the people are still inside."

I asked her if anybody had been hurt, referring to the house burnings. She took this as a generalized question regarding the overall conflict and began to list off many of the attacks that had occurred in Vunidawa in the past months. Naming those victims that she knew, in a monotone she described their injuries. "Bal Ram was attacked by men with a cane knife," she said, "and they cut his arm and tried to cut his head but cut his ear instead. Another man was also badly beaten. A woman who was seventy was "attacked . . ." here she paused and stared at me, ". . . by men. That woman is now here. They broke her ribs." Given the context of other conversations I had had, I realized she was referring to sexual assault.

What struck me most was how factual and seemingly devoid of emotion her account was. It seemed to me that the emotionless tone in which she discussed one tragedy after another was not an indication of the lack of emotional impact these events had on her, but rather attested to the overwhelming shock of finding herself in the midst of such circumstances.

We then talked about her children and she became more animated. Voicing some of her present concerns, she explained that she was sending her daughters to school again though at first it had been difficult to let them out of the house, as she herself was too terrified to walk half a block to the nearest corner store in case she was attacked.

When I went home to write up my notes from our conversation, I had trouble remembering the order of the events that Shanti had described because there was so little to link them together. Like many villagers who spoke of the attacks that were occurring against their relatives and acquaintances in the interior, she had offered a list of violent incidents, jumping from one event of brutality to the next. In a way, we had traveled full circle. Initially Shanti's own story had circulated through the neighborhood in the form of one of many events listed off in such an inventory—a woman in Vunidawa had been brutalized, her uncle had shot someone when he attempted to defend her, and then he himself was badly beaten. Slowly, as more details emerged, relatives and other residents of the village, including myself, attempted to sort these details together, piecing narratives together out of the fragments. It appeared to me that those of us who engaged in cobbling together Shanti's story had no illusions about producing a definitive account, but rather we were attempting to get as close as possible to reconstructing at least some of the events that had driven Shanti out of Vunidawa. For even Shanti could not, at least at that point in time, coherently relate what had happened to her. In her own words, she distanced the weapon that had been used against her, referring to it as "a knife at the throat" rather than admitting it had been held against her own body. The trauma that Shanti had undergone had made her desirous of telling the story of the attack but unable to represent herself as its victim.

Shanti's was not an exceptional circumstance. A similar situation is documented by Veena Das in her work on survivors of anti-Sikh riots in Delhi. In her discussion of women's and children's recoveries from communal violence directed against them and their kinfolk, Das (1990b) highlights how victims of violence must overcome numerous difficulties in remembering and understanding not only the events they have lived through but also to locate their own place in them. More recently, Agamben (2002), in his examination of Auschwitz, has interrogated how to reconcile the impossibility that a victim can ever fully voice his or her suffering with the crucial importance of the act of witnessing, however incompletely, the violence wrought on ourselves and others.

In Shanti's case, her reaction to the acute trauma caused by the attack resulted in an attempt to disembody her pain, casting it away from herself and into the disconnected image of "a knife at the throat," as if both the knife and the throat were nowhere near her own body. In her analysis of political and other cultural depictions of weapons, Scarry has suggested that images of weapons often transfer our perception of the agency of violence away from the persons involved and into the material object itself (1985, 17). It is as if the knife, or some other weapon, becomes the perpetrator of the act (Scarry 1985, 17). Likewise, Shanti's representation of her assault focused on the weapon and on the specific body part that was under attack, enabling her to elide the actual people involved. Her narrative thus allowed her to communicate to others the intensity of the attack without requiring her to recognize herself as its victim.

The Pragmatics of Circulating These Accounts

These sorts of accounts of violence spread like wildfire through villages, towns, and urban neighborhoods in the months between mid-May and August 2000. Many stories of brutality, such as Shanti's, were matter-of-factly related in order to account for the visible consequences of the violence, such as the closures of businesses, people's increasingly difficult financial situations due to loss of work and property, and the presence of new neighbors who had fled from areas of acute violence.

But in numerous cases, initial accounts, particularly when framed as part of longer inventories of violence, left it unclear *where* the attacks were taking place or *who* exactly had been assaulted. Confusion existed because of the overwhelming number of reports of violence, several of which were very similar. Many people felt driven to try to differentiate one attack from another and sort out who were the victims of these incidents so that they could respond appropriately.

This could lead to some disturbing conversations, as when my neighbor Subashni and I thought we were discussing the same story of an older woman who had been sexually assaulted only to discover that we might be talking about attacks against two different women.

One morning in early August, when I was visiting her, Subashni commented that the situation in the country was growing increasingly desperate. I asked her if she thought that things might soon get better. She shook her head and shrugged.

"Do you know a sixty-year-old woman got attacked . . . raped," Subashni said.

I nodded, thinking I knew the incident she was referring to. "In Tailevu?" I said.

"Yes," she said.

"And she lives here, now," I said.

"In Nausori? . . . No," Subashni replied.

"I thought she has relatives here," I said. "I thought she was actually seventy and they broke her ribs."

"No," said Subashni, "This woman is sixty and they . . ." She gestured silently with a chopping motion at her ear.

"Cut her ear?" I asked.

She nodded and said, "Can you *imagine*, at sixty?"

For a long time afterward, Subashni and I stared at each other in silence. Our conversation had stopped abruptly, as if we had both been suddenly hit by the realization that this wasn't some sort of intellectual puzzle, but a discussion of events that had had horrific consequences for those involved. What was so disturbing to me, and I think also for Subashni, was the way that we had become momentarily numb to the violence to the extent that we could coldly and clinically exchanged identifying features of various attacks, honing in our comparison of the two women's injuries until the force of the events, through Subashni's invocation that we *imagine* the rape, came down on us.

In the context of such an unprecedented level of violence, narratives of brutality acted as records of the rapidly changing nature of daily life. On a pragmatic level, people wanted to know where, how, and to whom the violence was occurring in order to assess their own safety and the safety of others in the village and in surrounding areas. These accounts forced audiences and narrators alike to constantly reassess what was at stake in the current situation. Telling such stories compelled people to cognitively and emotionally engage with the possibility of encountering events that it had previously been *unnecessary* for them to imagine.

Women in particular often shared accounts of violence against other women as a way of warning each other about the current situation. Toward the end of my pregnancy, I was at the receiving end of a number of such uncomfortable stories as other women grew concerned about what might happen when I went into labor. The same day that Subashni and I discussed the attack(s) on the older woman or women, I mentioned that I was worried about what I should do if the roadblocks and curfew were still in effect when I needed to get to the hospital to give birth. She nodded and told me the following story. "In 1987," she said, "during the few days of civil unrest following the first coup, there was an Indian woman who was in labor and was having trouble getting to CWM (the main hospital in Suva). The military said they would take her so some soldiers took her in their truck. They raped her and the baby died."

My impression was that Subashni did not intend to terrify me with this story, even though she did, but to implore me to seriously consider the various options that were available to me and to think through their possible consequences. In fact, I did end up going into labor during curfew. While the events that happened to me were nowhere near as horrific as Subashni's story, I was stopped on my way to the hospital and harassed by soldiers who questioned me in between contractions. Initially, they refused to allow me to pass through military checkpoints on the road to Suva. After a frighteningly long delay, they finally allowed me to continue on to the hospital.

As my own story demonstrates, one of the things that made accounts of violence, whether true or not, so compelling was that the boundary lines between victims, narrators, and audience members was porous. One moment, I listened to stories of pregnant women being detained while in labor. A few days later, I had a similar story of my own.

Collective Experiences of Pain

In addition to their pragmatic purposes of documenting the violence and preparing people for possible future attacks, violence narratives gave recognizable form to the physical and emotional distress of those who had been terrorized. In this respect, they can be thought of as therapeutic accounts. Indeed, many of the men and women I spoke with during the coup had gone through events of profound dislocation and used the act of conversing with others as a means of communicating their distress as well as of making sense of the events they had lived through, collaboratively piecing together events that would otherwise have remained confused or incoherent, as in the villagers' discussions of Shanti's attack.

There are, however, also conspicuous differences between stories of violence recounted primarily for therapeutic purposes and the effects of many of these circulations. These differences stemmed out of the potential interchangeability of the positions of victims, narrators, and audience members as well as the relationship between the event being recounted and the inescapable context of ongoing violence.

In a therapeutic setting the victim of violence is often encouraged to give voice to traumatic events in order to begin to understand and cope with their emotional and psychological impact. Regardless of the positioning of the violence in the client's life (i.e., whether the traumatic event is in the past, present, or is ongoing), the therapeutic space is, moreover, intended to provide a site outside of the conflict in which the client can, however momentarily, escape the violence in order to reflect on it. The stories told in Darshan Gaon engaged everyone—the victims (when present), narrators (including those who themselves had not been directly victimized), and audience members—in experiencing some relief at being able to make inchoate experiences narratable. At the same time, however, there was no sense of being able to escape the present situation. The effect of many of these accounts was thus to proliferate feelings of horror and panic, not only about what *had* happened, but because the violence was ongoing, about what might *still* happen. While the act of storytelling thus gave people a sense of agency over their lives (cf. M. Jackson 2002), allowing them to at least *attempt* to make sense of the violence, the perlocutionary effects of these accounts were not always positive. Indeed, the circulations of violence narratives were so powerful because they offered the potential of putting past events into rational order, while at the same time heightening people's fear and sense of panic over the violence yet to come. If we consider these narratives as therapeutic acts of "closure" providing emotional outlets and cognitive frameworks for past events, we must also consider how they acted as "openings," indicating the potential for further attacks, with no one sure of who might be the next victim.

The interchangeable quality of the victims, narrators, and audience members was made particularly vivid in the way that narrators, many of whom had not directly experienced violent assaults, located themselves in the position of victims. Often this was carried out by narrators placing their own bodies in the position of those who had been assaulted, physically mapping out the violence on themselves in order to enact the victims' pain and terror. While most of my examples thus far have focused on stories of violence against women, such gestures also occurred in depictions of attacks against men. In, for example, an account of the mugging of Indo-Fijian wedding guests in Korovou Town, which was first discussed in chapter 2, Krishna described to me how his friend Tej had been pulled out of the van in which he was traveling by men brandishing cane knives. Tej had just finished telling the story to the men assembled outside of the shop when John and I arrived there a few minutes later, but Krishna eagerly repeated it to us. "He was just sitting here [a few moments ago] drinking grog," Krishna explained, "but he had to go home for a rest. His heart was . . ." Krishna gestured a frantic pounding on his chest. "He could die!" Like Devi's repeated gesture of cutting her hand, Sangita's mimed cutting of her own throat in reference to Shanti's attack, and Subashni's silent chopping motion towards her ear, Krishna acted out Tej's distress on his own body in order to evoke its intensity to us.

In all of these cases, it was as if when faced with the horrifically unwanted but necessary task of trying to articulate another's pain, narrators attempted to simultaneously keep silent and to use their to bodies to break that silence. As Kendon and others have argued, gestures are not "symptoms of some struggle to attain verbal expression" (Kendon 2004, 359; also Haviland 2004) but a choice between modes of expression that must be analyzed as an integral component of the utterances in which they appear (Kendon 2004, 5). Gesture has, moreover, been noted for focusing attention onto the speaker and emphasizing his or her verbal disclosure (Goodwin 1986). Moreover, as Kendon further indicates, in some cases "a gestural action can be reminiscent of actual physical action, and it may derive some of its added forcefulness from this" (1995, 230). If we consider these gestures in such a light, we see that they acted as a mode of expression that highlighted the physicality of the attacks, drawing attention to both the body and its distress by using the body of the narrator to represent the body of the victim.

I would like to suggest that in addition to the forcefulness of the visual impact of the gesture of a throat being cut or a heart beating out of control, the refusal to use words to convey these images is meaningful in itself. Silence and the replacement of gesture for language often indicates sites where speech is regarded as inappropriate (Kendon 1995, 223), allowing one to make unquotable, off the record, remarks. In some cultural contexts, silence is moreover a marker for experiences and emotions that are considered to be so overwhelming that one can only respond to them without words (Basso 1970; Saville-Troike 1995).

In this case, narrators of violent accounts not only chose to use gestures but markedly refused to translate these gestures into words. This was particularly evident when I tried to orally interpret their gestures by supplying the "missing" words. Many would register their agreement with my interpretation but did not themselves engage in voicing the words *rape* or *cut her throat*. In fact, the one occurrence I recorded when someone other than myself verbally described the knife having been held against Shanti's throat occurred when Sunil related the incident to me on the telephone, an instance when he could not have used a gesture instead.

In expressing, but forcibly silencing aspects of violence, gestures not only communicate the force of physical violence, but also suggest that some things are beyond speech. To borrow a metaphor from Veena Das, they draw "fences" around certain kinds of events (2007, 11), not repressing them but communicating them, while at the same time placing them outside of the verbal realm and making them Other to ordinary communication. The move to another mode of expression, that is, to silent gesture, thus draws attention to the act as well as marks the disclosure as outside of language, making it unspeakable as it is "spoken" through the body rather than the voice.

The perlocutionary effect (Austin 1962) of these performances was such that audience members often responded by viscerally experiencing a small part of the terror that the attacks incited. Through retelling and physically reenacting the violence, narrators and audience members alike collectively engaged in the pain of the attacks. Akin to the panic inspired by the circulation of rumor (Bhabha 1994; Perice 1997), accounts of violence not only informed listeners of news of attacks and helped them delineate probable causes for these events but also resulted in audience members feeling emotionally and physically terrorized. While raising anger and hostility toward those seen as likely assailants, the overall feeling, both amongst women and men, was usually of fear and helplessness. Ironically, it was through the words of those speaking on behalf of the victim that the ability of the violence to terrorize was thus multiplied. One did not have to be at the receiving end of the assailants' blows to feel assaulted.

As I have noted, following Scarry's work on the incommunicability of pain (1985), much has been said of the alienating aspects of physical pain and the inability to communicate the sufferer's experience to others. Many scholars of violence have, however, also demonstrated that while a sufferer of intense pain might indeed struggle to come to terms with experiences that isolate them and that they cannot fully convey to another, there are a variety of linguistic and nonlinguistic means through which pain is communicated, comes to be shared, and sometimes embodied by others.[2] I do not want to discount the intensity of the victims' distress and am well aware of the impossibility of victims, much less of third parties, fully communicating to others the depth of their experiences (Agamben 2002; Das 1990b; Scarry 1985). But we must not overlook how violence and the fear it inspires physically and psychologically impact on not only victims but anyone who imaginatively inhabits the space of victim (cf. Mbembe 2003). In the case of anti-Indian violence during the 2000 coup, it was not only the specific individuals who were assaulted who then carried within them the pain of these events. The terror of these attacks was also embodied by those who imaginatively reconstructed the violence. My discussion here is intended not to diminish the psychological and physical effects of violence against those who directly experience it but to suggest some of the dynamics through which victims' communications with others and others' communications about victims resulted in the collectivization of the experiences of pain and terror.

Just as assertions of labor and evocations of bodily aches and pains to indicate productivity were lived out in the space of community relations, the narrative reconstructions of these brutal assaults became a community experience. It is important to reiterate, however, that the pain felt by Shanti should not be equated with the pain embodied by those who told and listened to her story, as these were radically different experiences. My point is a much simpler one; through the circulation of fragmentary accounts of the attack against her, Shanti's trauma became a collective experience in which other women and men participated not only by trying to help her and her kinfolk cope but by collaboratively placing the events in a coherent, meaningful form and, in the process, sharing some of the pain and terror.[3]

2. For an extended discussion of how Scarry's assertion that pain alienates the sufferer from society has influenced anthropology, see chapter 1.

3. No doubt, many of the indigenous Fijians who listened to similar accounts were also moved by them. During the coup, a number of Christian congregations were actively praying for an end to the violence, some of their members going on hunger strikes to promote their message. The outpouring of sentiment at religious gatherings, in the media, and in my own discussions with indigenous Fijians attested to the fact that many of them were deeply troubled and pained by the hostilities that were occurring. I am unaware, however, of the specific accounts that circulated among Fijians and was unable to document their responses to them.

Race, Gender, and Power: Bodies of Victims, Bodies of Assailants

In their struggle to articulate the violence, one popular framework that many Indo-Fijians used was that of racial differences between Indians and Fijians. But in comparison to accounts of urban looting or state-level violence, narratives of rural violence portrayed a more complex set of dynamics between Indian victims and their Fijian assailants.

As with urban looting, the most prevalent explanation for rural violence was that it was a fulfillment of indigenous Fijians' desires to acquire material goods. There was an abundance of stories that connected inter-ethnic physical attacks (current and past) with muggings and theft of material goods. The story of Bhābhī's attack is one illustration.

Other accounts told of Indo-Fijian property being destroyed "out of jealousy" as Indo-Fijians were chased out of their homes and forced to watch while their houses were set on fire. Farmers similarly spoke of having their crops destroyed before anyone could harvest them. These acts of destruction were recognized as having profound symbolic value, demonstrating Fijian power and relegating Indians to the position of victims who were reliant on Fijian goodwill for their livelihoods and for their lives. Such acts extended the dependence of the vulagi "guest" on his or her taukei "host" to the extreme.

Additional factors that were sometimes invoked alongside these included alcohol (either the assailants were drunk or were hoping to obtain alcohol by breaking into a house or shop) and political solidarity with the rebels, both of which were similarly described as adding extra incentive to the violence.

In addition to their discussions of the motivations that may have instigated the violence, a great deal of attention was spent on describing exactly who might constitute a victim or an assailant. While many narratives of rural violence, including both Devi's and Shanti's, depicted generic categories of "the Fijian" or "the Fijians" as responsible for the attacks, on closer examination, narrators of these accounts described a much more specific set of Fijians who they were afraid of. In accordance with the demographic details of assailants that appeared in the news media, "the Fijian" assailant that they described was generally an unemployed, rural, indigenous Fijian male youth. Narratives told by Darshan Gaon's residents, however, added characteristics that the newspapers often left out, endowing this image of the disaffected youth with great physical strength as well as sexual danger. The portrayal of victims also went beyond the broad category of "Indians," to specify particular concerns around the sexual vulnerability of older girls and young and middle-aged Indian women. Given the sexual dynamics at play, Indian men were portrayed as comparatively less vulnerable, and in a few cases, as heroically defending their female relatives.[4]

Both before and during the coup, many Indo-Fijians expressed an assessment of Fijian men as "naturally" stronger than Indian men. This notion of Fijians' exemplarily physiques was used to explain their accomplishments in the popular game of rugby and in other sports. During the coup, it was also sometimes used to explain how and why Indian men fell victim to attack. Many of these accounts furthermore echoed some of the images of Fijians as animals that occurred in racist jokes and responses to looting.

In the midst of an evening spent pouring over the latest political developments, my neighbor Rajesh made some generalized comments regarding how strong and agile he considered Fijians to be and then related how he had been mugged by a Fijian assailant a few years back. He told my husband and me,

> "There are two things Fijians are very good at. They are strong and they are fast. . . . They can run fast, like a horse. One time I was visiting my brother-in-law in Samabula [a neighborhood in Suva] and I was walking to my car when a Fijian tried to steal my wallet. I had only seventy dollars. He reached here," Rajesh patted his back pocket, "and I knew what he was doing but I was stupid and I reached too [to stop him]. And he was sitting on the ground so I grabbed his head and his legs but he pushed with his head and I fell and here . . ." Rajesh paused as he raised his shirt to show my husband a protrusion on his shoulder, "he hit me."
>
> "You dislocated your shoulder?" I asked.
>
> Rajesh nodded and continued his narrative, "My brother-in-law came running from the house. It was only so far from the car to the house," he paused to gesture what seemed like a few yards, "but the Fijian got up and ran and they could not catch him. He ran like a horse."

In Rajesh's narrative, the Fijian assailant is depicted as naturally physically stronger and faster than Rajesh or his brother-in-law. The consequences of resisting someone so powerful are serious, as illustrated by the misaligned shoulder from which Rajesh still suffers. Rajesh characterized himself as ridiculous but also as a bit brave to have tried to defend himself

---

4. There have been anecdotal accounts by NGO workers that some Indo-Fijian men were raped or otherwise sexually assaulted by Fijian men during the 2000 coup. As I have not found any documented cases of this nor did any of my interlocutors allude to such events, I am not considering such cases here.

against someone so much stronger than he is. However my husband and I may have actually responded, my impression was that the story was meant to leave us in awe of both the strength of his assailant and his own bravery in standing up to him even though he knew the odds were stacked against him.

In addition to images of Fijian strength, which were predominantly voiced by Indo-Fijian men, another attribute that appears in many of the rural violence narratives, frequently mentioned by both Indo-Fijian men and women, is of the Fijian assailant as a sexual predator. Rapes and threats of rape occurred during the coup, but even in cases where the threat was not explicitly made, there was a widespread assumption among many Indo-Fijians that when young Fijian men came into violent contact with Indo-Fijian women, there was the likelihood of rape. We see examples of this in Devi's concerns that her sister-in-law could have been raped, as well as in Shanti's fears for her daughters.

Concerns about rape were also reflected in who was perceived to be a likely target. Many Indo-Fijians' fears of potential victimization were primarily concentrated on women of childbearing age or a few years younger, who were seen as the most likely targets of sexual violence. The result was that women from this age group were subject to specific concern and safeguarding. On the night that Rajesh called to us that we must immediately leave our home due to reported mob of Fijians marching up the street with lighted torches, he declared to my husband, "I am sending [my] wife away. It's time to send Susanna out of the village." While I assume that Rajesh meant that both my four-year-old daughter and I should flee, it was myself and Rajesh's wife who, due to our perceived sexual vulnerability, were specifically pointed out as being a matter of concern.

Such specification of women of a certain age as potential victims was frequent throughout the months of the conflict. Indo-Fijian girls who had reached the age of puberty or just under were less likely to be sent to school than were their brothers. As one twenty-year-old woman told me, the schools were open but none of the girls were going out of fear that "Speight's people" would rape them. In discussions of various families' decisions to leave the interior, the ages of their daughters were often used to assess the possibilities of violence against them. Older women and very young children were not seen as potential targets as were older girls and young to middle-age women. When Devi's mother Chandra, who was in her seventies, was visiting Darshan Gaon and debating whether or not to go back to her home in Vunidawa during the height of the violence there, I asked her if she wasn't afraid of being attacked if she returned. She responded that she was not afraid as there were no "young daughters" in her house. Shanti similarly repeatedly mentioned the age of her daughters (ten and eleven) when she expressed her fears that they might be raped. Other women also commented that Shanti's daughters were of an age that merited such concern.

As, however, the conflict continued and violent attacks proceeded against people's expectations, there was confusion surrounding events that were contrary to many of these assumptions. Chandra returned to Vunidawa where her house, if not her person, was repeatedly attacked. News of rural attacks also revealed that some of the women who were being subject to physical and sexual assault were considerably older than villagers imagined potential victims to be, as reflected in my conversation with Subashni about the sixty-year-old and seventy-year-old victims.

While women such as Chandra were courageous enough to return to sites of violence, there were very few stories that portrayed women's agency, much less accounts of women standing up to their assailants.[5] Out of the dozens of violence narratives I documented, there was only one that depicted a woman actively defending herself, her family, or her belongings. This one was told in passing when Devi mentioned to me that one of her female relatives had been "clever" enough to hide some valuables under her skirt when she was forced out of her home by Fijian assailants. Otherwise, the generalized portrait was of Indo-Fijian women and girls as passive victims. In contrast, while Indian men were similarly depicted as victims, they were usually described as agentive subjects, removing their families from sites of violence or making arrangements to protect their properties. Moreover, despite the general emphasis on avoiding violence, there were a few accounts of Indian men fighting back, emphasizing their bravery in doing so. In addition to Rajesh's struggle with the mugger, there were also Bhābhī's husband and Shanti's uncle, both of whom attempted to fight off their assailants. In another account described in detail below, Rajesh also related how he rescued his wife's relatives from an ongoing assault. These distinctions reveal that while both Indo-Fijian men and women were victims of violent assaults, how these attacks were perceived was dependent on assumptions not only about "race," but also about age, sexuality, and gender.

Taken together, stories of rural violence suggest that when it came to responding to the violence, not all bodies were treated equally. Narratives and

5. For more on Indo-Fijian women, perceptions of gender, agency, and violence, including domestic violence (which many NGO workers noted was on the rise during the 2000 coup) see Adinkrah 1999; Lateef 1990; Trnka 2005d.

audience members' responses to them underscored that judgments regarding who might constitute potential assailants and potential victims revolved, in part, around attributes that were perceived to be inherent within the body—speed, physical strength, age, sexuality, and gender. What these racialized and gendered notions of the body do *not*, however, reveal are conceptions of Fijian (or Indian) bodies as inherently violent. While youth, speed, and agility might contribute to violence, no one suggested that the violence occurred *because* of innate, physical traits of either Fijians or Indians. Rather, these were seen as factors to be taken into account when attempting to assess which of "the Fijians" was a likely assailant and which of "the Indians" was their likely victim.

Beyond Ethnicity: Imagining Sociality in Times of Violence

At the same time as accounts of rural violence revolved around images of Fijians as assailants, numerous stories also demonstrated the possibilities of cooperative cross-ethnic endeavors. In fact, images of the "Fijian friend" were not an extraordinary occurrence but were frequently invoked, often by the same people and in some cases in the same narratives, as those that portrayed "the Fijians" as dangerous predators.

The phenomenon of the ethnic Other as both an aggressor and a savior is not unusual. Other studies of inter-ethnic violence have frequently remarked on this dual presence. Some scholars have gone no further than to note its occurrence,[6] while others have ascribed to the particular informant who tells such a tale the "remarkable" capacity to overcome prevailing anti-ethnic sentiment by recalling the help they received from a member of the antagonistic group (Kanapathipillai 1990, 327). One of the most extended commentaries on the ethnic Other as protector appears in Liisa Malkki's analysis of narratives told by victims of Hutu-Tutsi violence. Throughout her ethnography, Malkki paints a highly stylized portrait of Hutu conceptions of the " 'the Tutsi' as a homogenous category" (1995, 93). While her focus is firmly on Hutu assumptions of the Tutsi's Otherness, at one point she acknowledges that Hutu narratives of violence often diverted away from these stereotypes by invoking images of Tutsi individuals who assisted in their escapes from violent areas. Malkki explains that "the position of these accounts of individual Tutsi saviors in the mythico-history [of the

6. See, for instance, Das's description of Hindus who assisted Sikhs in fleeing anti-Sikh riots (1996b).

Hutu] is not clearly articulated, but they could be interpreted as a way of accounting for one's good fortune in being spared from death. . . . They did not seem to attenuate in the least the categorical distinction otherwise drawn between good and evil, Hutu and Tutsi—if anything, these exceptions seemed to strengthen the categories" (1995, 97). Unfortunately Malkki does not go far enough to explain how the exceptions proved the rule, nor does she take up the opportunity to use such exceptions to reflect further on the possible complexities of the otherwise "categorical" distinctions her interlocutors used. My concern here is with what might happen if rather than relegating these images of the ethnic Other as protector to the sidelines, we instead attempt to integrate an understanding of the "Fijian friend" with the abundance of negative ethnic stereotyping.

The "Good" Fijian

One very prevalent sentiment in Darshan Gaon was that the village would not experience the same sort of violence as was occurring in other villages and urban neighborhoods because the Fijians who lived there were "different." The Fijians here, a number of Indo-Fijian residents declared, are "good" unlike in so many other places. Sentiments of trust between Indo-Fijian and Fijian neighbors were furthermore demonstrated by the reliance Indo-Fijians placed in their Fijian neighbors to help them protect themselves and their families. As mentioned, in Darshan Gaon Indo-Fijian and Fijian men took part together in a neighborhood patrol whose duty was to police the neighborhood and frighten away the bands of youths who occasionally tried to attack the local school or private homes.

In the rural areas in the interior that were hardest hit by incidents of violence, the protective nature of affiliations between Fijians and Indo-Fijians was put more stringently to the test. "Good" relationships between Fijians and Indo-Fijians were often highlighted as the reason why people were able to escape violence. Newspaper reports of the violence in these areas made a point of describing how Indian victims of house burnings often fled to the homes of Fijians in surrounding koros. Likewise, in some of Devi's repeated remarks regarding the safety of her elderly mother in Vunidawa, she commented that it was her mother's Fijian neighbors who warned her that Fijians from a neighboring village were planning to burn down her house. Shanti likewise mentioned that if it wasn't for the older Fijian men who had surrounded Sunil's shop, it would have been burned down already.

Sometimes the same people who were victims of attacks had friendly relationships with those inflicting ethnically targeted violence on others. A few weeks after Shanti was attacked, Sunil's cousin Priya told me that

Shanti's uncle, who had been involved in defending her during the assault, had gone to visit some of the rebels in Parliament who were holding Chaudhry hostage. "But once he saw the scene down there," Priya added, "he got nervous and quickly left."

"But why did he go there in the first place?" I asked.

"He wanted to see what was going on," she replied. Sensing my confusion, she remarked, "He has lived with Fijians all his life."

Shanti's uncle was a dramatic example of what was actually commonplace, namely that in some cases strong bonds exist between Fijians and Indians. Both before and during the coup, a number of Indo-Fijians similarly asserted that in rural areas their relationships with Fijians were "good" either because they had known one another for a long time or because they exchanged food with each other. Repeatedly I was told that people who trade together and who are thus "friends" would not resort to violence against one another.

As ethnographers of friendship have noted, there exist various cultural understandings of what it means to be "friends." In many western contexts, friendship is conceptualized as a dyadic relationship that exists between equal and close intimates (Allan 1996; Paine 1969; Silver 1989). In popular opinion, such a bond is contrasted with business relations and it is thought best to keep apart one's friends from one's business dealings (Allan 1996; Y. Cohen 1961). In other contexts, however, friendship is not seen as inherently opposed to economic activities and the two spheres of business and friendship are sometimes inherently intertwined (Kong 2003; Wolf 1966). In Brazil, for example, friendship denotes relationships of care and affection that can develop out of unequal business exchanges, such as between housemaids and their employers (Rezende 1999). Elsewhere, as in Estonia and Finland, the emphasis is on "significant, positive and ideally longer term personal connections" in which the exchange of goods is viewed as fundamental to friendship (Abrahams 1999).

Bearing in mind such a variety of conceptualizations of friendship assists in understanding the depictions of the "Fijian friend" in these narratives. Most of the Indo-Fijian narrators who spoke of their Fijian friends did not see such friendships as particularly intimate or even as putting them on an equal footing. Rather, the term *friend* was often used to indicate a long-term, amicable bond based on trust, positive affects such as sociability and affability (as opposed to antagonism), as well as mutually beneficial exchange.

As we saw in the former girmitiyas' statements about their exchange relationships with indigenous Fijians in the previous chapter, such relations were not devoid of prejudice; the emphasis was not necessarily on shared

understanding but on assistance and reciprocity. There were of course exceptions. The fictional narrator of "The Story of the Haunted Line," whose
life was saved by his indigenous Fijian visitors is one early example. More
contemporary instances include the intimate and personal one-to-one relationships that are sometimes created at school, at church, in the workplace,
over the kava bowl, or on the sports field. But while deep and enduring ties
based on mutual intimacy and closeness, the characteristics often applied to
friendship in the West, certainly exist, often when Indo-Fijians referred to
their Fijian friends, they were not indicating such a level of intimacy.

Rather, frequently "friends" were people with whom one felt assured
that their interaction would be amicable, safe, and intended to bring both
sides benefit. Particular emphasis was furthermore placed on the importance of friendships created through the noncommercial exchange of
goods, reflecting the social value placed on exchanges outside of the monetary system. Just as Sanadhya's narrator creates a friendship with his Fijian
saviors through their exchange of food, Devi, in her story of Bhābhī's attack, emphasized that her brother and his Fijian friend "used to exchange
dalo and cassava" but "they did not pay him money. He was their friend."

In contrast to the emphatic assertions that indigenous Fijians who exchange goods without working for money or participating in commerce
will end up stealing from Indians, these accounts demonstrate how nonmarket exchanges were sometimes hailed as an indication of friendship
precisely because they do not involve money but are perceived as materially
beneficial to both parties. As we have seen, among Indo-Fijians in Darshan
Gaon and elsewhere, there exists a thriving nonmonetary exchange system
of both food and labor. Such exchanges are considered not only crucial for
village relations but are also valued as being the morally right thing to do.
When nonmonetary exchanges of goods or labor took place between Indo-
Fijians and Fijians, they were similarly valued and often described as mark-
ers of friendship. This suggests that Indo-Fijians' criticisms of indigenous
Fijian systems of communal production and nonmarket exchange are not
condemnations of nonmarket exchange per se. Rather, they refer to the importance of *balancing* exchange outside of markets, exchange that creates
"friends," with involvement in an investment-based, market system that is
perceived to move the nation "forward."

Friendship Gone Awry

Alongside the many narratives that evoked the importance of inter-
ethnic friendships, there were many stories of inter-ethnic friendships that
could not be relied on. These narratives pointed to a breakdown of friendly

relations between residential groups (an Indo-Fijian settlement and a neighboring koro, for example) as well as between individuals who once considered themselves to be friends. In attempting to understand which factors made for good and bad relationships, people often noted that the histories and length of their residence influenced their relations with neighbors, as well as the specificities of their land lease arrangements. But sometimes there was no telling how strong or weak friendship or more widely shared feelings of amity and neighborliness might be.

In early June, Saraswati, a teacher trainee who I knew mainly through an acquaintance with her brother, phoned me to ask if she could come stay with us in Darshan Gaon as the college dormitory she was staying at in Suva was unsafe. Her brother, who was a pandit in a temple in Suva and her only relative in the area, had likewise had to flee the temple in case he was attacked. Saraswati stayed in our home for about a week and later returned to her natal village in the farming area of Dreketi in Vanua Levu. During the 1987 coups there had been no trouble in Dreketi, she told me, and she was sure she would be safe there.

In late July, however, reports of some of the worst cases of violence originated from Dreketi. *The Fiji Times* reported on July 31, 2000, that "armed rebels forced people out of their homes and terrorized members of Indian families before taking males hostage in a rice farming community. Police confirmed the incident at Dreketi, 50 km from Labasa, saying the hostages had been moved to an unknown destination" (Maci 2000). When Saraswati and I met up again in October, she told me how she'd witnessed her cousins in Dreketi being forced at gunpoint to sign over deeds to their freehold land. I asked her if they knew the people who had attacked them and she replied that they did as they were all from neighboring koros. Her family had given a *sevusevu*, or a formal request for good relations, to the senior villagers. But, she asked, what is the purpose of giving a sevusevu to the elders when they cannot control the youths who commit the violence?

Another account I heard involved the breakdown of a friendship between residents in Muaniweni. In late June, following one of the rare widescale pūjās (devotional ceremonies) to be held in the village, Rajesh and Parvati invited my family and the pandit who had conducted the ceremony to share a meal with them. Given the tense climate, the men chose not to sit separately on the veranda as was usual, but to stay inside with the women. As the food was served, the family waited respectfully for the pandit to initiate conversation. The pandit began by repeating a story that had been told to him by one of Parvati's relatives, a farmer who had fled the violence in Muaniweni. The farmer had had a visit from one of his Fijian neighbors, the pandit told us. As they often did, on this occasion they drank grog (kava) together, an act usually taken as a sign of cooperation and amiability. They then ate together a big meal prepared by the Indian family. The pandit gestured toward our table to imply that it was the same as us sharing our food together now. But as the Fijian was leaving, he saw a bull outside. He turned to his host and said, "We used to be good friends but not now." He then violently slapped the man and took the bull away.

The pandit's story dramatically articulated the feeling that rural violence between Fijians and Indians was highly unpredictable. Even close friends, those who sit and drink grog and share food together, could turn into enemies. The question of how and when friendships might give way to enmities made for not only a poignant account of the betrayal that this entailed but was an issue of serious reflection as many Indo-Fijians, including the pandit and those seated around the table with him, had to judge the odds of their own safety.

Taking Risks—Uses of Ethnic Stereotypes and Local Knowledge

For many Indo-Fijians during the coup, one of the most difficult judgments they had to make was to assess the likelihood of whether they too might become victims of violence. Weighing who might be potential attackers and who might constitute a potential victim were serious issues for those who lived in especially violent areas, those who feared the spread of violence into their own neighborhoods, and those who traveled into violent areas in order to assist their family members.

The uncertain and confusing process by which such assessments of safety were made is well demonstrated by an account from Rajesh who told me how, at the height of the violence, he enlisted the aid of a Fijian friend to drive up to Muaniweni to rescue Parvati's relatives whose house was being stoned by Fijian youths. Like the pandit's story of the stolen bull, this narrative revolves around the question of the reliability of inter-ethnic friendship in the face of escalating levels of inter-ethnic violence. As a first-person account, Rajesh's narrative dramatically evokes some of the possible stakes involved in making these assessments, encouraging his audience to viscerally engage with his predicament, his fear, and ultimately his heroism.

"Yesterday," Rajesh told me, "the Nausori police rang me. The police in Muaniweni had radioed them. Some Fijians were throwing stones at the house (of my wife's relatives) so they asked if I could go up there in my van and get them. I rang them back, half an hour later and asked if it was safe for *ME* to drive up there and they said no. They said they'd give me one boy from the police but. . . . But then a Fijian I know, a *ratu* [chief] from Muaniweni came into the shop [that I own]. He said he would go up with me, but how would I get back? So we hired one carrier and drove up. I hid in the back." Rajesh gestured how he had completely covered himself up with a blanket or rug. "At the roadblocks [which were set up and manned by Fijian villagers] they saw the driver—a Fijian—and the ratu. I hid in the back. The ratu is well known there but I didn't know even with him if I'd be safe."

He went on to say how he brought the relatives back to his house in Nausori along with some of the Fijian relatives of the ratu who he invited over for the day. "When we got home, the Fijians went to the back room. You've seen the backroom?"

I shook my head.

"Oh, there is another settee there, so my wife came home and said, who are all those people in the back? So we spread out a mat and had them down here [in the front room], drinking grog [kava] and telling their stories, yarning, I don't know about what . . ." He gestured vaguely.

"But you know [how to speak] Fijian?" I asked.

"Yes, a lot, but I don't understand everything. . . ." He paused. "Up there [in the interior] it is very bad. Here . . ." he named some Fijian villages, "[those villages] are safe, safe for *me*. Not *everyone* can go there. But up there, it is very bad."

Rajesh's narrative demonstrates his perception of the complex role that ethnicity might play in rural conflict. On the one hand, he depicts the violence in the interior as ethnically motivated. A ratu, a Fijian driver, and what was most likely a young, junior police officer can all travel up there, but they also agree that Rajesh, by virtue of being Indian, would not be safe. And yet Rajesh was also acutely aware of the ways in which individualized relationships intersect with racial stereotypes. He noted that his friendship with the ratu grants him protection. There are furthermore other places, he asserted, in which he by virtue of his knowledge of the local Fijian dialect and his local connections to Fijian villagers, could travel unharmed. Like the account of the Fijian who mugged him, the story both details the fearful situation in which Rajesh found himself and his bravery in responding to it. But unlike the incident with the Fijian mugger, in this story the multitude of Rajesh's responses to violence demonstrated his ability, and it was an ability widely shared by many of Darshan Gaon's residents, to draw on both prevalent ethnic stereotypes and his personalized knowledge of Fijian individuals and particular local situations to gauge how he should respond to interpersonal violence.

The Police and the Politics of Violence

Rajesh's narrative, like many accounts of rural violence, also suggests that in addition to relationships between aggressors and victims, another factor in Indo-Fijians' responses to rural violence was that the violence was being played out in a context in which the police and the military, both of which are predominantly made up of indigenous Fijians, were either not present or not responding to the needs of local residents. Frequent references to the incapability of the police to halt the violence attested to the widely held sentiment that events of such explosive violence could not have happened outside of a political atmosphere conducive to them.

I have already described the general security situation in the country during the coup but it is worth noting again here that while much of the civilian violence in rural areas was carried out by bands of local Fijian youths, it could not have spread so rapidly and continued for so long without either the complicity of the state authorities or, in some cases, the inability of these forces to react due to internal struggles within their own ranks. In some areas, the numbers of police and military were likely ill-equipped in terms of arms and manpower to respond effectively. *The Fiji Times*' story of the attacks on Indians in Dreketi, for example, states that "a senior [police] officer said police units did not respond to reports [of the attack] after it was revealed that the hostage-takers were armed. He said no officers would be sent to Dreketi as there was a possibility unarmed police would be harmed in a confrontation" (Maci 2000). It is, however, unclear in a number of cases if arms really were unavailable to the police or if they were choosing not to intervene. In other parts of the country it appears from media reports and eyewitness accounts that the police and the military either turned a blind eye or actively participated in acts of violence.

Indo-Fijians' accounts of such incidents tended not to dwell on the local individuals involved but rather on the police and the military as state forces who were part of a widespread campaign to destabilize the country and terrorize Indian citizens. In contrast to situations where narratives of police involvement evoke specific members of the police involved and their local relationships (see Brass 1997; Das 1996b), Indo-Fijian narratives depicted the police and the military not as individuals with personal interests at stake but as state officials who actively inspired terror. By not specifying the actual individual police or police stations involved, Indo-Fijians thus continued to hold "the police," and by extension "the state," responsible for their protection and as therefore negligent in their duties.

These narratives of police and military involvement took a few weeks to emerge in Darshan Gaon. Initially, in the first few weeks following the coup, many villagers contrasted the violence of 2000, which they attributed to the behavior of Fijian civilians, with that of 1987 which they stated was conducted predominantly by the military. Stories were told of harassment, rape, and theft conducted by the military against Indians during 1987 in contrast to the present situation. But in later weeks, as more stories from rural areas started to circulate through Darshan Gaon, villagers began to comment on the complicity of the military and police in the violence of 2000. For example, when I asked Subashni why the police or the army were not protecting Indians in the interior, she angrily replied, "because they are mixed. . . . The police and the people doing it, they are mixed together, they are the same." When my husband and I met an elderly man who was among the relatives that Rajesh and the ratu had brought back from the interior, my husband asked him what the situation in Muaniweni was like now. "It's very bad," he said. "When do you think you can go back?" my husband asked. The man shook his head and replied, "There is no government [there]." He then described how a neighbor had had his bull shot and how the police had done nothing in response, vividly evoking the futility of relying on the government in times of crisis. Even Sunil's cousin Priya who proclaimed that the police and the military were doing a good job of keeping the peace in Vunidawa was irate over how much money Sunil was spending on food and beverages to ensure that he received their protection.

Given the political climate and lack of (or high cost of) police and military protection, it is clear why, even though numerous people were subjected to violence, comparatively few Indo-Fijians spoke out publicly about the violence or about the individuals and institutions responsible for it. The media and some political parties, most notably the National Federation Party and the deposed Fiji Labour Party, drew attention to the plight of victims of rural violence, but many of them were, or felt, further threatened due to this. The most famous case was that of Chandrika Prasad, the Muaniweni farmer who filed a lawsuit claiming that the interim government was illegal. Prasad's affidavit to the court detailed assaults that his family were subjected to following the May 19 coup, leading them to flee from Muaniweni and relocate to the refugee camp in Lautoka. In November 2000, Prasad won his case and thus put into question the legitimacy of the entire interim government and all of its decisions since its installation.[7]

7. Despite the interim government being declared illegal by both Justice Anthony Gates's High Court ruling in the Prasad case and the subsequent Court of Appeal ruling that followed

In a case of mistaken identity, another Indo-Fijian farmer also named Chandrika Prasad was physically assaulted on the day the verdict was announced. The result was that Chandrika Prasad—the farmer who was misidentified—was badly injured and Chandrika Prasad—the actual complainant in the court case—went into hiding, and within months of his victory, was preparing to flee to New Zealand, citing continued treats against his life (S. Singh 2001).

Prasad (the complainant) was unique in that his case made national and international headlines. The majority of Indo-Fijians in Fiji had few public forums within the country where they felt safe to voice their grievances. The images of police and military complicity that narratives of rural violence contained were one alternative in that they acted as a nonthreatening form of protest, allowing villagers to assign blame to the authorities without forcing them to further put their lives on the line.

Communicating through Terror

In his introduction to *The Anthropology of Violence,* David Riches writes that one of the essential characteristics of violence is that its legitimacy is questionable. Unless an action involving physical harm entails a struggle over legitimacy, Riches argues, it would not be deemed "violent." But violence also, he contends, acquires its potency from its ease of recognition. Regarding ethnic violence in particular, Riches states that "images of violence are among the few social images which are likely to be well understood across major ethnic divisions" (1986, 13). He considers violence "an excellent communicative vehicle" because of its visibility as well as "the probability that all involved—however different their cultural backgrounds—are likely to draw, at the very least, some basic common understanding from the acts and images concerned" (Riches 1986, 12).

While I agree that "some basic common understanding" of violence as a wrestle for power might be perceived by the various parties involved, what Riches fails, however, to adequately explore are the gaps in understanding and the struggles for meaning that characterize many violent situations. Indo-Fijians in Fiji did not apply to rural violence the straightforward meanings that Riches' theory suggests. Rather, their accounts of violence reveal the muddled, sometimes frantic, often contradictory, struggle to emotionally and cognitively cope with the violence that occurred. Those who had been directly

---

it, the People's Coalition government was, however, never returned to power. Instead fresh elections were held in September 2001.

victimized could not always coherently relate the events they had lived through. Others stepped into this space, attempting to piece together what had happened by recounting the terror of the attacks through both language and their own bodily reenactments. In the process, narrators and audiences bore witness to the pain of those who had been victimized by incorporating some of the horror of the attacks within their own physical being.

At the same time that the attacks and their narrations invoked racial divisions between attackers and victims, accounts of rural violence contained within them the radical potential to disrupt these stereotypes. Narrators of these accounts wrestled with a racial imaginary that attributed violence as stemming from Fijian jungliness but that also evoked the need to carefully assess the trustworthiness of each individual relationship in a social climate that promoted anti-Indian violence.

A Counterpoint to the Consolidation of Ethnic Identity through Ethnic Violence

What then is to be made of the suggestion proposed by so many case studies of "inter-ethnic violence" that violence which takes place between members of different ethnic groups precipitates a shift from local identities and relations to stereotyped ethnic identities?

Analysis of violence narratives in Darshan Gaon suggests that in a time of violence and social crisis, the perceptions and meanings of ethnicity were variously configured. Stories of urban violence and political upheaval tended to elicit a common set of reactions as urban looting, the hostage-taking, and the coup itself were generally blamed on Fijian cultural practices that were perceived as placing Fijians outside of capitalist exchange and its attendant modernizing capabilities.

Narratives and fragmentary accounts of rural violence were distinct from explanations of urban and state-level violence in the attention that they paid to specifying the circumstances in which violence was likely to occur. Rather than portraying an essentialized struggle between "the Fijians" and "the Indians," these narratives reveal that some Indians, particularly young and middle-aged women and older girls by virtue of their perceived sexual vulnerability, were considered more likely to be victimized. Other people, due to their personalities, friendships, local histories, and knowledge of Fijian culture—Rajesh's "*me*, not *everyone*"—were depicted as less likely to be victimized even in areas of the country that might be dangerous for others. Thus even when racial antagonisms were considered by Indo-Fijians as the primary factor in motivating attacks against them, the specific relationships between victims and potential assailants were also seen as crucial to assessing whether inter-ethnic attacks would take place.

This emphasis on describing the context of the violence reflects some of the differences in interpreting the faceless violence of an urban mob or of a rebel force versus that of assailants in rural areas who, even when they were masked, as was Bhābhī's attacker, were often known by their victims. Where the police and other government authorities could not be counted on, local social bonds created through networks of exchange and residential histories were evoked as stabilizing forces that, it was hoped, would—in some cases, if not in all—ensure trust and cooperation between those who might otherwise be separated by political and/or ethnic loyalties.

There was, however, also an ever-present awareness that one had to be ready to make judgments regarding which relationships—such as that of Rajesh and the ratu—could be relied on in potentially very violent situations and which ones—such as between the Indo-Fijian farmer in Muaniweni and the Fijian who stole his bull—were likely to fall to the wayside. In such situations, it was up to the individuals involved to make these decisions since the police and other state authorities were often unable or unwilling to ensure one's safety.

What occurred in narratives of rural violence was thus not a straightforward transformation of identities from local to ethnic, but a struggle to respond to events that overwhelmed people's psyches. Localized relationships were not forgotten but invoked as part of how people attempted to gauge their next move. Let me be clear that narratives of interpersonal violence that occurred in rural areas did not *dismiss* the factor of ethnicity but complicated it by employing racial stereotypes alongside assessments of the particular personalities, relationships, and histories that existed between victims and assailants, and victims and friends.

The emotional effects of these narratives were similarly multiple. At times they encapsulated the panic, fear, and helplessness evoked by the crisis. At other points, these sensations gave way to a numb, emotionless space in which people willingly exchanged and analyzed stories of attacks but appeared to be momentarily incapable of *feeling* any more of the effects of the violence. Such moments were, in turn, replaced by the visceral entanglement of multiple pains and multiple bodies as collective enactments of violent accounts reevoked the pain, fear, and in a few cases, the hope and heroism that encompassed victims, narrators, and their audiences in this time of profound crisis.

7 Restoring "Normalcy" in Postcoup Fiji

By late August 2000 the security situation across Fiji had settled down. The interim civilian government had been in place since the end of July. There had been mass arrests of the rebels after they quit Parliament as well as crackdowns on various rebel groups around the country. Speight and twelve of his leading men were ensconced on the newly created "Alcatraz" of Fiji, Nukulau Island. They were alternatively described as living in extremely Spartan conditions, suffering from a deluge of dengue-ridden mosquitoes, or as having an extended holiday on an island that had long been a popular picnicking spot for families from Suva. Ironically, Nukulau had in a previous incarnation acted as Fiji's "Ellis Island"; it had been the first stop for the indentured laborers where they were quarantined, sometimes for months at a time, while their health and physical fitness were assessed before they were released to join the plantation lines (Leckie 2002b, 119).

In 2000, Speight's removal to Nukulau heralded the beginning of a period that the military described as a return to "normalcy." Slowly, the violence in rural areas was quelled. Electricity was restored across Viti Levu. The curfew hour was pushed back and children started to regularly attend school again. Most people responded by eagerly attempting to put the events of the past few months behind them, but it was not always so easy to "forget," nor was everyone willing to do so.

The military had much at stake in promoting a perception of "normalcy." Not only would the return to "normalcy" legitimate the military's handling of the crisis, particularly its complicity in putting an end to any hope of the People's Coalition government returning to office, but it would also reinvigorate the economy. Furthermore, the military was banking on the fact that keeping the peace would encourage the cooperation of foreign governments to accept the interim civilian government led by Prime Minister Laisenia Qarase. The success of the military's effort depended on the widespread acceptance that stability was preferable to democracy and that the Fiji Labour Party simply could not return to office without endangering the fragile consensus that had been reached.

In order to achieve this, the interim government and the military worked together to mute possible criticisms of the stable, peaceful, indigenous-Fijian-led government that they promoted as the solution to Fiji's recent bout of anarchy. The military made clear its intolerance of negative coverage of state affairs through the detentions of journalists. In late October 2000, following reports that President Iloilo was going to be leaving the country for a routine medical check up and that while he was away Vice President Jope Seniloli (who had been Speight's choice for president) was going to be the acting head of state, Radio Fiji reported that unnamed senior army officers were unhappy with this situation. In response three of the station's journalists were detained by the military. The military justified its actions by claiming that the journalists' news coverage was "false" and "dangerous" as it might lead to divisions in the army (as quoted in *The Fiji Times*, Oct. 21, 2000, 1).

In a similar move, the government chose to have an unusually quiet commemoration of Fiji Day. An historic occasion that would normally have invited celebration as well as reflection on what nationhood means for Fiji, October 10, 2000 was the thirtieth anniversary of Fiji's independence from Great Britain. Instead of the usual fanfare on what had previously been celebrated as an event of national significance, this Fiji Day was a day of silence. The interim government chose not to celebrate the anniversary other than to encourage citizens to spend the day in prayer and quiet reflection.

According to a press release from the Fiji Government, Interim Prime Minister Qarase had the following message to the people of Fiji on Fiji Day (quoted in full):

> Normally on Fiji Day, 10th October, we remember important historical landmarks in our development as a nation.
>
> There is the Deed of Cession on 10th October, 1874 when our forefathers, the high chiefs of Fiji, ceded our country for safekeeping under the sovereignty of Her Majesty Queen Victoria of Great Britain and her heirs and successors.
>
> After ninety-six (96) years of British rule, Fiji gained full independence as a sovereign State on 10th October, 1970.

> This year marks the thirtieth (30th) year of our Independence, and it is the first year in this new Millennium.
>
> The People's Coalition Government had incorporated in its Budget for 2000 plans for celebrations of Fiji Day on a large [scale?—sic] covering our entire country.
>
> However, in light of the coup d'etat of May 19th and the serious and tragic consequences it has had on our country as a whole, with suffering to so many innocent people and their families, the Interim Administration has decided that it would be more appropriate that we celebrate this year's Fiji Day weekend as a period of reflection through prayer by all citizens, their families and communities, to think about our country, and in particular what we can all do together to rebuild and to restore it. Fiji will continue to be home to us all. We must not give up hope. We must not allow ourselves to be overcome by despair and hopelessness. (Fiji Government press releases 2000)

It was as if by sidestepping the holiday, Prime Minister Qarase's government hoped to circumvent the possibility of opening up public spaces in which contested meanings of the Fijian nation might be voiced.

But October 10, 2000, was also named "Blue Day," a day when trade unions around the country urged Fiji's citizens to express their support for the values of "peace," "justice," and "democracy" by wearing something blue. In the following days, there was considerable debate about whether or not the Blue Day protest action had been successful. The interim government's minister of information called it a "blue-less day" on which most people chose not to heed the protest (Fiji Government press releases 2000). In contrast, various trade union spokespeople stated that workers around the country wore blue and took part in a successful "silent protest" (Fijilive.com, October 10, 2000).

I encountered only a handful of people in Nausori who were wearing blue. I asked one, an Indo-Fijian taxi driver, what Blue Day was all about.

"It's the day when people wear blue in protest," he said. But he didn't say what they were protesting. Perhaps my question had breached the tacit agreement of a "silent protest" that allowed people to show their opposition to the current state of things without forcing them to be explicit about what they were protesting against.

Other than the military, government spokespeople, NGOs, and trade union leaders, no one else was talking much about "democracy" or "justice." Most people were interested in working out how to proceed with their everyday lives, given that the new "normalcy" wasn't quite the same as the old one. As one Indo-Fijian man explicitly put it to me, when it came to the government, the issue was no longer whether *democracy* was possible, but whether or not nationwide anarchy and chaos could be avoided. A minority, however, were clearly inspired to silently show where their allegiances lay, and a silent protest, while still risky, was the safest way.

The taxi driver had added that civil servants had been told by the government that they were not allowed to wear blue on Blue Day even if it was part of their regular office attire. I then pointed to his blue shirt, which seemed to be part of a civil servant's uniform, perhaps from a previous job. "So you are wearing blue today!" I remarked.

He laughed heartily, but did not say anything more.

A "Second Coup"

There had been rumors that October 10, 2000, might have yet a third historical significance for Fiji. It was widely reported that Fiji Day would be the probable date of "a second coup" (i.e., a second coup in 2000, which would actually have been Fiji's fourth coup). The rumors made it as far as the international media. The lead story on New Zealand's TV3 news broadcast on October 6, 2000, was that a well-placed Fiji military source had confirmed that a putsch against the leadership of military commander, Commodore Frank Bainimarama, was to take place on Fiji Day.

But on October 10, 2000, there was no sign of such unrest. And when the coup failed to materialize, the date on which a coup was expected was simply shifted forward. I had been told by residents of Darshan Gaon that the impending second coup would occur on October 10, 2000, and then, that it would happen by "the end of the week," and then, that it would happen on Diwali Day (October 27, 2000), when again, nothing happened. One university student complained that if she did not go into Suva every time she was warned that a second coup was imminent, then she would have missed almost every day of the term.

But if many feared that "normalcy" was not sustainable under the Qarase government, this did not necessarily mean that they thought that a second coup would be such a bad thing. In October 2000, many Indo-Fijians spoke of not only the possibility, but also the desirability of a second coup, hoping that it might return the country to the hands of a figure like Rabuka, if not to Rabuka himself. Such a person, they said, might actually know what he was doing and steer the country toward some kind of economic stability.

In the meantime, they cautiously returned to their everyday activities of juggling family life, work, and religious ceremonies, taking care to mute some of their more exuberant community celebrations out of fear of inciting further violence. We can glean a sense of this by looking at another quiet commemoration in 2000, this one from the Hindu calendar—the festival of Diwali.

Diwali 2000

Diwali, the celebration of the Hindu New Year, is usually a festive occasion, marked by sweets, bright lights, and fireworks. But Diwali in 2000 was a quiet affair. Community leaders throughout the country had advised Hindus to tone down their celebrations. Residents in Darshan Gaon were in full agreement. Many feared that too ostentatious a celebration would invite further victimization of Hindus. Others stated that the costs involved in hosting a *Ramayana* reading in their homes were too prohibitive given the economic downturn. The celebrations, which took place on October 27, 2000, were indeed low key. There were very few *Ramayana* readings in the weeks leading up to Diwali. In fact, in 2000 I was aware of only two *Ramayana* readings held in Darshan Gaon in the month of October. In the previous year there had sometimes been two on a single day. Also missing were the usual celebratory fireworks, as fireworks had recently been banned by the government. Maybe they are afraid they sound too much like gunshots, some villagers suggested. Many Hindus refrained from hanging up electric lights, something that had previously been lacking only from houses whose occupants were in mourning due to the death of a family member. In other respects, people tried their best to welcome in the New Year. Even though their finances were restricted, they put an enormous amount of effort into cleaning their houses, making sweets, and preparing a Diwali meal for themselves and for their non-Hindu neighbors.

On the evening of Diwali, I walked over to Rajesh and Parvati's house and followed Parvati up to their prayer room, a tiny but lavishly decorated room about the size of a walk-in closet, in which the Diwali pūjā, or devotional ceremony, was conducted. Afterward we sat with various villagers in Rajesh and Parvati's living room, chatting and watching videos of an even larger and more lavish prayer service their son had hosted in Sydney a few months before. In between comments the women made about how much work it took to put Diwali together, Rajesh and Parvati spoke with great pride about the Sydney pūjā, particularly of the fame of the pandit who was originally from Nausori. The Hindu ceremonies in Sydney were just like in Fiji, they told me, only better. I asked them if they too had thought of migrating. Parvati began to say yes, but Rajesh shook his head. Everything I have, everything I know is in Fiji, he told me. Aware that they had three other grown children who also lived overseas, I asked if their children would ever come back. They both shook their heads and laughed. They'll come to visit, Parvati suggested softly. Having seen the fascination and eagerness with which they watched the Sydney pūjā on video, I wondered what sort of a future they saw for themselves in Fiji.

"Helping You Forget"

As part of the effort to reestablish "normalcy" in late 2000, there was a strong reluctance among many Indo-Fijians to talk about what had happened during the coup. I first noted this active silencing when I returned to Fiji in October 2000. In mid-August 2000 I had to leave Fiji for eight weeks due to my newborn daughter's illness. When I returned, I was struck by how little the coup was talked about. The widespread need to assert the importance of Indian labor, to discuss the heinousness of the looting and destruction of Suva, and to share stories of physical violence was over. Now no one wanted to explicitly talk about the violence or the political events that had occurred so recently. In meeting close friends and neighbors from whom I had been apart for the past eight weeks, I found myself constantly thwarted in my attempts to catch up on what had happened over the intervening period. During the unrest of 2000, Saraswati had related to me detailed stories of how her brother had been attacked during the coups of 1987 and had openly spoken of how she had fled Suva, fearing the possibility of being attacked and raped in her college dormitory. Since I had last seen her, she had gone home to Dreketi, in Vanua Levu where she had witnessed her cousin being held at gunpoint and ordered to sign over his freehold land to neighboring indigenous Fijian landowners. When we met up again, Saraswati gave me the barest outline of the events that had occurred in Dreketi, shrugging off most of my questions about it. Even my closest companion Devi, whose mother had been at the heart of the violence in Vunidawa, likewise had little to say about it. The effects of the coup were clearly on their minds, but the events of the coup itself, both in terms of the political turbulence and the violence that had occurred, had become topics best left unspoken. In many ways this reluctance to talk about the 2000 crisis mirrored the previous reluctance to discuss the details of the events of the 1987 coups, up until the latest period of political unrest. In the midst of the turmoil of 2000, the violence of 2000 and of 1987 had been on everyone's lips. But barely five months after May 19, no one wanted to talk about it.

One way the coup *was* spoken about, and incessantly so, was as a historical marker. The date of May 19 had become an orientation point in people's sense of time. In all manner of conversation, the 2000 coup was a dividing line, separating political, economic, and social life into the time before and the time after. Such-and-such wedding, I was told, occurred *coup ke pehle* (before the coup) or so-and-so's school examinations were held *coup ke bād* (after the coup). Similar to oral and written references to *la violencia* in Guatemala (Warren 1993a, 32), *beeshanaya* (the terror) in Sri Lanka (Perera 2001), and the attack on the Twin Towers on September 11, 2001, the impact of the 2000 coup was continually recognized through the use of the coup as a historical marking point.

But no one wanted to actually reflect back on the events that they had just left behind, and they actively deflected any conversations that looked as if they might head in that direction. I don't think I could have understood the intensity of this reluctance had I not been going through another experience of silencing by members of the same community. When I returned with my baby daughter, I was immediately struck by how people actively avoided discussing the events of her medical evacuation. Whenever there was any reference to the fact that I had had to leave or that she had been critically ill, someone would quickly change the subject. At some points, I tried to talk about her illness with people I was close to, but I was always firmly stopped. I finally bluntly asked Ram, a close family friend, why this was so. He told me that it was precisely because of the pain that we needed to stay silent. "How can you want to talk about something like that?" Ram asked. "Isn't that something better *not* to talk about? These women have gone through so many things and they are trying to help you too to forget."

In retrospect, I realized that scars were slowly being formed. More precisely, they were being encouraged to form through a communitywide cultivation of silence. Rather than silence being considered an inhibitor of healing, as it is in much of Western medical, psychological, and cultural discourse, this was a case of a community encouraging silence as a means of promoting healing. To break the silence would be akin to breaking open the wound. Through silence, all of these events—be they the political overthrow that positioned Indo-Fijians as vulagi, or foreigners, in their own country, the terrifying violence that accompanied it, or my own family crisis—were firmly relegated into their place as things that *had been*, but were no longer. Silence was not only an effective means of communicating collective solidarity around one's pain (cf. Basso 1970) but also a political act that relegated an unbridgeable rupture between past and present. To break the silence would have been to bring these moments of trauma back into the present, something that the men and women of Darshan Gaon were not willing to do.

The Crisis Continues

There was no "second coup" on either Fiji Day or Diwali. But the villagers' guesses weren't too far off and their lives were soon plunged into renewed chaos. Less than a week after Diwali, on November 2, 2000, there was a bloody attempt to wrestle power away from Commodore Bainimarama. As discussed in chapter 2, a breakaway band of the armed forces mutinied against the commodore at the Queen Elizabeth Barracks. In terms of violence, it was the most intensive battle that had taken place at any point during the 2000 coup (or during the 1987 and 2006 coups). Suva and neighboring areas, including Darshan Gaon, were plunged into a two-day curfew as rebel and military shoot-outs took place in areas throughout the city. Eight soldiers were killed and several other soldiers and civilians were wounded. Under threat were not only Commodore Bainimarama's life and leadership, but the stability of the military and of the military-backed interim regime. Bainimarama, however, rode out the crisis with his position in the military intact. Within a few weeks the situation had restabilized, returning again to some variation of "normalcy." Six years later Bainimarama's coup of 2006 put the military's presence back into the forefront of people's lives. But the coup of 2006 was much less violent and disruptive than that of 2000 and as of this writing in mid-2008, there have been no further outbreaks of state-level violence, mass lootings, or military shoot-outs. Despite the fears of many, Indo-Fijians and Fijians alike, the violence in Fiji never escalated to the levels of comparable political and ethnic conflicts in Bougainville or the Solomon Islands.[1]

The issue of how to deal with the legacy of the events of 2000 continues, however, to divide Fijian society. Under the guidance of the then Fiji police commissioner Andrew Hughes, by January 2006 more than two thousand suspects had been investigated for their role in the 2000 coup. Out of these, 782 were charged and convicted (Republic of Fiji Islands Fiji Police Force 2006). But many of those who were found guilty of involvement in the coup served the briefest of jail sentences. As historian Brij V. Lal notes, some sentences were reduced to less than two weeks, with those convicted being quickly released under the Compulsory Supervision Order or on "dubious medical grounds" (2007, 3). Other figures who were suspected of involvement

---

1. The Bougainville conflict lasted nine years and estimates of the death toll vary widely, between 10,000 and 50,000 people. Estimates of deaths in the 2000 Solomon Islands conflict also vary, though many are in the vicinity of 70 or 80. The only estimates I am aware of for the death toll for the 2000 Fiji coup are 16 (Lakhan 2001) or "at least 20" (Field, Baba, and Nabobo-Baba 2005, 261).

in the 2000 coup, such as former police commissioner Isikia Savua and Ratu Inoke Kubuabola, were shuttled off on diplomatic postings overseas.

Prime Minister Qarase then followed up with his proposed Bill for the Promotion of Reconciliation, Unity, and Tolerance, offering amnesty to some of those found guilty of colluding in the coup. When it was first proposed in 2005, the Reconciliation bill raised some serious issues regarding what is at stake in the tactics of silencing. We have seen how attempts to silence pain might be employed by communities in the spirit of trying to move away from and thus help heal trauma. The Reconciliation bill was promoted on the similar idea that peace could be restored to the nation by moving away from the events of the past. As a result, many of those responsible for the violence of 2000 would never be made to face up to the consequences of their acts. But the bill raised more questions than it answered. Namely, what were the government's actual motivations for introducing the bill? Could amnesty result in anything other than papering over the political and social rifts that led up to the coup in the first place? Is this the kind of "reconciliation" and "unity" that the people of Fiji want?

In 2005, there was much public discomfort over the Reconciliation bill. When Fiji's citizens were explicitly asked by the Qarase government to make public their views, there was an outpouring of sentiment against the proposed amnesty. A variety of religious organizations, civic groups, trade unions, and NGOs spoke out against the bill on behalf of their indigenous Fijian and Indo-Fijian members. Some indigenous Fijian professionals I spoke with at the time questioned whether the bill was merely a vote-buying scheme, designed to keep Prime Minister Qarase in office. Many Indo-Fijians said that they had seen the court trials of those accused of involvement in the coup as a positive, albeit painstakingly slow, means of setting things straight without, it was hoped, inciting further unrest. But the proposed bill raised despair over the government's willingness to overlook the crimes committed against its citizens and fear over the government's responses to future violence. Even if people were earnestly endeavoring to forget and move on in their everyday lives, this did not mean they did not want to see those who were responsible for the crisis face justice.

Another Turning Point

Open, public debate over the Reconciliation bill and the appropriate response to the events of 2000 came to an abrupt halt in December 2006 when Commodore Bainimarama seized power. Bainimarama had no doubts over what should be done with the Reconciliation bill. As part of his justification for the 2006 coup, he asserted that the Qarase government's promotion of the Reconciliation, Tolerance, and Unity Bill was detrimental to the public good.[2] Many critics have also pointed out that the commodore also had a personal motivation in standing up against the bill, as the last thing he wanted to see was amnesty granted to the military personnel who took part in the November 2000 mutiny against his leadership, during which Bainimarama came close to being assassinated. Bainimarama himself preferred to portray his crusade as a defense of national morality. In the run up to his 2006 coup, he threatened, "If they [the Qarase government] lack the moral strength and the courage to continue the good fight, the military is willing to return and complete for this nation the responsibilities we gave this Government in 2000 and 2001" (as quoted in Berry 2006).

Bainimarama's takeover not only put the Reconciliation bill out of consideration, but also shifted some of the key terms in Fijian political debate. At issue, according to Bainimarama, was no longer the need to promote "indigenous rights" over and above democratic processes but the need to "clean up" corruption and set up a "truly democratic" democracy, albeit through nondemocratic means.

The military's fervor for "cleaning up" extended to "cleaning up" its critics by violently cracking down on antimilitary activism, curtailing reporting by local and, when possible, foreign journalists, and effectively muzzling much of public debate.[3] While dissent has been raised in internet blogs such as those of Fiji's "Freedom Bloggers" as well as through small-scale nonviolent protests, expressions of support for and against the current administration have mostly been the domain of recognized public authorities, such as NGO leaders, trades unions, and members of the Great Council of Chiefs, rather than by the grassroots citizenry. Although Bainimarama's government may deem such silence as necessary for moving the nation forward, it is clear by the number of citizens who continue to attempt to speak out against the regime that in this case many do not agree.

International outrage has, however, not been so easily stifled. Despite Bainimarama's repeated condemnations of foreign government's "misunderstandings" and intrusions into Fiji's internal politics, Australia, New

2. Commodore Bainimarama was also dissatisfied by Prime Minister Qarase's support of two other proposed bills. These were the similarly controversial Qoliqoli Bill, which would have granted indigenous Fijians exclusive rights over certain areas of beach, lagoon, and reef, and the Land Tribunal Bill, which addressed grievances over indigenous Fijian land rights but did not receive as much public debate (for details, see Lal 2007).

3. In June 2007, New Zealand journalist Michael Field was detained and barred entry when he arrived at Nadi airport. Journalists within Fiji have also reported harassment and intimidation by the military.

Zealand, the EU, Britain, and the United States have responded to Bainimarama's coup by imposing a range of sanctions, including restrictions on political contact, immigration, defense relationships, and development assistance. Soon after the 2006 takeover, New Zealand's prime minister Helen Clark and Australia's foreign minister Alexander Downer also called for Fiji's citizens to undertake acts of passive resistance against the military government. Despite continued international and domestic pressure on Bainimarama to move Fiji quickly toward democratic elections, the military leader has vacillated about how long he intends to remain in power, wavering between promises to return Fiji to parliamentary democracy in 2009, 2010, or possibly as late as 2020. In one public outburst that was widely reported in both local and international media, he threatened to keep the transitional military government in place for the next fifty years.[4] While the fifty-year time frame was not taken seriously, it reflects some of the volatility that Fiji's citizens must contend with in their new prime minister.

Reconstituting Social Life in Times of Political Crisis

As we have seen, the 2000 coup resulted in a radical rupture in Fiji's political, economic, and social life. Despite the various factors that contributed to the 2000 crisis, the 2000 coup itself was explained by many as a result of irreconcilable "racial" differences between Fiji's two major ethnic groups. As targets of coup-related violence, Indo-Fijians responded to the events following May 19, 2000, with shock and panic. But alongside their cries of despair and invocations of the fantastic, they shared more than a little humor, momentarily mastering the terror that engulfed them. They also intensified their concerns over the meanings of ethnic identity and the roles of different ethnic groups in the project of nation-making. In particular, physical labor was invoked as a crucial part of Indo-Fijians' understandings of themselves as both Hindus and as Indians. The destruction of shops and business enterprises came to symbolize Indian pain as Fijians were portrayed as dangerous junglis whose lawlessness, it was feared, would return Fiji to the dark ages. And yet, the all-encompassing racial stereotypes that

---

4. This incident occurred prior to the appointment of the interim government, when Bainimarama discovered that the Great Council of Chiefs was unlikely to approve his plan to reinstall Ratu Josefa Iloilo as president. Following his threats, Bainimarama finally received the GCC's grudging cooperation, but a few months later the GCC refused to agree to his choice of vice president. This time, Bainimarama responded with the unprecedented move of declaring that the GCC constituted a "security threat" and would no longer be allowed to meet ("Fiji's Council . . ." 2007). In 2008, Bainimarama revoked the ban against the GCC and, in a new strategy for asserting his control, made himself the organization's chairperson.

were used to explain much of coup-related violence were tempered when people began to relate stories of physical violence that they or those close to them had experienced. Turning inventories of violence into collective reenactments of pain, these narratives revealed moments of inter-ethnic friendship at the same time as they queried the role of the police and the military in allowing anti-Indian violence. The intense social and political turmoil shed light on the ambiguities of social relations as people collectively pondered the nature of inter-ethnic relations, the meanings of citizenship and the rights of citizens, and the security of local communities. In this book, we have explored some of the events that generated these conditions as well as how Indo-Fijians collectively attempted to cope with the emotional and psychological strains of struggling through and finding meaning in a world turned upside down by social and political chaos.

Important questions remain as to how everyday life is being reconstituted in the continuing aftermath of 2000. Some people, like Shanti, are still struggling with the emotional trauma of the violence. But even those who were not themselves victims of violence, shared in the widespread fear that they might lose their homes, their livelihoods, and their lives. Many Indians and Fijians have anxiously quit Fiji or are making plans to do so. Sera, the indigenous Fijian schoolteacher I befriended, has stayed but is actively trying to find scholarships or other means to get her teenage daughter out of the country. Out of the Indo-Fijians I got to know well in Darshan Gaon, Devi and her husband as well as Shanti and her family have remained in the village. Elizabeth resolutely declared that she would remain permanently in Fiji, until the 2006 coup propelled her and her husband to begin applying for overseas work visas. The families of Meena and Vijay, Saraswati, and half a dozen others have all followed their relatives overseas. Rajesh and Parvati, who in 2000 were divided on whether or not to leave, spent the next five years moving back and forth between their house in Darshan Gaon and their son's house in Australia until they too finally packed up and permanently resettled in Sydney.

Thousands of others, Indo-Fijians and indigenous Fijians, have stayed, either out of choice or out of necessity. Like those who have left, many of those who have remained are endeavoring to renew a sense of security and stability in their lives, hoping that one day they will truly witness the ushering in of a different kind of "normalcy" in Fiji.

Acknowledgments

A great many people contributed to making this book possible. First and foremost, I thank my husband John, without whose never-ending encouragement this project would never have been started, much less finished. He has enthusiastically engaged with my intellectual endeavors from my first days of undergraduate study up through my initial years as a professional academic. In Fiji, he shared the ups and downs of two years of fieldwork, always eager to share in both the joys and difficulties of life in the field. He has read and rigorously critiqued multiple drafts of this book and taken up the slack at home, changing more than his fair share of nappies, when writing deadlines loomed. I could not have asked for a more supportive partner. This book is dedicated to him.

Our daughters, Revena and Anika, were also central figures in both the fieldwork and writing process. Revena first journeyed to Fiji at the age of two and left at the age of four, her earliest memories being of gunshots and roadblocks. I hope in time she will have the opportunity to get to know a calmer, safer Fiji. Anika was born in Suva but spent only a few weeks there following her medical evacuation to New Zealand. Hopefully she too will have more of an opportunity to get to know the country of her birth. Our son, Lukáš, joined us just in time to provide welcomed company, and distraction, during the final stages of the writing process.

I also thank my parents and siblings who were the first to encourage me to take up a career in academia. My father promoted in me the desire to travel and see the world for myself, and my mother gave me the courage to fulfill my academic, and other, aspirations. My brother Peter and sister Irena similarly encouraged me to pursue a life of intellectual endeavor.

My initial teachers in anthropology at the University of California, Berkeley, in particular Lawrence Cohen, Nancy Scheper-Hughes, Ellen Lewin, and Alan Dundes, provided intellectual and practical guidance while fanning the enthusiasm of an eager undergraduate. Alena Heitlinger of Trent University was later crucial in providing me with my first professional research experience, in the Czech Republic, for which I will always be grateful.

At Princeton University, my intellectual debts to the faculty and my fellow graduate students at the time are numerous. Rena Lederman, Emily Martin, João Biehl, Isabelle Clark-Deces, and Jim Boon provided an intellectual environment equal to none. Rena Lederman in particular provided me with the support and sustained critical engagement necessary during my graduate studies. On the top floor of Aaron Burr Hall, Sarah Pinto, Kavita Misra, and Heiko Henkel provided comradeship and plenty of opportunity for intellectual debate. Stephen Jackson and Tisa Wenger helped keep the scholarly enthusiasm flowing. Since leaving Princeton, members of the Princeton Anthropology Graduate Cyberwriting Group—in particular, Sarah Pinto, Lisa Wynn, Rachel Newcomb, Tom Strong, Alex Edmonds, Kristi Latta, and Kirstin Sheid—have been crucial to keeping up a vibrant intellectual exchange.

In Fiji, I am indebted to many families for their care and support not only during the process of conducting field research but also during the difficult days of the coup and especially after my daughter's birth. While I cannot name many of those who were most instrumental in assisting with both my research and in making our lives as safe and comfortable as possible, I am intensely grateful to the residents of "Darshan Gaon," especially the families of "Devi," "Rajesh," and "Elizabeth" for their kindness. I'd also like to thank "Sera" for all her friendship and support during my pregnancy. Mike Davis of the University of the South Pacific, Scott MacWilliam and Brenda Love, Kimberly and Matthew Oman, and Meriea and Christian Carling were wonderful friends to have in the field, going out of their way to provide advice and support. Tej Ram Prem guided me through my initial days in Fiji and became not only a wonderful field adviser but also a close family friend.

I will always be extremely thankful to Howard H. Betts and other staff at the U.S. Embassy in Suva, administrators at the Suva Colonial War Memorial Hospital, and Dean Sandra Mawhinney of Princeton University for coming to our aid and enabling our newborn daughter's medical evacuation. I am especially grateful to the doctors at CWM who kept her alive so that she could be transferred overseas for more intensive medical care. My thanks also to the many nurses and matrons of the CWM maternity ward who offered their prayers and ceaseless cups of Milo. I will never forget the kindness and generosity of the women of "Darshan Gaon" and nearby settlements who fasted and prayed for us during this time.

While the early conceptualization of this book occurred at Princeton University, much of its development occurred at the University of Auckland. I am thankful to my colleagues in social anthropology, Cris Shore, Julie Park, Christine Dureau, Mark Busse, Phyllis Herda, Maureen Molloy, and Veronica Strang, in ethnomusicology, Greg Booth, and in development studies, Yvonne Underhill-Sem, for welcoming me into a vibrant intellectual community. As members of our departmental writing group, many of them have also read and provided vital feedback on various chapters of the book. Cris Shore was especially instrumental at various stages of the writing and publishing process. Alison and Greg Booth were most generous with friendship, food, and creative inspiration whenever it was needed. Also in Auckland, Sharyn Graham, Vivienne Elizabeth, and Relinde Tapp have provided great warmth and collegiality throughout the writing process. The women of the University of Auckland Women's Writing Group shared their insights into academic writing and kept my enthusiasm going. My graduate students, particularly those in my 2007 seminar "Violence and Pain," have also assisted in expanding my thinking on many of the issues explored here.

Various parts of the manuscript have benefited from the generous advice of a number of other colleagues and friends. Brij V. Lal and Matthew Tomlinson not only read and commented on previous drafts but were also ready to advise on any and all issues related to Fiji. Lisa Guenther and Lisa Wynn both provided crucial feedback on an earlier version of the manuscript. My sister, a practicing psychotherapist, kindly read chapter 6 and shared her thoughts on therapeutic approaches to violence with me.

Peter Wissoker and Teresa Jesionowski of Cornell University Press have both been much welcomed sources of encouragement and support during the preparation of the book manuscript. I also thank the two anonymous reviewers for their input on how to rework and strengthen a previous draft.

I have received permission to reprint the following: figures 6 and 9 were previously published in *Oceania* 75, no. 4 (September/December 2005). Sections of chapter 4 were previously published as part of "Foreigners at Home: Discourses of Difference, Fiji Indians, and the Looting of May 19," in *Pacific Studies* 25, no. 4 (2002): 69–92. A previous version of chapter 6 was published as "Between Victims and Assailants, Victims and Friends: Sociality and the Imagination in Indo-Fijian Narratives of Rural Violence during the May 2000 Fiji Coup," in *Terror and Violence: Imagination and the Unimaginable,* edited by Andrew Strathern, Pamela Stewart, and Neil Whitehead (London: Pluto, 2005), 117–141.

Financial support at various stages of this project has come from a variety of sources. A Mellon grant from Princeton University made my graduate studies all the easier. The Social Science Research Council Predissertation Fellowship enabled me to travel to Fiji and begin my research there. At the University of Auckland, I have received a series of Faculty of Arts Research grants that were vital for conducting research on the post-2000 coup situation in Fiji. A grant from the Green Foundation was also instrumental in enabling follow-up research in Fiji. Finally, the Faculty of Arts Research Fellowship allowed me time off from teaching to focus on completing the manuscript.

To all of these individuals and institutions, my sincerest thanks.

Susanna Trnka

Auckland, New Zealand

References

Abrahams, Ray. 1999. "Friends and Networks as Survival Strategies in North-East Europe." In *The Anthropology of Friendship,* edited by Sandra Bell and Simon Coleman, 155–68. Oxford: Berg.

Abramson, Allen. 2000. "Bounding the Unbounded: Ancestral Land and Jural Relations in the Interior of Eastern Fiji." In *Land, Law, and Environment: Mythical Land, Legal Boundaries,* edited by Allen Abramson and Dimitrios Theodossopoulos, 191–210. London: Pluto Press.

Adinkrah, Mensah. 1999. "Uxoricide in Fiji: The Sociocultural Context of Husband-Wife Killings." *Violence against Women* 5, no. 11: 1294–1320.

Agamben, Giorgio. 1998. *Homo Sacer: Sovereign Power and Bare Life.* Translated by Daniel Heller-Roazen. Stanford, CA: Stanford University Press.

———. 2002. *Remnants of Auschwitz: The Witness and the Archive.* Translated by Daniel Heller-Roazen. New York: Zone Books.

———. 2005. *State of Exception.* Translated by Kevin Attell. Chicago: University of Chicago Press.

Akram-Lodhi, A. Haroon, ed. 2000. *Confronting Fiji Futures.* Canberra: Asia Pacific Press.

Ali, Ahmed. 1979. *Girmit: The Indenture Experience.* Suva: Fiji Museum.

———. 1980a. "Fiji Indians: A Historical Perspective." In *Girmit: A Centenary Anthology, 1879–1979,* edited by Jai Ram Reddy, 11–17. Suva: Ministry of Information.

———. 1980b. *Plantation to Politics: Studies on Fiji Indians.* Suva: University of the South Pacific.

Allan, Graham. 1996. *Kinship and Friendship in Modern Britain.* Oxford: Oxford University Press.

Allport, Gordon, and Leo Postman. 1947. *The Psychology of Rumor.* New York: Henry Holt.

Alonso, Ana Maria. 1994. "The Politics of Space, Time, and Substance: State Formation, Nationalism, and Ethnicity." *Annual Review of Anthropology* 23: 379–405.

Amnesty International. 2001. "Fiji." Annual reports. Online version available at http://web.amnesty.org/web/ar2001.nsf/webasacountries/FIJI?OpenDocument.

Appadurai, Arjun. 1998. "Dead Certainty: Ethnic Violence in the Era of Global Uncertainty." *Public Culture* 10, no. 2: 225–47.

———. 2006. *Fear of Small Numbers: An Essay on the Geography of Anger.* Durham, NC: Duke University Press.

Arendt, Hannah. 1958. *The Human Condition.* Chicago: University of Chicago Press.

Aretxaga, Begoña. 1995. "Dirty Protest: Symbolic Overdetermination and Gender in Northern Ireland Ethnic Violence." *Ethos* 23, no. 2: 123–48.

———. 1997. *Shattering Silence: Women, Nationalism, and Political Subjectivity in Northern Ireland.* Princeton, NJ: Princeton University Press.

Arno, Andrew. 1993. *The World of Talk on a Fijian Island: An Ethnography of Law and Communicative Causation.* Norwood, NJ: Ablex.

Austin, John Langshaw. 1962. *How to Do Things with Words: The William James Lectures Delivered at Harvard University in 1955.* Oxford: Clarendon Press.

Barth, Fredrik, ed. 1969. *Ethnic Groups and Boundaries: The Social Organization of Cultural Difference.* Boston: Little, Brown.

———. 1994. "Enduring and Emerging Issues in the Analysis of Ethnicity." In *The Anthropology of Ethnicity: Beyond "Ethnic Groups and Boundaries,"* edited by Hans Vermeulen and Cora Grovers, 11–32. The Hague: Het Spinhuis.

Basso, Keith. 1970. " 'To Give Up on Words': Silence in Western Apache Culture." *Southwestern Journal of Anthropology* 26, no. 3: 213–30.

Bauman, Richard. 1986. *Story, Performance, and Event: Contextual Studies of Oral Narrative.* Cambridge: Cambridge University Press.

———. 1992. "Contextualization, Tradition, and the Dialogue of Genres: Icelandic Legends of the Kraftaskald." In *Rethinking Context: Language as an Interactive Phenomenon,* edited by Charles Goodwin and Alessandro Duranti, 125–45. Cambridge: Cambridge University Press.

Bax, Mart. 1997. "Mass Graves, Stagnating Identification, and Violence: A Case Study in the Local Sources of 'The War' in Bosnia Hercegovina." *Anthropological Quarterly* 70, no. 1: 11–19.

Becker, Anne. 1995. *Body, Self, and Society: The View from Fiji.* Philadelphia: University of Pennsylvania Press.

Belshaw, Cyril. 1964. *Under the Ivi Tree: Society and Economic Growth in Rural Fiji.* Berkeley: University of California Press.

Berry, Ruth. 2006. "NZ Cautions Fiji Military over Threats." *New Zealand Herald,* Online edition, January 10.

Bhabha, Homi K. 1994. *The Location of Culture.* London: Routledge.

Birtles, Terry G. 1997. "First Contact: Colonial European Preconceptions of Tropical Queensland Rainforest and Its People." *Journal of Historical Geography* 23, no. 4: 393–417.

Blueprint for the Protection of Fijian and Rotuman Rights and Interests, and the Advancement of Their Development. 2000. Presentation to the Great Council of Chiefs by the Interim Prime Minister, Mr. Laisenia Qarase. July 13.

Bourdieu, Pierre, and Alain Accardo. 1999. *The Weight of the World: Social Suffering in Contemporary Society.* Translated by Priscilla Parkhurst Ferguson. Cambridge: Polity Press.

Bourgois, Philippe. 1996. *In Search of Respect: Selling Crack in El Barrio.* Cambridge: Cambridge University Press.

Bowman, Glen. 1994. "Xenophobia, Fantasy, and the Nation: The Logic of Ethnic Violence in Former Yugoslavia." In *The Anthropology of Europe: Identity and Boundaries in Conflict,* edited by Victoria Goddard, Josep Llobera, and Cris Shore, 143–71. Oxford: Berg.

Brass, Paul R. 1997. *Theft of an Idol: Text and Context in the Representation of Collective Violence.* Princeton, NJ: Princeton University Press.

Brenneis, Donald. 1978. "The Matter of Talk." *Language in Society* 7, no. 2: 159–70.

———. 1983. "The Emerging Soloist: Kavvali in Bhatgaon." *Asian Folklore Studies* 42: 67–80.

———. 1984. "Grog and Gossip in Bhatgaon: Style and Substance in Fiji Indian Conversation." *American Ethnologist* 11, no. 3: 487–506.

———. 1990a. "Dramatic Gestures: The Fijian Indian Pancayat as Therapeutic Event." In *Disentangling Conflict Discourse in Pacific Societies,* edited by Karen Ann Watson-Gegeo and Geoffrey M. White, 214–38. Stanford, CA: Stanford University Press.

———. 1990b. "Shared and Solitary Sentiments: The Discourse of Friendship, Play, and Anger in Bhatgaon." In *Language and the Politics of Emotion,* edited by Catherine Lutz and Lila Abu-Lughod, 113–25. Cambridge: Cambridge University Press.

———. 1991. "Aesthetics, Performance, and the Enactment of Tradition in a Fiji Indian Community." In *Gender, Genre, and Power in South Asian Expressive Traditions,* edited by Arjun Appadurai, Frank Korom, and Margaret Mills, 362–78. Philadelphia: University of Pennsylvania Press.

———. 1995. " 'Caught in the Web of Words': Performing Theory in a Fiji Indian Community." In *Everyday Conceptions of Emotion: An Introduction to the Anthropology, Psychology, and Linguistics of Emotion,* edited by James A. Russel, Jose-Miguel Fernandez-Dols, Antony Manstead, and J. C. Wellenkemp, 241–50. Dordrecht: Kluwer Academic.

Briggs, Charles L. 2003. *Stories in the Time of Cholera: Racial Profiling during a Medical Nightmare.* Berkeley: University of California Press.

Brodwin, Paul. 1992. "Symptoms and Social Performances: The Case of Diane Reden." In *Pain as Human Experience: An Anthropological Perspective,* edited by Mary-Jo Delvecchio Good, Byron Good, Arthur Kleinman, and Paul Brodwin, 77–99. Berkeley: University of California Press.

Burma, John H. 1990. "Humor as a Technique in Race Conflict." In *Mother Wit from the Laughing Barrel: Readings in the Interpretation of Afro-American Folklore,* edited by Alan Dundes, 620–27. Jackson: University Press of Mississippi.

Burton, John Weir. 1910. *The Fiji of Today.* London: C. H. Kelly.

"Cabinet Post for Ratu Naiqama Says PM." 2005. Fijilive website, www.fijilive.com, September 20.

Carmichael, Cathie. 2006. "Violence and Ethnic Boundary Maintenance in Bosnia in the 1990s." *Journal of Genocide Research* 8, no. 3: 283–93.

Chatterjee, Partha. 1993. *The Nation and Its Fragments: Colonial and Postcolonial Histories.* Princeton, NJ: Princeton University Press.

Chatterjee, Piya. 2001. *A Time for Tea.* Durham, NC: Duke University Press.

Cohen, Abner. 1974. *Urban Ethnicity.* London: Tavistock.

Cohen, Lawrence. 2004. "Operability: Surgery at the Margin of the State." In *Anthropology in the Margins of the State,* edited by Veena Das and Deborah Poole, 165–90. Santa Fe: School of American Research Press.

Cohen, Ronald. 1978. "Ethnicity: Problem and Focus in Anthropology." *Annual Review of Anthropology* 7: 379–403.

Cohen, Yehudi A. 1961. "Patterns of Friendship." In *Social Structure and Personality: A Casebook,* edited by Yehudi Cohen, 351–86. New York: Holt, Rinehart, and Winston.

Cole, Jennifer. 2004. "Painful Memories: Ritual and the Transformation of Community Trauma." *Culture, Medicine, and Psychiatry* 28, no. 1: 87–105.

Comaroff, Jean, and John Comaroff. 1991. *Of Revelation and Revolution: Christianity, Colonialism, and Consciousness in South Africa.* Chicago: University of Chicago Press.

Comaroff, John. 1987. "Of Totemism and Ethnicity." *Ethnos* 3–4: 301–23.

Daniel, E. Valentine. 1996. *Charred Lullabies: Chapters in an Anthropography of Violence.* Princeton, NJ: Princeton University Press.

Das, Veena, ed. 1990a. *Mirrors of Violence: Communities, Riots and Survivors in South Asia.* Delhi: Oxford University Press.

——. 1990b. "Our Work to Cry: Your Work to Listen." In *Mirrors of Violence: Communities, Riots, and Survivors in South Asia,* edited by Veena Das, 345–98. Delhi: Oxford University Press.

——. 1995. *Critical Events: An Anthropological Perspective on Contemporary India.* Delhi: Oxford University Press.

——. 1996a. "Language and Body: Transactions in the Construction of Pain." *Daedalus* 125, no. 1: 67–91.

——. 1996b. "The Spatialization of Violence: Case Study of a 'Communal Riot.' " In *Unravelling the Nation: Sectarian Conflict and India's Secular Identity,* edited by Kaushik Basu and Sanjay Subrahmanyam, 157–203. New Delhi: Penguin Books India.

——. 1998. "Official Narratives, Rumour, and the Social Production of Hate." *Social Identities* 4, no. 1: 109–30.

——. 2004. "The Signature of the State: The Paradox of Illegibility." In *Anthropology in the Margins of the State,* edited by Veena Das and Deborah Poole, 225–52. Santa Fe: School of American Research Press.

——. 2007. *Life and Words: Violence and the Descent into the Ordinary.* Berkeley: University of California Press.

Das, Veena, Arthur Kleinman, Margaret Lock, Mamphela Ramphele, and Pamela Reynolds, eds. 2001. *Remaking a World: Violence, Social Suffering, and Recovery.* Berkeley: University of California Press.

Das, Veena, Arthur Kleinman, Mamphela Ramphele, and Pamela Reynolds, eds. 2000. *Violence and Subjectivity.* Berkeley: University of California Press.

Das, Veena, and Deborah Poole, eds. 2004a. *Anthropology in the Margins of the State.* Santa Fe: School of American Research Press.

——. 2004b. "State and Its Margins." In *Anthropology in the Margins of the State,* edited by Veena Das and Deborah Poole,

Dean, Eddie, and Stan Ritova. 1988. *Rabuka: No Other Way.* Sydney: Doubleday.

Desjarlais, Robert. 1992. *Body and Emotion: The Aesthetics of Illness and Healing in the Nepal Himalayas.* Philadelphia: University of Pennsylvania Press.

Dormandy, Thomas. 2006. *The Worst of Evils: The Fight against Pain.* New Haven, CT: Yale University Press.

Douglas, Mary. 1966. *Purity and Danger: An Analysis of Concepts of Pollution and Taboo.* London: Routledge and Kegan Paul.

———. 1968. "The Social Control of Cognition: Some Factors in Joke Perception." *Man* 3, no. 3: 361–76.

Dundes, Alan. 1987. *Cracking Jokes: Studies of Sick Humor Cycles and Stereotypes.* Berkeley, CA: Ten Speed Press.

Dundes, Alan, and Roger D. Abrahams. 1987. "On Elephantasy and Elephaticide: The Effect of Time and Place." In *Cracking Jokes: Studies of Sick Humor Cycles and Stereotypes,* edited by Alan Dundes, 51–54. Berkeley, CA: Ten Speed Press.

Dundes, Alan, and Thomas Hauschild. 1987. "Auschwitz Jokes." In *Cracking Jokes: Studies of Sick Humor Cycles and Stereotypes,* edited by Alan Dundes, 19–28. Berkeley, CA: Ten Speed Press.

Fassin, Didier, and Paula Vasquez. 2005. "Humanitarian Exception as the Rule." *American Ethnologist* 32, no. 3: 389–405.

Feldman, Allen. 1991. *Formations of Violence: The Narrative of the Body and Political Terror in Northern Ireland.* Chicago: University of Chicago Press.

———. 1994. "From Desert Storm to Rodney King via ex-Yugoslavia: On Cultural Anesthesia." In *The Senses Still: Perception and Memory as Material Culture in Modernity,* edited by Nadia Seremetakis, 45–62. Boulder: Westview.

Ferme, Mariane. 2004. "Deterritorialized Citizenship and the Resonances of the Sierra Leonean State." In *Anthropology in the Margins of the State,* edited by Veena Das and Deborah Poole, 81–116. Santa Fe: School of American Research Press.

Feuchtwang, Stephan. 2006. "Images of Sub-humanity and Their Realization." *Critique of Anthropology* 26, no. 3: 259–78.

Field, Michael, Tupeni Baba, and Unaisi Nabobo-Baba. 2005. *Speight of Violence: Inside Fiji's 2000 Coup.* Auckland: Reed.

Fiji Government press releases. 2000. Speech by Interim Prime Minister Qarase on Fiji Day and Blue Day statement by minister of information, October 10, available at www.fiji.gov.fj.

Fiji Islands Bureau of Statistics. 1996. Census of Fiji. General Tables—Population. Suva.

Fiji Times, The, various dates, 1999–2006.

Fiji Women's Crisis Centre (FWCC). 2001. *The Impact of the May 19 Coup on Women in Fiji.* Report by the Fiji Women's Crisis Centre, Suva.

"Fiji's Council of Chiefs Sacked." 2007. *New Zealand Herald,* Online edition, April 3.

Fijilive.com. 2000–2006. News reports.

FM 96 radio. 2000. News reports, May 20.

FM 101 radio. 2000. News reports, July 16.

Foster, Robert J. 1995. *Nation Making: Emergent Identities in Postcolonial Melanesia.* Ann Arbor: University of Michigan Press.

———. 2002. *Materializing the Nation: Commodities, Consumption, and Media in Papua New Guinea.* Bloomington: Indiana University Press.

France, Peter. 1969. *The Charter of the Land: Custom and Colonization in Fiji.* Melbourne: Oxford University Press.

Freud, Sigmund. 1963. [1905] *Jokes and Their Relation to the Unconscious [Der Witz und Seine Beziehung zum Unbewussten].* Translated by James Strachey. New York: W. W. Norton.

Geertz, Clifford. 1973. *The Interpretation of Cultures: Selected Essays.* New York: Basic Books.

———. 1988. "Being There." In *Works and Lives: The Anthropologist as Author*, 1–24. Stanford, CA: Stanford University Press.

Gill, Kuldip. 1988. "Health Strategies of Indo-Fijian Women in the Context of Fiji." Ph.D. diss., University of British Columbia.

Gillion, K. L. 1977. *The Fiji Indians: Challenge to European Dominance, 1920–1946.* Canberra: Australian National University Press.

Goldstein, Donna. 2003. *Laughter Out of Place: Race, Class, Violence, and Sexuality in a Rio Shantytown.* Berkeley: University of California Press.

Goneyali, Eloni. 1986. "Who Wants to Stay on the Farm?" In *Fijians in Town*, edited by Michael Monsell-Davis and Chris Griffen, 1–7. Suva: Institute of Pacific Studies, University of the South Pacific.

Good, Byron J. 1992. "A Body in Pain: The Making of a World of Chronic Pain." In *Pain as Human Experience: An Anthropological Perspective*, edited by Mary-Jo Delvecchio Good, Byron Good, Arthur Kleinman, and Paul Brodwin, 29–48. Berkeley: University of California Press.

———. 1994. *Medicine, Rationality, and Experience: An Anthropological Perspective.* Cambridge: Cambridge University Press.

Good, Mary-Jo Delvecchio, Byron Good, Arthur Kleinman, and Paul Brodwin, eds. 1992. *Pain as Human Experience: An Anthropological Perspective.* Berkeley: University of California Press.

Goodwin, Charles. 1986. "Gesture as a Resource for the Organization of Mutual Orientation." *Semiotica* 62, no. 1–2: 29–49.

Government Printing Office. 1990. *Constitution of the Sovereign Democratic Republic of Fiji (Promulgation) Decree, 25 July 1990.* Suva.

Government Response to Statements by the National Federation Party and the Fiji Kisan Sangh—Need for Just and Fair Rent for Land Leases. 2000. Press Release by the Prime Minister's Office. As printed in *The Sunday Times*, August 13, 25.

Greenhouse, Carol J., Elizabeth Mertz, and Kay B. Warren, eds. 2002. *Ethnography in Unstable Places: Everyday Lives in the Contexts of Dramatic Political Change.* Durham, NC: Duke University Press.

Griffen, Arlene, ed. 1997. *With Heart and Nerve and Sinew: Postcoup Writing from Fiji.* Suva, Fiji: Christmas Club.

Griffin, Chris, and Mike Monsell-Davis, eds. 1986. *Fijians in Town.* Suva: Institute of Pacific Studies, University of the South Pacific.

Guha, Ranajit. 1999. *Elementary Aspects of Peasant Insurgency in Colonial India.* Durham, NC: Duke University Press.

Gupta, Akhil, and James Ferguson. 1992. "Beyond 'Culture': Space, Identity, and the Politics of Difference." *Cultural Anthropology* 7, no. 1: 6–23.

Haviland, John B. 2004. "Gesture." In *A Companion to Linguistic Anthropology*, edited by Alessandro Duranti, 197–221. Malden, Mass.: Blackwell.

Hayden, Robert. 1996. "Imagined Communities and Real Victims: Self-Determination and Ethnic Cleansing in Yugoslavia." *American Ethnologist* 23, no. 4: 783–801.

Heitlinger, Alena, and Susanna Trnka. 1997. *Young Women of Prague.* London: Macmillan Press.

———. 1999. "Formuje se Nova Generace. Vysledky Studie 'Zivoty Mladych Prazskych Zen' " (A New Generation in the Making? The Results of the Study 'Young Women of

Prague'). In *Ceska Spolecnost na Konci Tisicileti* (Czech Society towards the End of the Millennium), edited by Martine Potucek, 55–73. Prague: Karolinum Press.

Hereniko, Vilsoni. 1995. *Woven Gods: Female Clowns and Power in Rotuma.* Honolulu: University of Hawai'i Press.

Hermann, Elfriede, and Wolfgang Kempf, eds. 2005. *Relations in Multicultural Fiji: The Dynamics of Articulations, Transformations, and Positionings.* Special issue of *Oceania* 75, no. 4.

Herzfeld, Michael. 2005. *Cultural Intimacy: Social Poetics in the Nation-State.* New York: Routledge.

Hooper, Helen, and Bie Nio Ong. 2005. "When Harry Met Barry, and Other Stories: A Partner's Influence on Relationships in Back Pain Care." *Anthropology and Medicine* 12, no. 1: 47–60.

Iloilo, Ratu Josefa. 2000. "Address to the Nation by the President of the Public [*sic*] of the Fiji Islands." July 21, 2000. As printed in *The Sunday Times* July 23, 25.

Jackson, Jean E. 1992. " 'After a While No One Believes You': Real and Unreal Pain." In *Pain as Human Experience: An Anthropological Perspective,* edited by Mary-Jo Delvecchio Good, Byron Good, Arthur Kleinman, and Paul Brodwin, 138–69. Berkeley: University of California Press.

———. 1994. "Chronic Pain and the Tension between the Body as Subject and Object." In *Embodiment and Experience: The Existential Ground of Culture and Self,* edited by Thomas Csordas, 201–28. Cambridge: Cambridge University Press.

———. 2005. "Stigma, Liminality, and Chronic Pain: Mind-Body Borderlands." *American Ethnologist* 32, no. 3: 332–53.

Jackson, Michael 2002. *Politics of Storytelling: Violence, Transgression, and Intersubjectivity.* Copenhagen: Museum Tusculanum Press.

Jansen, Steff. 2003. " 'Why Do They Hate Us?' Everyday Serbian Nationalist Knowledge of Muslim Hatred." *Journal of Mediterranean Studies* 13, no. 2: 215–37.

Jayawardena, Chandra. 1980. "Culture and Ethnicity in Guyana and Fiji." *Man* 15, no. 3: 430–50.

Johansen, R. Elise. 2002. "Pain as a Counterpoint to Culture: Toward and Analysis of Pain Associated with Infibulation among Somali Immigrants in Norway." *Medical Anthropology Quarterly* 16, no. 3: 312–40.

Jordens, J. T. F. 1998. *Gandhi's Religion: A Homespun Shawl.* Houndsmills, Basingstoke, UK: Palgrave.

Kanapathipillai, Vali. 1990. "July 1983: The Survivor's Experience." In *Mirrors of Violence: Communities, Riots and Survivors in South Asia,* edited by Veena Das, 321–44. Delhi: Oxford University Press.

Kapferer, Jean-Noel. 1990. *Rumors: Uses, Interpretations, and Images.* New Brunswick, NJ: Transaction.

Kaplan, Martha. 1988. "The Coups in Fiji: Colonial Contradictions and the Postcolonial Crisis." *Critique of Anthropology* 8, no. 3: 99–116.

———. 1990. "Christianity, People of the Land, and Chiefs in Fiji." In *Christianity in Oceania: Ethnographic Perspectives,* edited by John Barker, 127–47. Lanham, MD: University Press of America.

———. 1993. "Imagining a Nation: Race Politics and Crisis in Postcolonial Fiji." In *Contemporary Pacific Societies: Studies in Development and Change,* edited by Victoria S.

Lockwood, T. Harding, and Ben Wallace, 34–54. Englewood Cliffs, NJ: Prentice Hall.

———. 1995. *Neither Cargo nor Cult: Ritual Politics and the Colonial Imagination in Fiji.* Durham, NC: Duke University Press.

———. 2003. "Promised Lands." In *Law and Empire in The Pacific: Fiji and Hawaii,* edited by Sally Engle Merry and Donald Brenneis, 153–86. Santa Fe: School of American Research Advanced Seminar Series.

———. 2004. "Fiji's Coups: The Politics of Representation and the Representation of Politics." In *Globalization and Culture Change in the Pacific Islands,* edited by Victoria Lockwood, 72–85. Upper Saddle River, NJ: Prentice Hall.

Kaplan, Martha, and John Kelly. 1994. "Rethinking Resistance: Dialogics of 'Disaffection' in Colonial Fiji." *American Ethnologist* 12, no. 1: 123–51.

Kelly, John D. 1988a. "Fiji Indians and Political Discourse in Fiji: From the Pacific Romance to the Coups." *Journal of Historical Sociology* 1, no. 4: 399–422.

———. 1988b. "From Holi to Diwali in Fiji: An Essay on Ritual and History." *Man* 23: 40–55.

———. 1990. "Discourses about Sexuality and the End of Indenture in Fiji." *History and Anthropology* 5: 19–61.

———. 1991a. *A Politics of Virtue: Hinduism, Sexuality, and Counter-colonial Discourse in Fiji.* Chicago: University of Chicago Press.

———. 1991b. "Introduction to My Twenty-One Years in the Fiji Islands." In *My Twenty-One Years in the Fiji Islands.* Translated and edited by John D. Kelly and Uttra Kumari Singh, 1–31. Suva: Fiji Museum.

———. 1992. "Fiji Indians and 'Commoditization of Labor.'" *American Ethnologist* 19, no. 1: 97–120.

———. 1993. "'Coolie' as a Labour Commodity: Race, Sex, and European Dignity in Colonial Fiji." *Journal of Peasant Studies* 19, no. 3–4: 246–67.

———. 1995a. "*Bhakti* and Postcolonial Politics: Hindu Missions to Fiji." In *Nation and Migration: The Politics of Space in the South Asian Diaspora,* edited by Peter van der Veer, 43–72. Philadelphia, University of Pennsylvania Press.

———. 1995b. "Diaspora and World War: Blood and Nation in Fiji and Hawaii." *Public Culture* 7: 475–97.

———. 1995c. "Threats to Difference in Colonial Fiji." *Cultural Anthropology* 10, no. 1: 64–84.

———. 1998. "Aspiring to Minority and Other Tactics against Violence." In *Making Majorities: Constituting the Nation in Japan, Korea, China, Malaysia, Fiji, Turkey, and the United States,* edited by Dru C. Gladney, 173–97. Stanford, CA: Stanford University Press.

———. 2001. "Fiji's Fifth Veda: Exile, Sanatan Dharm, and Countercolonial Initiatives in Diaspora." In *Questioning Ramayanas: A South Asian Tradition,* edited by Paula Richman, 329–51. Berkeley: University of California Press.

Kelly, John D., and Martha Kaplan. 1999. "Race and Rights in Fiji." *Research in Politics and Society* 6: 237–57.

———. 2001a. "Constituting Fiji: Communities, the Nation-State, and the Coup of 2000." In *Represented Communities: Fiji and World Decolonization,* 143–200. Chicago: University of Chicago Press.

———. 2001b. *Represented Communities: Fiji and World Decolonization.* Chicago: University of Chicago Press.

Kendon, Adam. 1995. "Some Uses of Gesture." In *Perspectives on Silence,* edited by Deborah Tannen and Muriel Saville-Troike, 215–34. Norwood, NJ: Ablex.

———. 2004. *Gesture: Visible Action as Utterance.* Cambridge: Cambridge University Press.

Kleinman, Arthur. 1986. *Social Origins of Distress and Disease: Depression, Neurasthenia, and Pain in Modern China.* New Haven, CT: Yale University Press.

———. 1992. "Pain and Resistance: The Delegitimation and Relegitimation of Local Worlds." In *Pain as Human Experience: An Anthropological Perspective,* edited by Mary-Jo Delvecchio Good, Byron Good, Arthur Kleinman, and Paul Brodwin, 169–97. Berkeley: University of California Press.

Kleinman, Arthur, Veena Das, and Margaret Lock, eds. 1997. *Social Suffering.* Berkeley: University of California Press.

Koli, Erich, and Hermann Muckler, eds. 2002. *Politics of Indigeneity in the South Pacific: Recent Problems of Identity in Oceania.* Hamburg: LIT-Verlag.

Kong, Kenneth C. 2003. " 'Are You My Friend?': Negotiating Friendship in Conversations between Network Marketers and Their Prospects." *Language and Society* 32: 487–522.

Lakhan, Asha. 2001. "A Year On, Ousted Fiji PM Still Bitter over Racist Coup." *Agence France-Presse* May 19.

Lal, Brij V. ed. 1990. "As the Dust Settles: Impact and Implications of the Fiji Coup." Special Issue of *Contemporary Pacific* 2: 1.

———. 1992. *Broken Waves: A History of the Fiji Islands in the Twentieth Century.* Honolulu: University of Hawai'i Press.

———. 1995. "Managing Ethnicity in Colonial and Postcolonial Fiji." In *Lines across the Sea: Colonial Inheritance in the Postcolonial Pacific,* edited by Brij V. Lal and Hank Nelson, 37–48. Brisbane: Pacific History Association.

———. 1998. *Another Way: The Politics of Constitutional Reform in Post-Coup Fiji.* Canberra: Asia Pacific Press, Australian National University.

———. 1999. "The Voice of the People: Ethnic Identity and Nation Building in Fiji." *New Pacific Review: Pacific Identities, Proceedings from the Noumea Symposium* 1, no. 1: 127–44.

———. 2000a. "A Time for Change: The Fiji General Elections of 1999." In *Fiji before the Storm,* edited by Brij V. Lal, 21–48. Canberra: Asia Pacific Press, Australian National University.

———. 2000b. *Chalo Jahaji: On a Journey through Indenture in Fiji.* Canberra: Research School of Pacific and Asian Studies.

———. 2000c. "Chiefs and Thieves and Other People Besides: The Making of George Speight's Coup." *The Journal of Pacific History* 35, no. 3: 281–93.

———. 2000d. "Madness in May: George Speight and the Unmaking of Modern Fiji." In *Fiji before the Storm,* edited by Brij V. Lal, 175–94. Canberra: Asia Pacific Press.

———. 2002a. "The Debris." In *Communities in Crisis: Ethnographies of the May 2000 Fiji Coup,* edited by Susanna Trnka. Special issue of *Pacific Studies* 25, no. 4: 109–16.

———. 2002b. "In George Speight's Shadow." *The Journal of Pacific History* 37, no. 1: 87–101.

———. 2002c. "Making History, Becoming History: Reflections on Fijian Coups and Constitutions." *Contemporary Pacific* 14, no. 1: 148–67.

———. 2003a. "Fiji's Constitutional Conundrum." *Round Table* 372: 671–85.

———. 2003b. "Heartbreak Islands." In *Law and Empire in the Pacific: Fiji and Hawaii,* edited by Sally Engle Merry and Donald Brenneis, 261–80. Santa Fe: School of American Research Advanced Seminar Series.

———, ed. 2004a. *Bittersweet.* Canberra: Pandanus Books.

———. 2004b. "Girmit, History, Memory." In *Bittersweet,* edited by Brij V. Lal, 1–29. Canberra: Pandanus Books.

———. 2007. " 'Anxiety, Uncertainty, and Fear in Our Land': Fiji's Road to Military Coup, 2006." Paper presented at the workshop The Fiji Coup—Six Months On. Canberra: The Australian National University, June 5, 2007. Available on the Fijilive website, www.fijilive.com.

Lal, Brij V., and Michael Pretes, eds. 2001. *Coup: Reflections on the Political Crisis in Fiji.* Canberra: Pandanus Books.

Lal, Padma. 2000. "Land, Lome, and the Fiji Sugar Industry." In *Fiji before the Storm,* edited by Brij V. Lal, 111–33. Canberra: Asia Pacific Press.

Lal, Victor. 1990. *Fiji Coups in Paradise: Race, Politics, and Military Intervention.* London: Zed Books.

Lateef, Shireen. 1990. "Rule by the *Danda*: Domestic Violence among Indo-Fijians." *Pacific Studies* 13, no. 3: 43–62.

Lawson, Stephanie. 1991. *The Failure of Democratic Politics in Fiji.* Oxford: Clarendon Press.

Leavitt, Stephen. 2002. "Chiefly Politics in the First Reactions in Rakiraki to the May 2000 Coup in Fiji." In *Communities in Crisis: Ethnographies of the May 2000 Fiji Coup,* edited by Susanna Trnka. Special issue of *Pacific Studies* 25, no. 4: 29–46.

Leckie, Jacqueline. 2000. "Women in Post-Coup Fiji: Negotiating Work through Old and New Realities." In *Confronting Fiji Futures,* edited by A. Haroon Akram-Lodhi, 178–201. Canberra: Asia Pacific Press.

———. 2002a. "Race Has Nothing to Do with Anything." In *Nations under Siege: Globalization and Nationalism in Asia,* edited by Roy Starrs, 243–67. New York: Palgrave.

———. 2002b. "Return to Nukulau: The Troubled Waters of Ethno-Nationalism in Fiji." In *Politics of Indigeneity in the South Pacific: Recent Problems of Identity in Oceania,* edited by Erich Koli and Hermann Muckler, 119–42. Hamburg: LIT-Verlag.

Lienhardt, Peter. 1975. "The Interpretation of Rumour." In *Studies in Social Anthropology: Essays in Memory of E. E. Evans-Pritchard,* edited by J. H. M. Beattie and R. G. Lienhardt, 105–31. Oxford: Clarendon Press.

Linnekin, Jocelyn, and Lin Poyer, eds. 1990. *Cultural Identity and Ethnicity in the Pacific.* Honolulu: University of Hawai'i Press.

Lockwood, Victoria, ed. 2004. *Globalization and Culture Change in the Pacific Islands.* Upper Saddle River, NJ: Prentice Hall.

Loizos, Peter. 1988. "Intercommunal Killing in Cyprus." *Man* 23, no. 4: 639–53.

Maci, Ruci. 2000. "Rebels Seize Rural Group." *The Fiji Times,* July 31, 1.

Madraiwiwi, Jona. 2007. "Mythic Constitutionalism: Whiter Fiji's Course in June 2007?" Paper Presented at the workshop The Fiji Coup—Six Months On. Canberra: The Australian National University, June 5. Available on the Fijilive website, www.fijilive.com.

Malkki, Liisa. 1995. *Purity and Exile: Violence, Memory, and National Cosmology among Hutu Refugees in Tanzania.* Chicago: University of Chicago Press.

Manoa, Pio. 1979. "Across the Fence." In *The Indo-Fijian Experience,* edited by Subramani, 184–207. St. Lucia, Queensland: University of Queensland Press.

Manueli, Irene. 2000. "A Soldier's Toughest Mission." *The Fiji Times,* July 31, 7.

Marau, Mereseini. 2005. "We've Lost 18 Yrs." *The Fiji Times,* May 20, 1.

Mayer, Adrian. 1963. *Indians in Fiji.* London: Oxford University Press.

———. 1973. *Peasants in the Pacific: A Study of Fiji Indian Rural Society.* 2d ed. Berkeley: University of California Press.

Mbembe, Achille. 2003. "Necropolitics." Translated Libby Meintjes. *Public Culture* 15, no. 1: 11–40.

Mbembe, Achille, and Janet Roitman. 1995. "Figures of the Subject in Times of Crisis." *Public Culture* 7, no. 2: 323–52.

McMillan, A. W. 1929. "Fiji: Where Three Continents Meet." *Pacific Affairs* 2, no. 7: 397–405.

Megoran, Nick. 2007. "On Researching 'Ethnic Conflict': Epistemology, Politics, and a Central Asian Boundary Dispute." *Europe-Asia Studies* 59, no. 2: 253–77.

Mehta, Deepak, and Roma Chatterji. 2001. "Boundaries, Names, Alterities: A Case Study of a 'Communal Riot' in Dharavi, Bombay." In *Remaking a World: Violence, Social Suffering, and Recovery,* edited by Veena Das, Arthur Kleinman, Margaret Lock, Mamphela Ramphele, and Pamela Reynolds, 201–49. Berkeley: University of California Press.

Merry, Sally Engle, and Donald Brenneis, eds. 2003. *Law and Empire in the Pacific: Fiji and Hawaii.* Santa Fe: School of American Research Advanced Seminar Series.

Mimica, Jadran. 1996. "On Dying and Suffering in Iqwaye Existence." In *Things as They Are: New Directions in Phenomenological Anthropology,* edited by Michael Jackson, 213–37. Bloomington: Indiana University Press.

Ministry of Education. 1990. *Merī Pāmcvāmī Pustak* [My Fifth Book]. Suva: Government of Fiji.

Mishra, Vijay. 1979. "Introduction" to *Rama's Banishment: A Centenary Tribute to the Fiji Indians 1879–1979,* 1–11. London: Heinemann Education Books.

Mitchell, William E., ed. 1992. *Clowning as Critical Practice: Performance Humor in the South Pacific.* Pittsburgh: University of Pittsburgh Press.

Moag, Rodney F. 1977. *Fiji Hindi: A Basic Course and Reference Grammar.* Suva: Australian National University Press and Extension Services, University of the South Pacific.

Morreall, John, ed. 1987. *The Philosophy of Humor.* Albany: State University of New York Press.

Nandan, Satendra. 1991. *The Wounded Sea.* New South Wales, Australia: Simon and Schuster.

Nayacakalou, R. R. 1963. "The Urban Fijians of Suva." In *Pacific Port Towns and Cities: A Symposium,* edited by Alexander Spoehr, 33–41. Honolulu: Bishop Museum.

Neofotistos, Vasiliki P. 2004. "Beyond Stereotypes: Violence and the Porousness of Ethnic Boundaries in the Republic of Macedonia." *History and Anthropology* 15, no. 1: 1–36.

Nordstrom, Carolyn, and Antonius Robben, eds. 1995. *Fieldwork under Fire: Contemporary Studies of Violence and Survival.* Berkeley: University of California Press.

Norton, Robert. 1990. *Race and Politics in Fiji.* 2d ed. St Lucia, Australia: University of Queensland Press.

———. 2000a. "Reconciling Ethnicity and Nation: Contending Discourses in Fiji's Constitutional Reform." *The Contemporary Pacific* 12, no. 1: 83–122.

———. 2000b. "Understanding the Results of the 1999 Fiji Elections." In *Fiji before the Storm*, edited by Brij V. Lal, 49–72. Canberra: Asia Pacific Press.

Oakley, A. 1974. *The Sociology of Housework.* Oxford: Oxford University Press.

Paine, Robert. 1969. "In Search of Friendship: An Exploratory Analysis in 'Middle-Class' Culture." *Man* 4, no. 4: 505–24.

Pandey, Gyanendra. 2001. *Remembering Partition.* Cambridge: Cambridge University Press.

Pandolfo, Stefania. 2005. "Eschatological Imaginations and Life Experiments." Paper presented at the American Anthropological Association 104th Annual Meeting. December 3. Washington, DC.

Perera, Sasanka. 2001. "Spirit Possessions and Avenging Ghosts: Stories of Supernatural Activity as Narratives of Terror and Mechanisms of Coping and Remembering." In *Remaking a World: Violence, Social Suffering, and Recovery,* edited by Veena Das, Arthur Kleinman, Margaret Lock, Mamphela Ramphele, and Pamela Reynolds, 157–200. Berkeley: University of California Press.

Perice, Glen A. 1997. "Rumors and Politics in Haiti." *Anthropological Quarterly* 70, no. 1: 1–10.

Pillai, Raymond. 1979. "Labourer's Lament." In *The Indo-Fijian Experience,* edited by Subramani, 160–61. St. Lucia, Queensland: University of Queensland Press.

Ponter, Elizabeth. 1986. "The Growth of Wage Labour and Its Consequences for a Fijian Village." In *Fijians in Town,* edited by Michael Monsell-Davis and Chris Griffen, 29–49. Suva: Institute of Pacific Studies, University of the South Pacific.

Poole, Deborah. 1994. "Peasant Culture and Political Violence in the Peruvian Andes: Sendero Luminoso and the State." In *Unruly Order: Violence, Power, and Cultural Identity in the High Provinces of Southern Peru,* edited by Deborah Poole, 247–81. Boulder: Westview.

Premdas, Ralph R. 1995. *Ethnic Conflict and Development: The Case of Fiji.* Hants, England: Avebury.

Premdas, Ralph R., and Jeffrey Steeves. 1993. "Ethnic Politics and Inequality in Fiji: Understanding the New Constitution." *Journal de la Société des Océanistes* 96 (1): 63–75.

Rabuka, Sitiveni. 2000. "The Fiji Islands in Transition: Personal Reflections." In *Fiji before the Storm,* edited by Brij V. Lal, 7–20. Canberra: Asia Pacific Press.

Rakuita, Tui. 2002. "Taukei-Vulagi Philosophy and the Coup of May 19, 2000." In *Communities in Crisis: Ethnographies of the May 2000 Fiji Coup,* edited by Susanna Trnka. Special issue of *Pacific Studies* 25, no. 4: 93–108.

Ramesh, Sanjay. 2001. "The Race Bandwagon." In *Coup: Reflections on the Political Crisis in Fiji,* edited by Brij V. Lal and Michael Pretes, 117–25. Canberra: Pandanus Books.

Ravuvu, Asesela. 1991. *The Facade of Democracy: Fijian Struggles for Political Control.* Suva: Reader Publishing House.

Reddy, Jai Ram, ed. 1980. *Girmit: A Centenary Anthology, 1879–1979.* Suva: Ministry of Information, Government of Fiji.

Reddy, Mahendra, and Padma Lal. 2002. "State Land Transfer in Fiji." *Pacific Economic Bulletin* 17, no. 1: 146–53.

Republic of Fiji Islands Fiji Police Force. 2006. "Media Update: January 5, 2006, Coup Investigations." Online version available at http://www.police.gov.fj/release5ajan.html.

Rezende, Claudia. 1999. "Building Affinity through Friendship." In *The Anthropology of Friendship,* edited by Sandra Bell and Simon Coleman, 79–97. Oxford: Berg.

Riches, David, ed. 1986. *The Anthropology of Violence.* Oxford, England: Basil Blackwell.

Rika, Netani. 2000. "Get Off Your Backside." *The Fiji Times,* June 4, 10.

Robertson, Robbie, and William Sutherland. 2001. *Government by the Gun: The Unfinished Business of Fiji's 2000 Coup.* Annandale: Pluto Press Australia.

Robie, David. 2001. "Coup Coup Land: The Press and the Putsch in Fiji." *Asia Pacific Media Educator* 10: 1148–62.

Romero, Mary. 1992. *Maid in the USA.* New York: Routledge.

Rutz, Henry. 1995. "Occupying the Headwaters of Tradition: Rhetorical Strategies of Nation Making in Fiji." In *Nation Making: Emergent Identities in Postcolonial Melanesia,* edited by Robert J. Foster, 71–93. Ann Arbor: University of Michigan Press.

Sahlins, Marshall. 1962. *Moala: Culture and Nature on a Fijian Island.* Ann Arbor: University of Michigan Press.

———. 1981. *Historical Metaphors and Mythical Realities: Structure in the Early History of the Sandwich Islands Kingdom.* Ann Arbor: University of Michigan Press.

Sanadhya, Totaram. 1991a. *My Twenty-One Years in the Fiji Islands.* Translated and edited by John D. Kelly and Uttra Kumari Singh. Suva: Fiji Museum.

———. 1991b. "The Story of the Haunted Line." In *My Twenty-One Years in the Fiji Islands,* translated and edited by John D. Kelly and Uttra Kumari Singh, 115–27. Suva: Fiji Museum.

Saville-Troike, Muriel. 1995. "The Place of Silence in an Integrated Theory of Communication." In *Perspectives on Silence,* edited by Deborah Tannen and Muriel Saville-Troike, 3–18. Norwood, NJ: Ablex.

Scarr, Deryck. 1980. *Viceroy of the Pacific.* Part II. *The Majesty of Colour—A Life of Sir John Bates Thurston.* Canberra: The Australian National University.

———. 1988. *Fiji Politics of Illusion: The Military Coups in Fiji.* Kensington, NSW: New South Wales University Press.

Scarry, Elaine. 1985. *The Body in Pain: The Making and Unmaking of the World.* Oxford: Oxford University Press.

Scheper-Hughes, Nancy. 1992. *Death without Weeping: The Violence of Everyday Life in Brazil.* Berkeley: University of California Press.

Scott, James C. 1985. *Weapons of the Weak: Everyday Forms of Peasant Resistance.* New Haven, CT: Yale University Press.

"The Seeds Were Sown over One Hundred Years Ago." 1999. *The Fiji Times,* August 21, 11.

Sekulíc, Duško, Garth Massey, and Randy Hodson. 2006. "Ethnic Intolerance and Ethnic Conflict in the Dissolution of Yugoslavia." *Ethnic and Racial Studies* 29, no. 5: 797–827.

Seremetakis, C. Nadia. 1990. "The Ethics of Antiphony: The Social Construction of Pain, Gender, and Power in the Southern Peloponnese." *Ethos* 18, no. 1: 481–511.

Sharma, Seema. 2000. "Slaves of the Economy." *The Fiji Times,* June 4, 12.

Sharpham, John. 2000. *Rabuka of Fiji: The Authorized Biography of Major-General Sitiveni Rabuka.* Rockhampton, Queensland: Central Queensland University Press.

Shibutani, Tamotsu. 1966. *Improvised News: A Sociological Study of Rumor.* Indianapolis: Bobbs-Merrill.

Silver, Allan. 1989. "Friendship and Trust as Moral Ideals: An Historical Approach." *Archives Européennes de Sociologie* 30, no. 2: 274–97.

Singh, Anirudh. 1992. *Silent Warriors.* Suva: Fiji Institute of Applied Studies.

Singh, Shailendra. 2001. "After Beating Govt. in Court, Fiji Farmer Seeks to Flee." *Indiaabroaddaily.com,* March 4.

Singh, Vijay. 2000a. "Forgotten Milestones." *The Fiji Times,* May 16, 17.

——. 2000b. "Living in Unusual Times." *The Fiji Times,* June 29, 7.

Stoller, Paul. 1995. *Embodying Colonial Memories: Spirit Possession, Power, and the Hauka in West Africa.* New York: Routledge.

Strathern, Andrew, Pamela Stewart, and Neil Whitehead. 2005. *Terror and Violence: Imagination and the Unimaginable.* London: Pluto.

Subramani. 1997. "Captive in Liberated Bush." In *With Heart and Nerve and Sinew: Postcoup Writing from Fiji,* edited by Arlene Griffen, 244–67. Suva: Christmas Club.

——, ed. 1979. *The Indo-Fijian Experience.* St. Lucia: University of Queensland Press.

Suguta, Aloesi. 1986. "The Dilemma of Tradition." In *Fijians in Town,* edited by Michael Monsell-Davis and Chris Griffen, 185–88. Suva: Institute of Pacific Studies, University of the South Pacific.

Sutherland, William. 1992. *Beyond the Politics of Race: An Alternative History of Fiji to 1992.* Canberra: Department of Political and Social Change, Research School of Pacific Studies, Australian National University.

——. 2000. "The Problematics of Reform and the 'Fijian' Question." In *Confronting Fiji Futures,* edited by A. Haroon Akram-Lodhi, 205–25. Canberra: Asia Pacific Press.

Tambiah, Stanley J. 1989. "Ethnic Conflict in the World Today." *American Ethnologist* 16, no. 2: 335–49.

——. 1996. *Leveling Crowds; Ethnonationalist Conflicts and Collective Violence in South Asia.* Berkeley: University of California Press.

Taussig, Michael. 1987. *Shamanism, Colonialism, and the Wild Man: A Study in Terror and Healing.* Chicago: University of Chicago Press.

Teaiwa, Teresia. 2000. "An Analysis of the Current Political Crisis in Fiji." *Pacific Islands Report,* May 22. Reprinted in *The Fiji Times* under the title "Nationalism with No Nation," May 25, 16.

Thomas, Larry. 2002. *A Race for Rights.* Suva: University of the South Pacific.

Thomas, Nicholas. 1989. "Tin and Thatch: Identity and Tradition in Rural Fiji." *Age Monthly Review* 8, no. 11: 15–18.

——. 1990a. "Regional Politics, Ethnicity, and Custom in Fiji." *Contemporary Pacific* 2, no. 1: 131–46.

——. 1990b. "Sanitation and Seeing: The Creation of State Power in Early Colonial Fiji." *Comparative Studies in Society and History* 32: 149–70.

——. 1992. "The Inversion of Tradition." *American Ethnologist* 19: 213–32.

——. 1997. *In Oceania.* Durham, NC: Duke University Press.

Thomson, Peter. 1999. *Kava in the Blood.* Auckland: Tandem Press.

"Thugs Raid Party Bus." 2000. *The Fiji Times,* July 12, 8.

Thurston, Basset. 1924. "The First Crossing of Fiji." *Geographical Journal* 64, no. 5: 393–403.

Tinker, Hugh. 1974. *A New System of Slavery: The Export of Indian Labour Overseas, 1830–1920.* London: Oxford University Press.

Tomlinson, Matthew. 2002a. "Sacred Soil in Kadavu, Fiji." *Oceania* 72, no. 4: 237–57.

——. 2002b. "Speaking of Coups before They Happen." In *Communities in Crisis: Ethnographies of the May 2000 Fiji Coup,* edited by Susanna Trnka. Special issue of *Pacific Studies* 25, no. 4: 9–28.

——. 2004. "Ritual, Risk, and Danger: Chain Prayers in Fiji." *American Anthropologist* 16, no. 1: 6–17.

Toren, Christina. 1988. "Making the Present, Revealing the Past: The Mutability and Continuity of Tradition as Process." *Man* 23, no. 4: 696–717.

——. 2005. "Laughter and Truth in Fiji: What We May Learn from a Joke." *Oceania* 75, no. 3: 268–84.

Trnka, Susanna, ed. 1993. *Bodies of Bread and Butter: Reconfiguring Women's Lives in the Post-Communist Czech Republic.* Prague: Gender Studies Center.

——. 1999. "Global Spaces, Local Places: The Body and Imagination in Indo-Fijian Fiction." *SPAN (Journal for the South Pacific Association for Commonwealth Literature and Language Studies (SPACLALS)* (University of Waikato, New Zealand) 48–49: 40–52.

——, ed. 2002a. *Communities in Crisis: Ethnographies of the May 2000 Fiji Coup.* Special issue of *Pacific Studies* 25, no. 4.

——. 2002b. "Foreigners at Home: Discourses of Difference, Fiji Indians, and the Looting of May 19." *Ethnographies of the May 2000 Fiji Coup,* edited by Susanna Trnka. Special issue of *Pacific Studies* 25, no. 4: 69–92.

——. 2002c. *God Only Listens to Those Who Sweat: Violence, the Body, and Community in Sanatan Hindu Dialogues of the May 2000 Fiji Coup.* Ph.D. diss., Princeton University.

——. 2002d. "Introduction: Communities in Crisis." In *Communities in Crisis: Ethnographies of the May 2000 Fiji Coup,* edited by Susanna Trnka. Special issue of *Pacific Studies* 25, no. 4: 1–8.

——. 2004. "Upahar Gaon." In *Bittersweet: The Indo-Fijian Experience,* edited by Brij V. Lal, 135–50. Canberra: Pandanus Books.

——. 2005a. "Between Victims and Assailants, Victims and Friends: Sociality and the Imagination in Indo-Fijian Narratives of Rural Violence during the May 2000 Fiji Coup." In *Violence and Terror: Imagination and the Unimaginable,* edited by Andrew Strathern, Pamela J. Stewart, and Neil L. Whitehead, 117–41. London: Pluto.

——. 2005b. "Bodily Translations: The Politics of Pain Expression among Indo-Fijian Women." In *Translations, Treaties, and Testimonies,* edited by Cris Shore. Special issue of *Sites* 2, no. 2: 119–40.

——. 2005c. "Land, Life, and Labour: Indo-Fijian Claims to Citizenship in a Changing Fiji." In *Relations in Multicultural Fiji: The Dynamics of Articulations, Transformations and Positionings,* edited by Elfriede Hermann and Wolfgang Kempf. Special issue of *Oceania* 75, no. 4: 354–67.

——. 2005d. "Violence, Agency, and Freedom of Movement: Issues Emerging out of the Lata Sisters' Disappearance." *Fijian Studies* 3, no. 2: 277–94.

——. 2007. "Languages of Labor: Negotiating the 'Real' and the Relational in Indo-Fijian Women's Expressions of Body Pain." *Medical Anthropology Quarterly* 21, no. 4: 388–408.

Verdery, Katherine. 1994. "Ethnicity, Nationalism, and State-making." In *The Anthropology of Ethnicity: Beyond "Ethnic Groups and Boundaries,"* edited by Hans Vermeulen and Cora Grovers, 32–58. The Hague: Het Spinhuis.

Volkan, Vamik. 2006. *Killing in the Name of Identity: A Study of Bloody Conflicts.* Charlottesville: Pitchstone.

Warren, Kay B. 1993a. "Interpreting *La Violencia* in Guatemala: Shapes of Mayan Silence and Resistance." In *The Violence Within: Cultural and Political Opposition in Divided Nations,* edited by Kay B. Warren, 25–56. Boulder: Westview.

——, ed. 1993b. *The Violence Within: Cultural and Political Opposition in Divided Nations*. Boulder: Westview.

Weismantel, Mary. 2001. *Cholas and Pishtacos: Stories of Race and Sex in the Andes*. Chicago: University of Chicago Press.

White, Luise. 2000. *Speaking with Vampires: Rumor and History in Colonial Africa*. Berkeley: University of California Press.

"Why Fijians Hate Indians." 2000. Interview with Sitiveni Rabuka. *Daily Post*, August 10, 3.

Williams, Brackette F. 1989. "A Class Act: Anthropology and the Race to Nation across Ethnic Terrain." *Annual Review of Anthropology* 18: 401–44.

——. 1991. *Stains on My Name, War in My Veins: Guyana and the Politics of Cultural Struggle*. Durham, NC: Duke University Press.

——. 1995. "Classification Systems Revisited." In *Naturalizing Power: Essays in Feminist Cultural Analysis*, edited by Sylvia Yanagisako and Carol Delaney, 201–238. New York: Routledge.

Williams, Robin M., Jr. 2003. *The Wars Within: Peoples and States in Conflict*. Ithaca: Cornell University Press.

Williams, Thomas. 1982 [1858]. *Fiji and the Fijians*. Vol 1. *The Islands and Their Inhabitants*. Suva: Fiji Museum.

Wittgenstein, Ludwig. 1958. *The Blue and Brown Books: Preliminary Studies for the "Philosophical Investigations."* New York: Harper and Row.

Wolf, Eric. 1966. "Kinship, Friendship, and Patron-Client Relations in Complex Societies." In *The Social Anthropology of Complex Societies*, edited by Michael Banton, 1–22. London: Tavistock.

Young, John M. R. 1984. *Adventurous Spirits: Australian Migrant Society in Pre-Cession Fiji*. St. Lucia, Queensland: University of Queensland Press.

Yule, Henry, and A. C. Burnell. 1985 [1886]. *Hobson-Jobson: A Glossary of Colloquial Anglo-Indian Words and Phrases, and of Kindred Terms, Etymological, Historical, Geographical, and Discursive*. London: Routledge and Kegan Paul.

Index

Page numbers in **bold** refer to illustrations.